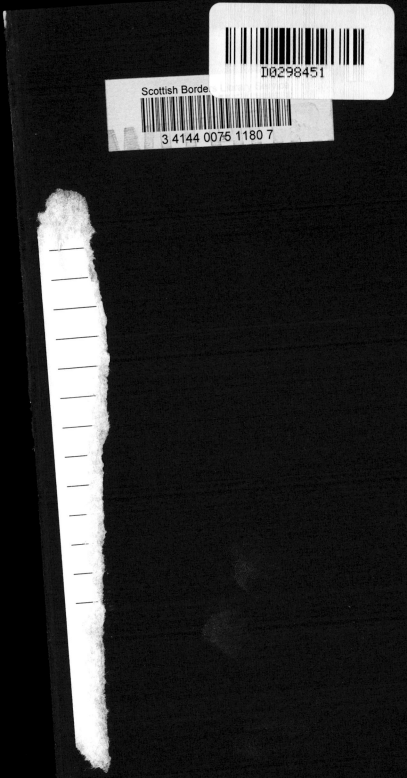

THE LITERARY TRAVELLER IN SCOTLAND

This book is for Harry Winslow: ace researcher, photographer and friend; and with whom Glasgow is always 'a 24-hour cabaret'.

THE LITERARY TRAVELLER IN SCOTLAND

A Book Lover's Guide

Allan Foster

MAINSTREAM
PUBLISHING

EDINBURGH AND LONDON

Scottish
Arts Council

Copyright © Allan Foster, 2007
The moral right of the author has been asserted

First published in Great Britain in 2007 by
MAINSTREAM PUBLISHING COMPANY
(EDINBURGH) LTD
7 Albany Street
Edinburgh EH1 3UG

ISBN 9781845961893

A catalogue record for this book is available
from the British Library

Typeset in Apollo and Univers

Printed in Great Britain by
Scotprint, Haddington

I'm going back to Scotland which I left when just
a boy,
For my pooch is full o' money and my heart is full
of joy,
And I'm longin' for the moment when I'll hear the
porter cry,
All change for Auchtermuchty, Eccelfechan and
Mulguy.

Robert Service, Bard of the Yukon,
from *Bath-Tub Ballads* (1939)

Acknowledgements

Sincere thanks to Harry Winslow, Chris Foster, Ian Nimmo, the Scottish Arts Council, Jason Cycling William Patient, Noël Donoghue, Elaine Greig and the staff of Edinburgh's Writers' Museum, Harry Kane, Ali Bowden and Anna Burkey of Edinburgh UNESCO City of Literature, Lis Lee, Tom Bryan, Walter Elliot, Dougie Munro, Bob and Pat Watt, Alex Goick, Maureen and Arthur Still, Dawn and Tony Greaves, Lucy Foster, Jack Foster, Chloe Foster, Kit Foster, Cissie Riddles, Wilson Ogilvie, Dumfries and Galloway Council, Burns Festival Trust, Elaine Kennedy and Dumfries and Galloway Museums Service, Matt Welsh and the staff of Poosie Nansies, Pat and Adam Dagg, Izzy Whitfield, Deborah Buchan, Joan Sanderson and the staff of Duns Library, David Weir and the staff of Paisley Library, Pam Beasant, Kathryn Berthon and the staff of Dundee Central Library, the Mitchell Library and the staff of the Glasgow Room, the staff of Kelso Library, Lorna Munson, David Fowler and Mary Fergusson of Stornoway Library, Sarah Kelly, Jane Murray-Flutter, David Robertson and the staff of Kirkcaldy Library, Alison Tait, Rab Steele, John Henderson, Jacquie Wright and the staff of Abbotsford House, Tom Ramage, Ali Brown and the staff of Inverness Library, Stewart Conn, Isla Robertson and the National Trust for Scotland, Ida Glendinning and the staff of Dundee Library, Laura Esslemont and Birlinn Publishing, Robert Bain and the staff of Wick Library, Alison Tait and the staff of Peebles Library, Jim McAllister and the Friends of Ellisland Farm, and my editor Paul Murphy at Mainstream Publishing.

Contents

Introduction

This is a wee book about a huge subject. It dips its toe in the water, but doesn't go for a swim. It's not a history of Scottish literature, but a guide to many of its sites, haunts and landscapes. It leans towards the classic and the traditional rather than the contemporary, and I've tried my best to squeeze it between the covers of an easy-to-read guidebook. I have given more emphasis to writers than to their writings, because the majority of them we have lost. If their roots stretch too far back into history, it's likely their origins are patchy or elusive, and therefore nothing tangible connected to them exists to go and see any more. Those wishing a more in-depth study of literary Edinburgh should consult my book, *The Literary Traveller in Edinburgh* (Mainstream Publishing, 2005).

There is so much I wanted to get in that didn't make it; nonetheless the true legacy of Scottish literature over the centuries lies within the book's pages. That pleases me enormously, but it is still only in embryo. I hope others will follow in my footsteps along the roads and over the hills that I have travelled, and I also hope they'll find as much pleasure and beauty as I have wandering through the landscapes of Scottish literature. Saint Augustine once said, 'The world is a book, and those who do not travel read only a page.' The same could be said about the literary landscapes of Scotland.

Allan Foster

Borders

Chirnside

Ninewells
Childhood home of David Hume (1711–76), moral philosopher, historian and political thinker

> A man who has so much conceit as to tell all mankind that they have bubbled for ages, and he is the wise man who sees better than they – a man who has so little scrupulosity as to venture to oppose those principles which have been thought necessary to human happiness – is he to be surprised if another man comes and laughs at him?
>
> Doctor Johnson on David Hume

Doctor Johnson's reaction to Hume was typical for his time. As a celebrated atheist, sceptic, believer in civil liberties, opponent of 'divine right' and a political thinker who greatly influenced European thought, it's not surprising that many thought that David Hume was in league with the Devil. Even the binge-drinking, whoring and gonorrhoea-ridden James Boswell (1740–95) thought his character might be besmirched by associating with Hume, commenting, 'I was not clear that it was right in me to keep company with him.' German philosopher Immanuel Kant, however, was not so blinkered, reporting in the *Prolegomena* that Hume 'first interrupted my dogmatic slumber', and Jeremy Bentham said Hume 'caused the scales to fall' from his eyes. Charles Darwin considered him a central influence, and history now rightfully ranks Hume as one of the great men of genius of the eighteenth century.

Born in Edinburgh on 7 May 1711, Hume spent his childhood at Ninewells, his family's estate near Chirnside in the Scottish Borders. After the death of his father, an Edinburgh lawyer, his mother brought him up at the family's Borders estate. He went to school in Chirnside until he was 12, when he left to attend Edinburgh University, although he did not graduate. He spent much of his teens at Ninewells, where he reputedly experienced a religious conversion influenced by the local minister. He later studied law and was briefly employed as a clerk for a Bristol sugar importer before entering the Jesuit College at La Flèche in 1734, where for three years he read French and other European literature. It was here, between 1734 and 1737, that he drafted his first and most important work, *A Treatise of Human Nature*, which he published anonymously in 1739. Its hostile reception prompted Hume to describe it as falling 'dead-born from the press'. He produced two more popular volumes of *Essays, Moral*

and Political in 1741 and 1742. He applied for the Chair of Moral Philosophy at Edinburgh in 1744, but his religious scepticism ruled against him. For the next seven or eight years he held various posts as tutor, secretary and minor diplomat, returning to Edinburgh in 1751 to take up a post as librarian to the Faculty of Advocates.

Hume's first Edinburgh home was at Riddles Close, 322 High Street, 'in the first court reached on entering the close, and it is approached by a projecting turret stair'. Hume described his household as 'consisting of a head, viz. myself, and two inferior members – a maid and a cat. My sister has since joined me, and keeps me company.' It was in this house that Hume wrote his *Political Discourses* (1752) and started on his monumental *History of England* (5 volumes, 1754–62). In 1753 he moved to Jack's Land, now renumbered 229 Canongate, where he lived for nine years, and where he completed his *History*, a work which became a bestseller and at last made him financially independent. From 1763 to 1765 he acted as secretary to the British Ambassador in Paris, where he was fêted by the French court. He befriended Rousseau and returned to London with him in 1766, but they later quarrelled bitterly. In 1767 he became undersecretary of state for the Northern Department, returning to Scotland in 1768, where he lived out the rest of his life as a man of letters at his house on the corner of St Andrew Square – a then unnamed street. One day his maid informed him that someone had chalked 'St David's Street' on the wall. 'Never mind, lassie, mony a waur man has been made a saint o' before.'

David Hume died aged 65 of intestinal cancer on 25 August 1776 and is buried in Old Calton Burial Ground, Waterloo Place, Edinburgh.

FURTHER INFORMATION: Ninewells is located on the left bank of Whitadder Water, just under a mile south-west of Chirnside village in Berwickshire, and was Hume's occasional residence throughout his life. It is not open to the public. During the 1960s the southern edge of George Square in Edinburgh was demolished to make way for the new buildings of Edinburgh University. The tall tower built to the east of the library was named David Hume Tower, and a better example of an architectural monstrosity will not be found anywhere. Robert Garioch immortalised the tower in his poem 'A Wee Local Scandal'. A statue to David Hume was erected in 1997 on the corner of Edinburgh's Bank Street and the Lawnmarket by the Saltire Society to mark its 60th anniversary. Due to the statue's low height, Hume's head can often be seen sporting a jaunty traffic cone.

FURTHER READING: R. Graham, *The Great Infidel* (Tuckwell Press, 2005); A.J. Ayer, *Hume* (Oxford Paperbacks, 1980); N.K. Smith, P. Jones, *Hume's Sentiments* (Edinburgh University Press, 1982).

Duns

Duns Castle
Birthplace of Duns Scotus (c. 1266–1308), theologian, philosopher and logician

> Of realty the rarest-veinèd unraveller . . .
> Gerard Manley Hopkins, from *Duns Scotus's Oxford* (1918)

John Duns Scotus was one of the most significant thinkers in the history of Christian thought, and he rivalled Thomas Aquinas as the greatest theologian of the Middle Ages. Details of his life are patchy, but he was probably born in Duns. Known more as a philosopher today, he became a Franciscan and was ordained priest in St Andrews Church, Northampton, in 1291, studying and teaching in Oxford, Cambridge, Paris and Cologne, where he died and is buried. The inscription on his sarcophagus reads, '*Scotia me genuit. Anglia me suscepit. Gallia me docuit. Colonia me tenet.*' (Scotland brought me forth. England sustained me. France taught me. Cologne holds me.) He was beatified by Pope John Paul II on 20 March 1993.

His works are mainly commentaries on the Bible, Aristotle and Italian theologian Peter Lombard, and he reacted fiercely against the philosophy of Aristotle and Thomas Aquinas. He set forth the primacy of the individual and the freedom of the individual will. Faith to him was an essential foundation of Christian theology, but he saw this as a practical commitment, not abstract or theoretical. He also developed the doctrine of the Immaculate Conception and was known by his followers and contemporaries as 'Doctor Subtilis' because of his merging of contradictory views. Scotists were derided by later philosophers and dubbed 'Dunses', from which is derived the modern word 'dunce'.

Duns Scotus was reputedly prone to fits, during which he could be assumed dead. He died in Cologne and was buried after one of these fits. Tragically, his servant, who had been instructed to prevent this happening, was elsewhere at the time and arrived after the burial. When his body was exhumed, the corpse's hands were seen to have clawed the interior of the coffin. A plaque once marked Duns Scotus's tomb with a Latin inscription, which translated reads:

> Mark this man's demise, o traveler,
> For here lies John Scot, once interr'd
> But twice dead; we are now wiser
> And still alive, who then so err'd.

SEE ALSO: David Hume.
FURTHER INFORMATION: The house in which Duns Scotus was born stood near the more westerly lodge, now called the Pavilion Lodge, of Duns Castle. In 1966 members of the Franciscan Order erected a stone cairn near the lodge marking the spot of his birth and also erected a bronze sculpture to him in the public park near the Murray Street entrance.
FURTHER READING: T. Williams (ed.), *The Cambridge Companion to Duns Scotus* (Cambridge, 2003).

Ednam

Memorial to Rev. Henry Francis Lyte (1793–1847), poet and hymnologist who wrote 'Abide with me'

Abide with me; fast falls the eventide;
The darkness deepens; Lord with me abide.
When other helpers fail and comforts flee,
Help of the helpless, O abide with me.

Rev. H.F. Lyte, from 'Abide with me' (1847)

The great Victorian hymnologist Rev. Henry Francis Lyte was born in the village of Ednam, just outside Kelso, on 1 June 1793. His family hailed from Somerset, and his father was a naval officer. The family moved to Ireland, where he was educated in Enniskillen, Co. Fermanagh, and Trinity College, Dublin. He took Anglican holy orders in 1815 and met his wife Ann when he was a curate in Cornwall. His last parish was the fishing village of Lower Brixham in Devon, where he wrote 'Abide with me', apparently while walking along the beach. Plagued by consumption for most of his life, he wintered frequently in southern Europe to escape Britain's damp climate. Lyte's first published work was *Tales in Verse Illustrative of Several of the Petitions in the Lord's Prayer* (1826), but his best-known hymns are 'Abide with me', 'Jesus, I my cross have taken', 'Praise my soul the King of Heaven' and 'Pleasant are thy courts above'.

The circumstances surrounding the birth of 'Abide with me' were related by his daughter, Anna Maria Maxwell Hogg:

> The summer was passing away, and the month of September (that month in which he was once more to quit his native land) arrived, and each day seemed to have a special value as being one day nearer his departure. His family were surprised and almost alarmed at his announcing his intention of preaching once more to his people. His weakness and the possible danger attending the effort, were urged to prevent it, but in vain . . . He did preach, and amid the breathless attention of his hearers [they] had no reason to believe it had been hurtful to him. In the evening of the same day he placed in the hands of a near and dear relative the little hymn, 'Abide with me . . .'

Sadly, this legendary hymn was the last he ever wrote. Ten weeks after preaching his farewell sermon, and while wintering in Europe for his health, he sent the finished manuscript to his wife from Avignon and died shortly afterwards of tuberculosis in Nice, where he is buried in the English Cemetery of the Holy Trinity Church. The original tune of 'Abide with me', composed by Lyte and his daughter, was replaced by William Henry Monk's (1823–89) 'Eventide' in 1861.

SEE ALSO: James Thomson.

Kelso

Maxwell Lane
Waverley Lodge
**Former home of Walter Scott's aunt, and where he lodged in
the summer of 1783**

> To this period I can trace the awakening of that delightful
> feeling for the beauties of natural objects which has never
> since deserted me. The neighbourhood of Kelso, the most
> beautiful if not the most romantic village in Scotland, is
> eminently calculated to awaken these ideas. It presents
> objects not only grand in themselves, but venerable from their
> associations.
>
> Sir Walter Scott, Ashestiel, 26 April 1808

Scott's praise for Kelso is not misplaced even today, though his
'romantic village' has now grown into a thriving town of 7,000
residents. But despite its increased size, the heart of the town,
centred around its French-style cobbled square, remains much the
same as it was in his day.

After leaving Edinburgh's Royal High School in the spring of
1783, and not due to start college until the autumn, Scott's father
sent him to live with his Aunt Janet for six months in Kelso, where
she had moved from nearby Sandyknowe. Young Wattie would
spend many holidays in Kelso during his youth, but this trip was
his first real introduction to Border village life, and he seemed to
forever remain under its spell. Much of his time that year was spent
exploring his aunt's large garden with its mazes and bowers leading
down to the banks of the Tweed. A bust of Scott and a statue of his
dog Maida can be seen on the gable end of the house.

Scott reminisced about his Kelso days in 1808:

> [My] health had become rather delicate from rapid growth,
> and my father was easily persuaded to allow me to spend
> half a year at Kelso with my kind aunt, Miss Janet Scott,
> whose inmate I again became. At this time she resided in a

10 Bridge Street, former premises of the *Tory Kelso Mail*.

small house, situated very pleasantly in a large garden, to the eastward of the churchyard of Kelso, which extended down to the Tweed. It was then my father's property, from whom it was afterwards purchased by my uncle. My grandmother was now dead, and my aunt's only companion, besides an old maid-servant, was my cousin, Miss Barbara Scott, now Mrs Meik.

He attended the old grammar school, adjoining the abbey (a site now occupied by the Abbey Row Community Centre):

[My teacher] was Mr Lancelot Whale, an excellent classical scholar, a humorist, and a worthy man. He had a supreme antipathy to the puns which his very uncommon name frequently gave rise to; inasmuch, that he made his son spell the word Wale, which only occasioned the young man being nicknamed the Prince of Wales by the military mess to which he belonged. As for Whale senior, the least allusion to Jonah, or the terming him an odd fish, or any similar quibble, was sure to put him beside himself. In point of knowledge and taste, he was far too good for the situation he held, which only required that he should give his scholars a rough foundation in the Latin language. My time with him, though short, was spent greatly to my advantage and his gratification.

It was also at the old grammar school that he befriended the Ballantyne brothers, James and John, who would become lifelong friends and business partners. The elder brother James went on to study law, but in 1797 he set up as a printer and launched the *Tory Kelso Mail*, from premises which can still be seen in Bridge Street, and in 1802 printed the first two volumes of Scott's *Minstrelsy of the Scottish Border* (1802–03) from here. Scott encouraged James to move to Edinburgh, and in 1805 he bought a quarter share in Ballantyne's printing business. Four years later, he set up both brothers in a publishing enterprise, an involvement which eventually led to his financial downfall.

Waverley Lodge.

SEE ALSO: Dryburgh Abbey, Abbotsford, Ashestiel, County Hotel, Clovenfords Hotel, Gordon Arms, Dryburgh Abbey, Scott's View, Smailholm Tower, Scott's Courtroom and Statue, Traquair House, Minchmoor, Newark Castle, Tibbie Shiel's Inn, St Ronan's Well, Melrose Abbey, College Wynd, George Square, North Castle Street, Scott Monument, Loch Katrine.

FURTHER INFORMATION: Waverley Lodge is on the corner of Maxwell Lane at the south-east corner of the Knowes car park. Walton Hall, a villa built and occupied by the Ballantyne brothers in the 1820s, can be seen in Roxburgh Street. Beardie's House, the home of Scott's Jacobite great-grandfather Walter Scott, who derived his nickname from an enormous beard, which he wore 'in token of his regret for the banished dynasty of Stuart', can be seen opposite Kelso Old Church, facing The Butts. None of these properties is open to the public. Kelso Tourist Information 0870 608 0404.

Smailholm

Sandyknowe Farm and Smailholm Tower
Childhood home of Sir Walter Scott (1771–1832)

In 1773, when he was about 18 months old, Walter Scott contracted poliomyelitis, which left him with a limp for the rest of his life. He then lived with his family at 25 George Square in Edinburgh, but after medical advice he was sent to live with his paternal grandfather at Sandyknowe Farm, where it was hoped fresh air and exercise would improve his health. Amongst his earliest memories were being wrapped in the newly flayed skin of a sheep to attempt a cure and being carried by the ewe-milkers to the crags above the house, where he was once forgotten about and left there during a thunderstorm, only to be found again clapping his hands at the lightning and crying 'Bonny, bonny!' Up on the crags the cow-bailie would blow a particular note on his whistle, alerting the maid-servants at the house that he needed to be carried home again. On winter evenings he would listen to his grandmother's tales around the fireside or to his Aunt Janet reading from the Bible, and it was at Sandyknowe that he was given his first pony, a Shetland mare named Marion. Thus began young Wattie's lifelong love affair with the Border country, a love he recalled in the introduction to Canto III of *Marmion* in 1808:

> And well the lonely infant knew
> Recesses where the wall-flower grew,
> And honey-suckle loved to crawl
> Up the low crag and ruined wall.
> I deemed such nooks the sweetest shade
> The sun in all his round surveyed;
> And still I thought that shattered tower
> The mightiest work of human power.

Smailholm Tower.

17

It would remain his world, apart from a trip to take the waters at Bath for a year in 1775–76, until his return two years later to the family home at George Square when he was between seven and eight years old. 'I felt the change,' he wrote, 'from being a single indulged brat, to becoming a member of a large family, very severely.'

SEE ALSO: Dryburgh Abbey, Abbotsford, Ashestiel, County Hotel, Clovenfords Hotel, Gordon Arms, Dryburgh Abbey, Scott's View, Scott's Courtroom and Statue, Traquair House, Minchmoor, Waverley Lodge, Newark Castle, Tibbie Shiel's Inn, St Ronan's Well, Melrose Abbey, College Wynd, George Square, North Castle Street, Scott Monument, Loch Katrine.

FURTHER INFORMATION: Smailholm Tower was built in the early fifteenth century and is open to the public, offering magnificent views of the Cheviots, the Eildons and the Lammermuirs. The tower was also the setting for 'The Eve of St John', one of Scott's earliest ballads featured in the *Minstrelsy of the Scottish Border*, and the inspiration for Avenel Castle in *The Monastery* (1820). From St Boswells on the A68 take the B6404 signposted for Kelso. About three miles further on, Smailholm Tower will appear on your left set back from the road. Follow the Historic Scotland signs to the tower, which will lead you through the farmyard of Sandyknowe. Open daily April to September. December to March weekends only. Tel: 01573 460365.

Dryburgh

Dryburgh Abbey
The tomb of Sir Walter Scott

> The court-yard and all the precincts of Abbotsford were crowded with uncovered spectators as the procession was arranged; and as it advanced through Darnick and Melrose, and the adjacent villages, the whole population appeared at their doors in like manner – almost all in black. The train of carriages extended, I understand over more than a mile; the yeomanry followed in great numbers on horseback; and it was late in the day ere we reached Dryburgh . . .
> The wide enclosure at the Abbey of Dryburgh was thronged with old and young; and when the coffin was taken from the hearse, and again laid on the shoulders of the afflicted serving-men, one deep sob burst from a thousand lips. Mr. Archdeacon Williams read the Burial Service of the Church of England; and thus, about half-past five o'clock in the evening of Wednesday the 26th September 1832, the remains of Sir Walter Scott were laid by the side of his wife in the sepulchre of his ancestors.
>
> J.G. Lockhart, *The Life of Sir Walter Scott* (1837–38)

Nestling on the banks of the River Tweed, this imposing twelfth-century monastic ruin seems a fitting resting place for 'the mighty minstrel'. Scott's tomb is situated in one of the ruined aisles that once belonged to his forbears – the Haliburtons of Merton, an ancient baronial family and from whom his paternal grandmother was descended. Lady Scott was buried there in May 1826; Sir Walter himself on 26 September 1832; his son, Colonel Sir Walter Scott, in February 1847; and John Gibson Lockhart, 'his son-in-law, biographer, and friend', in November 1854.

In his *Minstrelsy of the Scottish Border* Scott recounts the tale of the Nun of Dryburgh, who lived in a vault amid the ruined abbey, leaving it only when darkness had fallen in search of food:

> But it was believed that it was occasioned by a vow that, during the absence of a man to whom she was attached, she would never look upon the sun. Her lover never returned. He fell during the civil war of 1745–46, and she never more beheld the light of day.

The north transept of Dryburgh Abbey, the last resting place of Sir Walter Scott.

SEE ALSO: Abbotsford, Ashestiel, County Hotel, Clovenfords Hotel, Gordon Arms, Scott's View, Sir Walter Scott Way, Smailholm Tower, Scott's Courtroom and Statue, Traquair House, Minchmoor, Waverley Lodge, Newark Castle, Tibbie Shiel's Inn, St Ronan's Well, Melrose Abbey, College Wynd, George Square, North Castle Street, Scott Monument, Loch Katrine.

FURTHER INFORMATION: Dryburgh Abbey (01835 822381) is situated five miles south-east of Melrose, near the village of St Boswells. From the A68 take the B6404, St Boswells to Kelso road, and turn off at the B6356, signposted to Dryburgh Abbey.

Robert Burns (1759–96) visited the ruins of Dryburgh on 10 May 1787, as did William and Dorothy Wordsworth on 20 September 1803.

Temple of the Muses
A memorial to James Thomson (1700–48), dramatist and poet, best remembered for writing 'Rule Britannia'

> So long, sweet Poet of the year!
> Shall bloom that wreath thou well hast won;
> While Scotia, with exulting tear,
> Proclaims that Thomson was her son.
>> Robert Burns, from 'Address to the
>> Shade of Thomson' (1791)

It's ironic that two Scotsmen should have written a poem which is now recognised the world over as the unofficial English national anthem. James Thomson and David Mallet's (c.1705–65) 'Rule Britannia', put to music by Thomas Arne around 1740, is now indelibly stamped on the psyche of every patriotic Englishman. Although both gained reputations as formidable poets in their day, it was James Thomson who would become revered as one of the great Scottish poets and become regarded as the first nature poet and forerunner of British Romanticism, inspiring Robert Burns, William Wordsworth, Samuel Taylor Coleridge and the English romantic painter J.M.W. Turner. Today he is all but forgotten. He was born on 11 September 1700 in the Borders village of Ednam, near Kelso, the third son and fourth child of Beatrix Trotter and Thomas Thomson, a minister. Shortly after his birth the family moved to Southdean, near Jedburgh. In 1715 he attended Edinburgh University, where he studied divinity. He left Edinburgh in 1725, without a degree, and headed for London seeking success as a poet and dramatist.

In London he worked as a tutor and rubbed shoulders with Sir Robert Walpole, John Arbuthnot, Alexander Pope and Thomas Gray. Soon he began publishing poetry – *The Seasons* (1726–30) and *The Castle of Indolence* (1748) are generally regarded as his finest work – but it was as a dramatist that he would become best known in his own lifetime, thanks notably to the musical entertainment *Alfred* (1740), which contains the famous 'Rule Britannia'. His tragedies include *Sophonisba* (1729), *Agamemnon* (1738), *Edward and Eleonora* (1739) and *Coriolanus* (1748). He died in Richmond in 1748 and is buried in the local churchyard. In 1817 the 11th Earl of Buchan erected the Temple of the Muses as a tribute to James Thomson on Bass Hill, near the village of Dryburgh.

SEE ALSO: Robert Burns.

FURTHER INFORMATION: The Temple of the Muses is located on Bass Hill next to the suspension bridge. The temple originally contained a statue of Apollo, but this disappeared years ago. A new sculpture was erected in 2002 by local sculptor Siobhan O'Hehir, inspired by Thomson's *The Seasons*. An obelisk also commemorates Thomson just outside Kelso on the Ednam road. James Thomson's memory is also honoured by a memorial in the Poets' Corner of Westminster Abbey.

Bemersyde

Scott's View
Favourite view of Sir Walter Scott

The stunning view of the Eildon Hills from Bemersyde, with the River Tweed meandering in the foreground, was said to be one of Sir Walter Scott's favourite Border views. Scott's funeral cortège passed this spot in the late afternoon of Wednesday, 26 September 1832, and legend has it that the horse pulling the hearse taking him to his interment at nearby Dryburgh Abbey halted here, as was its custom to do during their outings together. However, the real reason for the hold-up is explained by Scott's son-in-law, J.G. Lockhart, in *The Life of Sir Walter Scott* (1837–38):

> Some accident, it was observed, had caused the hearse to halt for several minutes on the summit of the hill at Bemersyde – exactly where a prospect of remarkable richness opens, and where Sir Walter had always been accustomed to rein up his horse.

SEE ALSO: Dryburgh Abbey, Abbotsford, Ashestiel, County Hotel, Clovenfords Hotel, Gordon Arms, Dryburgh Abbey, Sir Walter Scott Way, Smailholm Tower, Scott's Courtroom and Statue, Traquair House, Minchmoor, Waverley Lodge, Newark Castle, Tibbie Shiel's Inn, St Ronan's Well, Melrose Abbey, College Wynd, George Square, North Castle Street, Scott Monument, Loch Katrine.

FURTHER INFORMATION: From the B6404, St Boswells to Kelso road, turn off along the B6356, signposted to Dryburgh Abbey. About one mile along this road there is a junction signposted for Scott's View to the right. Follow this road for about two miles. OS ref: NT594343.

Denholm

3 Main Street
Birthplace of James Murray (1837–1915), philologist, lexicographer and inspirational editor of the *Oxford English Dictionary*

> James Boswell: What would you say, sir, if you were told that in a hundred years' time a bigger and better dictionary than yours would be compiled by a Whig?
> Samuel Johnson: A Dissenter? A Scotsman?
> James Boswell: And that the University of Oxford would publish it.
> Samuel Johnson: Sir, in order to be facetious it is not necessary to be indecent!
>> From a dream of James Murray's, no doubt of dubious authenticity, but oft quoted by him in his dotage

The *Oxford English Dictionary* (*OED*) had several editors during its colourful 71-year gestation period, but it was Scottish philologist James Murray who saved this monumental enterprise from turning turtle, culminating with the publication of the first edition in 1928 and described by Prime Minister Stanley Baldwin as 'The greatest enterprise of its kind in history.' Today the *OED* still towers above its competitors, and the name of James Murray remains synonymous with its triumph.

Born 7 February 1837, the son of a linen draper, he left school at 14, as his family were too poor to send him to college. He immersed himself in local geology, botany, wildlife and archaeological digs, and taught himself astronomy, phonetics, bookbinding and how to illuminate manuscripts, leaving no stone unturned in his quest for knowledge. He even taught ten-year-old Alexander Graham Bell the

basic principles of electricity and can therefore lay claim to having been a catalyst for the invention of the electric telephone. He became an assistant schoolmaster when he was seventeen, in the nearby town of Hawick, graduating to headmaster within three years. 'A day away from Hawick is a day wasted' runs a local saying. Murray obviously took this literally and remained in his post for ten years, but rural anonymity was not to be his destiny.

In 1861, aged 25, he married local music teacher Maggie Scott, with whom he had a baby girl. Within three years both mother

3 Main Street, birthplace of James Murray.

21

and daughter had died, leaving James, who by this time was living in London and working as a humble bank clerk, alone. Shortly afterwards he married Ada Ruthven, a woman much more his social and intellectual equal, in a union which produced 11 children. He left the bank and took up a teaching post at Mill Hill School in north London, and in 1873 published *The Dialect of the Southern Counties of Scotland*, a work which established his reputation as a serious philological scholar.

He was now a member of the exclusive Philological Society, whose distinguished, and often eccentric, members included Henry Sweet, the phonetician on whom George Bernard Shaw based his character Henry Higgins in *Pygmalion*, and Frederick Furnivall, secretary of the Philological Society and Kenneth Grahame's inspiration for the water rat in *The Wind in the Willows*. Furnivall became one of the early editors of the great dictionary and was instrumental in persuading James Murray to take the helm of the gargantuan project, which had its beginnings on 5 November 1857, when the eminent Victorian divine Richard Chenevix Trench gave a speech at the London Library 'On Some Deficiencies in Our English Dictionaries'. What Trench outlined in his speech would basically become the blueprint for all modern dictionaries, emphasising that the lexicographer's job was not about being selective with words, but about including all words, stating that they were historians, not critics. This basic principle was the key to the success of the great dictionary, but what it proposed was a monumental undertaking, outwith the ability of any one individual.

It took another year before the Philological Society set the wheels in motion, and on 7 January 1858 the official go-ahead was given to begin a new dictionary. The society called it *A New English Dictionary on Historical Principles*, which was later to be known as the *Oxford English Dictionary*. Its first editor was Herbert Coleridge (the poet's grandson), who was succeeded by the outlandish Frederick Furnivall, lover of life and pretty young ladies. Had Furnivall remained editor, it's likely that the great enterprise would have hit the rocks, or at best wallowed in mediocrity and muddle, and it was only with the engagement of James Murray as third editor in 1879 that new impetus and energy really began to grip the enterprise. Murray edited the dictionary from a corrugated-iron shed he built in the grounds of Mill Hill School, which became known as the Scriptorium. Material for the dictionary was acquired by collating around five million contributed quotations supplied by nearly two thousand volunteer readers, who had undertaken to scrutinise the literature of English throughout its history under the direction of Murray. Many of these learned contributors were equally as eccentric and peculiar as the members of the Philological Society, and included American army surgeon William Chester Minor, a homicidal lunatic confined to Broadmoor Asylum for murder, and the hermit and self-taught philologist Fitzedward Hall.

Everyone, including Murray, underestimated the time required to complete the great work. The first instalment was published in 1884, covering 'A' to 'ant', and was three hundred and fifty-two pages in length; by 1900 four and a half volumes had been published, reaching the letter 'H'. Seventy years after the Philological Society's resolution to start work on a new dictionary, the final section was issued in 1928. Much to his regret, James Murray never saw the complete *OED*, as he died from prostate cancer on 26 July 1915. He would have had good reason to rest on his laurels, though, as the end

James Murray and assistants in the Oxford Scriptorium.

result ran to 12 volumes, defining 414,825 words, with 1,827,306 illustrative quotations. He lost only one word: 'bondmaid'. It was mislaid by Murray, but history will forgive him.

FURTHER INFORMATION: Murray's birthplace faces onto the village green and is marked by a plaque. In the middle of the green is an obelisk erected to the memory of John Leyden (1775–1811), the son of a local shepherd who did not follow in his father's footsteps, but mastered many oriental languages, became a successful poet and assisted Walter Scott in his ballad-collecting expeditions for his *Minstrelsy of the Scottish Border*. After various appointments in India and the Far East, he died of fever in Java. His birthplace is the low, thatched, whitewashed cottage in the north-east corner of the village green, diagonally opposite Murray's birthplace.

FURTHER READING: S. Winchester, *The Meaning of Everything* (Oxford University Press, 2003); S. Winchester, *The Surgeon of Crowthorne* (Viking, 1998); K.M.E. Murray, *Caught in the Web of Words: James A.H. Murray and the Oxford English Dictionary* (Yale University Press, 1977).

Bedrule

The Kirkyard
Grave of Jean Elliot (1727–1805), author of 'The Flowers of the Forest'

In 1513 King James IV of Scotland declared war on England to honour the Auld Alliance between Scotland and France, and to divert Henry VIII's troops from their war with Louis XII. Scotland lost over 10,000 men to the English army, commanded by Thomas Howard, Earl of Surrey. Over a third of the Scottish army was killed, including nobles from almost every family, and the king himself was amongst the slain. Written in Scots, 'The Flowers of the Forest' is a lament for the Scottish defeat at Flodden and conveys the grief of those who lost their young men. Solo bagpipe versions of the song are still played at services of remembrance and funerals today.

It was written by Jean Elliot, third daughter of Sir Gilbert Elliot, Second Baronet of Minto. Not much is known about Jean Elliot, but she has been described as having an aristocratic bearing and

23

Bedrule Kirkyard.

of 'possessing a sensible face, a slender and well shaped figure'. Border legend claims she wrote the ballad for a bet with her elder brother Gilbert, who challenged her to write a song about Flodden after they returned home from a party one night. The prize he offered was said to be a pair of gloves or coloured ribbons. Gilbert, thankfully, lost the bet, but for many years his retiring sister tried to disown the song and many took it for an ancient ballad. Robert Burns called it a 'fine ballad . . . the manners are indeed old, but the language is of yesterday'.

The ballad was first published by David Herd in 1776 and uses a tune which appears in the Skene Manuscript of 1630 as 'The Flowres of the Forrest'. There are actually three songs from the same period called 'The Flowers of the Forest', all written by women, but only Jean Elliot's ballad is about the Battle of Flodden. None of Jean Elliot's other work has survived. She remained unmarried all her life and died at her brother's home at Mount Teviot on 29 March 1805. She went to her grave a one-hit wonder, but more likely she was an undiscovered poetic genius.

The Flowers of the Forest

I've heard them lilting, at the ewe-milking,
Lasses a' lilting before dawn of day;
But now they are moaning on ilka green loaning;
The flowers of the forest are a' wede awae.

As bughts, in the morning, nae blythe lads are scorning;
Lasses are lonely, and dowie, and wae;
Nae daffing, nae gabbing, but sighing and sabbing;
Ilk ane lifts her leglin, and hies her awae.

In har'st, at the shearing, nae youths now are jeering;
Bandsters are runkled, and lyart or gray;
At fair, or at preaching, nae wooing, nae fleeching;
The flowers of the forest are a' wede awae.

At e'en, in the gloaming, nae younkers are roaming
'Bout stacks wi' the lasses at bogle to play;
But ilk maid sits dreary, lamenting her deary –
The flowers of the forest are a' wede awae.

Dool and wae for the order, sent our lads to the Border!
The English for ance, by guile wan the day:
The flowers of the forest that fought aye the foremost,
The prime of our land, are cauld in the clay.

We'll hae nae mair lilting, at the ewe-milking;
Women and bairns are heartless and wae,
Sighing and moaning on ilka green loaning –
The flowers of the forest are a' wede awae.

Melrose

Abbotsford
Home of Sir Walter Scott

Another twenty minutes or half-hour brought us to Abbotsford, the well-known residence of Sir Walter Scott. It lies low and looks rather gloomy . . . They showed us the part of the house in which Sir Walter lived, and all his rooms – his drawing-room with the same furniture and carpet, the library where we saw his MS of Ivanhoe, and several others of his novels and poems in a beautiful handwriting with hardly any erasures, and other relics which Sir Walter had himself collected. Then his study, a small dark room, with a little turret in which is a bust in bronze, done from a cast taken after death, of Sir Walter. In the study we saw his journal, in which Mr. Hope Scott asked me to write my name (which I felt it to be a presumption in me to do so) . . . We went through some passages into two or three rooms where were collected fine specimens of old armour, etc., and where in a glass case are Sir Walter's last clothes. We ended by going into the dining-room, in which Sir Walter Scott died, where we took tea . . .

From the diary of Queen Victoria, Thursday, 22 August 1867

Scott was appointed sheriff-depute of Selkirk Sheriff Court in 1799, and in the spring of 1804 he began looking for a house in the Borders. His first residence was Ashestiel, near Selkirk, but in 1811 he bought a small farm of about a hundred acres near Melrose called Cartley Hole (nicknamed Clarty Hole) and began building himself what can only be described as a fake castle. He named it

Abbotsford, since there was a ford in the Tweed below it and the land had once belonged to Melrose Abbey. In 1823 Maria Edgeworth visited Abbotsford and afterwards wrote, 'All the work is so solid you would never guess it was by a castle-building romance writer and poet.' Sir Walter lived at Abbotsford with his French wife, Charlotte Charpentier, and their four children, and died at home on 21 September 1832. The property is set in the heart of the Borders, on the banks of the River Tweed. Designed by the architect William Atkinson, it took six years to build and was completed in 1824. The house opened to the public in 1833, five months after Scott's death, and contains his collections of historic relics, weapons and armour, including Rob Roy's gun and Montrose's sword. Visitors can wander through his study, library (containing 9,000 rare volumes), drawing room, armouries and the dining room where he died.

Scott entertained many literary greats at Abbotsford, including William Wordsworth, Thomas Moore and Washington Irving, but his reception towards some visitors, 'especially foreigners', could be slightly on the frosty side:

> Talking of Abbotsford it begins to be haunted by too much company of every kind. But especially foreigners. I do not like them. I hate fine waistcoats and breast pins upon dirty shirts. I detest the impudence that pays a stranger compliments and harangues about his works in the Author's house, which is usually ill breeding. Moreover they are seldom long of making it evident that they know nothing about what they are talking of excepting having seen the Lady of the Lake at the Opera.
>
> Sir Walter Scott,
> Journal entry, 23 November 1825

SEE ALSO: Ashestiel, County Hotel, Clovenfords Hotel, Gordon Arms, Dryburgh Abbey, Scott's View, Sir Walter Scott Way, Smailholm Tower, Scott's Courtroom and Statue, Traquair House, Minchmoor, Waverley Lodge, Newark Castle, Tibbie Shiel's Inn, St Ronan's Well, Melrose Abbey, College Wynd, George Square, North Castle Street, Scott Monument, Rosslyn Chapel, Loch Katrine, Fettercairn.

FURTHER INFORMATION: Abbotsford is approximately two miles from Melrose. Travelling on the A68, take the A6091 Melrose bypass, heading north towards Galashiels. Turn left at the second roundabout onto the B6360. Car parking facilities can be found a quarter of a mile on the left opposite Abbotsford. Open daily from March to October, and Monday to Friday from November to February. Tea room and gift shop. Abbotsford, Melrose, Roxburghshire, TD6 9BQ. Tel: 01896 752 043.
Email: enquiries@scottsabbotsford.co.uk
Website: www.scottsabbotsford.co.uk

Abbotsford is undergoing a period of change following the death of the last member of the family to live there, Dame Jean Maxwell Scott. The Abbotsford Trust – an independent charitable trust – has been formed to secure the future of the house and gardens. The Trust will be seeking to raise funds to develop innovative projects within the Abbotsford estate.

Abbey Street
Melrose Abbey
Setting for many of the works of Sir Walter Scott

If thou wouldst view fair Melrose aright,
Go visit it by the pale moonlight;
For the gay beam of lightsome day
Gild but to flout the ruins gray
    Sir Walter Scott, from the *Lay of the Last Minstrel* (1805)

In the north-east corner of this picturesque Border town stands the Abbey of Melrose – almost midway between the Eildon hills and the River Tweed – Sir Walter Scott's inspiration for the monastery of Kennaquhair in his novel *The Monastery* (1820) and its sequel *The Abbot* (1820), set in the reign of Elizabeth. Scott and his family were frequent visitors to the town, as his home at Abbotsford was only a couple of miles away, and his daughter and her husband lived in neighbouring Chiefswood. All that remains of the Abbey today is the ruins of the church, but it was founded in 1136 when David I granted 'the lands of Melros' to a Cistercian order of monks from Rievaulx in Yorkshire. Beneath the site of the high altar is thought to be the burial place of the heart of Robert the Bruce, and like most historic abbeys it has been repeatedly restored and destroyed over the centuries. The ruins were repaired in 1822 at the expense of the Duke of Buccleuch, supervised by Scott, who was disgusted by years of litter and the removal of stonework by locals for their own use – a charge which was laid at Scott's own door by Washington Irving, who accused him of carrying off 'morsels from the ruins of Melrose Abbey' to be incorporated in Abbotsford. What Irving actually saw was probably plaster-cast copies. Scott was a collector of curious mementoes of the past, but he was no vandal.

A doorway that opens off the north aisle is the 'steel-clenched postern door' by which Scott makes the old monk introduce William of Deloraine to the church in the *Lay of the Last Minstrel*, and it leads to where the cloisters would have stood. The walls have a number of false Gothic arches, beautifully preserved. In the wall, above the site of the high altar, are the remains of the tracery of the east window where Scott described the moon shining 'through slender shafts of shapely stone'.

Robert Burns visited the abbey in 1787 during his Border tour, describing it as 'that far-famed glorious ruin'. Scott guided William

and Dorothy Wordsworth over the ruins during their Scottish tour of 1803, but Dorothy was not particularly impressed:

> [It] is of considerable extent, but unfortunately it is almost surrounded by insignificant houses, so that when you are close to it you see it entirely separated from many rural objects; and even when viewed from a distance the situation does not seem to be particularly happy, for the vale is broken and disturbed and the abbey at a distance from the river, so that you do not look upon them as companions to each other.

Queen Victoria, on the other hand, thought it looked 'very ghostlike'.

SEE ALSO: Dryburgh Abbey, Abbotsford, Ashestiel, County Hotel, Clovenfords Hotel, Gordon Arms, Dryburgh Abbey, Scott's View, Smailholm Tower, Scott's Courtroom and Statue, Traquair House, Minchmoor, Waverley Lodge, Newark Castle, Tibbie Shiel's Inn, St Ronan's Well, College Wynd, George Square, North Castle Street, Scott Monument, Sir Walter Scott Way, Loch Katrine.

FURTHER INFORMATION: Abbey Street is just off the Market Square. Tel: 01896 822562. Open all year.

FURTHER READING: Bower, *Description of the Abbeys of Melrose* (Kelso, 1813); Morton, *Monastic Annals of Teviotdale* (Edinburgh, 1832).

Old Newton Road
The Eildon Tree Stone
Where Thomas the Rhymer was transported to Elfland

> True Thomas lay on the Huntlie Bank;
> A ferlie he spied wi his ee;
> And there he saw a lady bright,
> Come riding down by the Eildon tree

Traditional

From the fourteenth century to the early seventeenth century the Borderlands were awash with the plundering and pillaging of feuding families on both sides of the border. Known as reivers (robbers, freebooters), they came from all strata of society, from shepherd to local laird, from labourer to earl. They were not empire builders or out for riches; it was simply their way of enduring the struggle to survive. This wild and troubled backdrop created a rich oral tradition of ballads and storytelling, known collectively as the 'Border Ballads': songs and stories of love, great battles, local heroes, mystery and the supernatural, all by unknown authors and travelling minstrels. The people who composed them were mostly illiterate, but the strength of the stories probably derives from the fact that they could not read or write. The Border Ballads cover a vast area, too vast for this small volume, but the 'further reading' section will open up its riches for you if you wish to dig deeper. A good start, however, would be to visit the Eildon Tree Stone, where Thomas Learmont of Ercildoune, known as Thomas the Rhymer, met the Queen of Elfland. He is often described as the 'Father of Scottish poetry' and is probably the author of *Sir Tristram* and *Prophecy*, best known in its ballad versions. These tell how, as he lay on Huntly Bank, the Fairy Queen rode by on a

The Eildon Tree Stone.   Tam Wight, the 'Pig Man'.

milk-white palfrey and how, having kissed her under the Eildon Tree, he was taken by her to Elfland, where through the bite of an apple he gained a perilous guerdon, the tongue that could never lie. Seven years he tarried in Elfland, and then he was permitted to revisit earth only on the condition that he should, when summoned, return to his mistress the queen. And so, as he sat one evening carousing in his tower with some friends, a messenger rushed in, in breathless haste, to beg him to come forth and break the spell of a portent which troubled the village. Straightaway the Rhymer obeyed the summons, and hurrying out saw a hart and a hind from the neighbouring forest pacing slowly and stately up and down the street. The animals at sight of him quietly made off for the forest; and, with a last farewell to Ercildoune, True Thomas followed them, thenceforth to 'dree his weird' (endure his fate) in Fairyland.

This folklore survived orally for hundreds of years, until the early nineteenth century when it was collected (sometimes 'improved') and printed by Sir Walter Scott in his three-volume *The Minstrelsy of the Scottish Border*. Scott had distinguished help in this massive undertaking, notably from James Hogg (1770–1835), John Leyden and Robert Shortreed. When Scott's *Minstrelsy* was published in 1802, it came in for severe criticism from James Hogg's mother Margaret. 'There was never ane o' my sangs prentit till ye prentit them yoursel', and ye have spoilt them awthegither. They were made for singin' and no' for readin', but ye have broken the charm now, an' they'll never be sung mair.'

But Scott's *Minstrelsy* was not definitive, and 200 years later, in 2006, *The New Minstrelsy of the Scottish Border* was collected and compiled by Border poet Walter Elliot, a descendant of James Hogg. It is a history seen through the eyes of ordinary Borderers who express their feelings in poetry – the dykers, shepherds, housewives, ministers, shoemakers, doctors, farmers, bakers, drunkards, land girls, poachers, soldiers, mill workers, teachers, sailors and tramps. One of these ordinary Borderers with an extraordinary talent for words was Tam the 'Pig Man' from Morebattle:

> Late yin Sunday efternin, I happened tae espy,
> Sae cleverly was she concealed, I nearly passed her by.
> But, as luck or fate might have it, I turned aside ma heid,
> There wis nature's camouflage, strivin' tae mislead.

Under the Eildon Tree . . .

Where I might have clapped ma clumsy fit, her sma een
    sair distressed,
Wis a brave wee mother paitrick sittin' tightly on her
    nest.
'Now dinna fash yer anxious heid', says I 'ma bonnie
    bird.
Settle doon, and dinna fret, mine is a freendly word.'

Yer a brave yin no tae scoot awa' on lightnin' little legs,
Prepared tae gie yer life, it seems, tae save yer precious
    eggs.
I grieve tae think sic men exist tae fell ye wi' a stane,
Wi' nae thought for yer labour lost, and nae thought for
    yer pain.

          Tam Wight (1926–74), from 'The Little Paitrick'

SEE ALSO: Sir Walter Scott, James Hogg, John Leyden.

FURTHER INFORMATION: To find the Eildon Tree Stone take the road
out of Melrose past the Ship Inn, turn left onto the A6091 and
almost immediately turn right at the signpost to the cemetery.
You will find the stone at the road end.

Ercildoune was the old name for Earlston, situated about
seven miles north-east of Melrose on the A68, and a fragment of
the 'Rhymer's Tower' still stands between the town and Leader
Water. A stone in the wall of Earlston Parish Church bears the
inscription 'Auld Rhymer's race lies in this place'.

FURTHER READING: Walter Elliot, *The Ballads Trail* (Scottish
Borders Tourist Board, 2000); Sir Walter Scott, *The Minstrelsy of
the Scottish Border* (1802–03); Walter Elliot, *The New Minstrelsy
of the Scottish Border, 1805–2005* (Deerpark Press, 2006); *Poems by
Tam Wight* (compiled and published by the Wight family, 2005
– Tel: 01573 225664); E. Kushner, *Thomas the Rhymer* (Spectra
Books, 2005); Dr J.A.H. Murray, *Romance and Prophecies of
Thomas of Ercildoune* (Early English Text Society, 1875); J. Reed,
The Border Ballads (Athlone Press, 1973).

Selkirk

Market Place
Statue of Sir Walter Scott and Scott's Courtroom

A statue of 'The Great Unknown', Sir Walter Scott, was erected in Market Place in 1839. Sculpted by Handyside Ritchie, it stands almost eight-feet high and represents Scott in his robes as sheriff-depute of Selkirkshire. Selkirk's old courtroom, which also served as Selkirk's town hall, was built between 1803 and 1804, and it was from this building that Sir Walter Scott, sheriff-depute, dispensed justice to the people of Selkirkshire. Now refurbished as a museum, the courtroom explores Scott's life and those of his contemporaries.

Scott was sheriff-depute for 33 years and doggedly manipulated his legal career with that of author. Writing in his journal for 3 August 1826, Scott emphasises his duty to both:

> From eleven till half-past eight in Selkirk taking precognitions about a row, and came home famished and tired. Now, Mrs. Duty, do you think there is no other Duty of the family but yourself? Or can the Sheriff-depute neglect his Duty, that the author may mind his? The thing cannot be; the people of Selkirk must have justice as well as the people of England books. So the two Duties may go pull caps about it. My conscience is clear.

SEE ALSO: Dryburgh Abbey, Abbotsford, Ashestiel, County Hotel, Clovenfords Hotel, Gordon Arms, Dryburgh Abbey, Scott's View, Smailholm Tower, Traquair House, Minchmoor, Waverley Lodge, Newark Castle, Tibbie Shiel's Inn, St Ronan's Well, Melrose Abbey, College Wynd, George Square, North Castle Street, Scott Monument, Sir Walter Scott Way.

FURTHER INFORMATION: Relics of James Hogg, 'The Ettrick Shepherd', can also be seen in the courtroom.

The Scott's Selkirk weekend festival takes place every December, when this royal and ancient burgh celebrates the work of Scott with two days of readings, dramatisations, re-enactments, processions and general mayhem.

Open April to October. Admission free. Tel: 01750 20096. Website: www.scottsselkirk.com

3–5 High Street
The County Hotel
Patronised by Sir Walter Scott

Formerly a historic coaching inn, the County Hotel was patronised regularly by Walter Scott and his cronies, including James Hogg and Robert Southey. Scott's daughter Sophia was prevailed upon by her father to sing the Souters' song to a gathered throng here.

SEE ALSO: Dryburgh Abbey, Abbotsford, Ashestiel, Clovenfords Hotel, Gordon Arms, Dryburgh Abbey, Smailholm Tower, Scott's View, Scott's Courtroom and Statue, Traquair House, Minchmoor, Waverley Lodge, Newark Castle, Tibbie Shiel's Inn, St Ronan's Well, Melrose Abbey, College Wynd, George Square, North Castle Street, Scott Monument, Sir Walter Scott Way.

West Port
Site of the Old Forest Inn
Where Robert Burns wrote his epistle to Willie Creech

> [Burns] coming up Leith Walk brandishing a sapling and with much violence in his face and manner. When asked what was the matter, Burns replied, 'I am going to smash that shite, Creech.'
>
> Related to John Grierson

William Creech (1745–1815) was a bookseller and publisher who published the second edition of Burns's poems (the Edinburgh edition) in 1787. Burns rashly sold the copyright to him for one hundred guineas 'to be payable on demand', but getting money out of Creech was an art in itself, and Burns had to wait over six months to be paid. During his Border tour, Burns penned an epistle to Creech at the Forest Inn on 13 May 1787:

> May I be slander's common speech;
> A text for infamy to preach;
> And lastly, streekit out to bleach
> In winter snaw;
> When I forget thee! Willie Creech,
> Tho' far awa!

Corner of Back Row and High Street
Statue of Mungo Park (1771–1806), Scottish explorer and
author of *Travels into the Interior Districts of Africa* (1799)

Sculptor Andrew Currie's monument to this intrepid Scot was erected in 1859, commemorating a man who lived and died in the true spirit of the great explorers. Born in nearby Foulshiels, Mungo Park studied medicine at Edinburgh University, and his first voyage was to Sumatra in 1793 as assistant ship's surgeon. In 1795 he led an expedition to determine the direction of the flow of the Niger in West Africa, a trip from which he was lucky to escape with his life, encountering as he did tribal feuds, famine, slavery, imprisonment, starvation and fever. On his return he retold the story of his daring exploits in one of the greatest books ever written about African exploration: *Travels in the Interior Districts of Africa*, the only British travel book never to have been out of print since it was first published in 1799. He married the same year and settled down to the life of a country doctor in Peebles, but in 1805 he again set sail for Africa on a doomed government

mission to chart the full course of the Niger. By the time he reached the banks of the Niger, only five of his forty-four-man expedition were still alive. Writing to Lord Camden back in England, Park was still hopeful of success:

I am afraid your lordship will be apt to consider matters as in a very hopeless state, but I assure you I am far from desponding . . . I shall set sail to the east with the fixed resolution to discover the termination of the Niger or perish in the attempt.

And perish he did when his boat reached Boussa, 800 miles downstream, where he was attacked by natives and drowned. Only one survivor lived to tell the tale.

SEE ALSO: Minchmoor, David Livingstone.

FURTHER READING: Mungo Park, *Travels into the Interior of Africa* (Eland, 2004); R. Tames, *Mungo Park* (Newbury Books, 1973).

Viewfield Lane
Birthplace of Andrew Lang (1844–1912), folklorist, historian and poet

There was once a woman who had three daughters, of whom the eldest was called Little One-eye, because she had only one eye in the middle of her forehead; and the second, Little Two-eyes, because she had two eyes like other people; and the youngest, Little Three-eyes, because she had three eyes, and her third eye was also in the middle of her forehead. But because Little Two-eyes did not look any different from other children, her sisters and mother could not bear her. They would say to her, 'You with your two eyes are no better than common folk; you don't belong to us.' They pushed her here, and threw her wretched clothes there, and gave her to eat only what they left, and they were as unkind to her as ever they could be . . .

From 'Little One-Eye, Little Two-Eyes, and Little Three Eyes',
The Green Fairy Book (1892)

What better way to send a Victorian child to sleep in their candlelit, shadow-strewn bed chamber than with a story dripping with emotional angst, fear of abandonment and parental abuse? No better examples of the essence of the fairy-tale genre can be found than those of Andrew Lang. He is best remembered today for his 12-book series of 'coloured' fairy-tale collections – *The Blue Fairy Book* (1889), *The Red Fairy Book* (1890), *The Green Fairy Book* (1892), etc. – in which he collected memorable fairy tales from all over the world, featuring witches, princes, glass mountains, golden birds and other classic elements of the fairy-tale world. The fairy-tale genre was no longer fashionable in the late nineteenth century, but the compilations of Andrew Lang, assisted by his wife Leonora, did much to resurrect it.

Born in Selkirk, he was the son of the sheriff-clerk of Selkirkshire and was educated at Edinburgh Academy, St Andrews University and at Oxford, where he studied myth, ritual and totemism. He moved to London in 1875 to pursue a career in journalism and his columns in *Longman's Magazine* were extremely influential. He became a fellow of Merton College, Oxford, and a distinguished Greek scholar translating Homer and several volumes of verse. His other books included *Myth, Ritual and Religion* (1887), *Modern Mythology* (1897), *History of Scotland* (three volumes, 1899–1904), *History of English Literature* (1912) and *Letters to Dead Authors* (1886). Lang was also a prolific and multifaceted writer in other fields, as a poet, essayist, reviewer, biographer, bibliographer, historian, translator, editor and anthropologist.

Much of his work is now largely forgotten but was remarkably persuasive in its day, encouraging contemporaries like Robert Louis Stevenson (1850–94), H. Rider Haggard and George Douglas Brown, but it is as a folklorist and for his collections of tales of magical and imaginary beings in far-off lands that he will be remembered by children of all ages. He died on 20 July 1912 in Banchory.

SEE ALSO: George Douglas Brown, Robert Louis Stevenson.

FURTHER INFORMATION: A plaque marking the site of Andrew Lang's birthplace is erected on a gatepost at the start of Viewfield Lane.

FURTHER READING: Roger Lancelyn Green, *Andrew Lang: A Critical Biography* (Edmund Ward, 1946).

Vale of Yarrow

Gordon Arms Hotel
Where Sir Walter Scott and James Hogg parted for the last time

In the picturesque Yarrow valley, where the lower reaches of the River Yarrow begin, is situated the Gordon Arms, a former coaching inn. It is here that Sir Walter Scott, en route from Drumlanrig to Abbotsford, said goodbye to the Ettrick Shepherd, James Hogg, for the last time in the autumn of 1830:

> I accordingly waited at the inn and handed him out of the carriage. His daughter was with him, but we left her at the inn, and walked slowly down the way as far as Mount Benger Burn. He then walked very ill indeed, for the weak limb had become almost completely useless; but he leaned on my shoulder all the way, and did me the honour of saying that he never leaned on a firmer or a surer. We

talked of many things, past, present, and to come, but both his memory and onward calculation appeared to me then to be considerably decayed. I cannot tell what it was, but there was something in his manner that distressed me. He often changed the subject very abruptly, and never laughed. He expressed the deepest concern for my welfare and success in life more than I had ever heard him do before, and all mixed with sorrow for my worldly misfortunes. There is little doubt that his own were then preying on his vitals. When I handed him into the coach that day, he said something to me which, in the confusion of parting, I forgot; and though I tried to recollect the words the next minute, I could not, and never could again. It was something to the purport that it was likely it would be long ere he leaned as far on my shoulder again. But there was an expression in it, conveying his affection for me, or his interest in me, which has escaped my memory for ever.

This two-storey hostelry was built in the early nineteenth century by John Gordon, who according to a licence application dated 21 May 1828, which can still be seen in the hotel, 'always behaved civilly and honourably to his customers'. James Hogg was his referee.

SEE ALSO: James Hogg, Sir Walter Scott.

FURTHER INFORMATION: The Gordon Arms Hotel is situated on the A708 ten miles west of Selkirk. Gordon Arms Hotel, Yarrow Valley, Yarrow, TD7 5LE. Tel: 01750 82222.

Newark Castle
Visited by Walter Scott and William Wordsworth

> Once more by Newark's Castle-gate
> Long left without a warder,
> I stood, looked, listened, and with Thee
> Great Minstrel of the Border.
> William Wordsworth, from *Yarrow Revisited* (1831)

This ruinous Border stronghold, standing on the banks of Yarrow Water, 520 feet above sea level, was visited twice by Wordsworth in 1814 and 1831. His last visit was in the company of Sir Walter Scott, and the same year he penned his 14-verse tribute to his beloved Yarrow valley in *Yarrow Revisited*. It was also at Newark that the 'Last Minstrel' is made to sing his 'lay' (a narrative poem meant to be sung) to the sorrowing Duchess, in Scott's *Lay of the Last Minstrel*:

> He pass'd where Newark's stately tower
> Looks out from Yarrow's birchen bower:
> The Minstrel gazed with wishful eye –
> No humbler resting-place was nigh

Newark is basically a massive square tower, four storeys high, built in the early fifteenth century. It was a royal hunting seat in Ettrick Forest, and the royal arms can be seen carved on the west gable. Like most Border strongholds, Newark has a bloody history. Hundreds of prisoners from the nearby battle of Philiphaugh were shot in its courtyard in 1645, and after the battle of Dunbar it was occupied by Cromwell's army in 1650. The scene of the old Border ballad 'The Sang of the Outlaw Murray' is set at Newark Castle, and Mary Scott, the flower of Yarrow, is supposed to have been born here.

SEE ALSO: Dryburgh Abbey, Abbotsford, Ashestiel, County Hotel, Clovenfords Hotel, Gordon Arms, Dryburgh Abbey, Scott's View, Smailholm Tower, Scott's Courtroom and Statue, Traquair House, Minchmoor, Waverley Lodge, Tibbie Shiel's Inn, St Ronan's Well, Melrose Abbey, College Wynd, George Square, North Castle Street, Scott Monument, Loch Katrine.

FURTHER INFORMATION: Newark Castle is situated in the Yarrow valley, four miles west-north-west of Selkirk on the A708. Open May to August.

Ettrick Valley

Ettrick
Birthplace and grave of James Hogg, the Ettrick Shepherd

> Pray, who wishes to know anything about his [Hogg's] life? Who indeed cares a single farthing whether he be at this blessed moment dead or alive? Only picture yourself a stout country lout with a bushel of hair on his shoulders that had not been raked for months, enveloped in a coarse plaid impregnated with tobacco, with a prodigious mouthful of immeasurable tusks, and a dialect that sets all conjecture at defiance . . .
> John Wilson (Christopher North), *Noctes Ambrosianae,*
> *Blackwood's (Edinburgh) Magazine*

Ettrick will be forever associated with the poetic gifts of the Ettrick Shepherd, who was a distinct oddity in the fashionable literary world of the early nineteenth century. A Border poet with a shepherd's plaid slung across his shoulders, his crudeness and outspokenness sent shockwaves through the salons and conventions of the literati. Initially, they were charmed and reverential, but eventually they tired of him and often ridiculed him as the novelty of the artistic bumpkin wore thin. A similar reception had greeted the 'Ploughman Poet', Robert Burns, a generation earlier. But

Ettrick Kirkyard.

Monument marking the birthplace of
James Hogg at Ettrick.

Hogg was no transient performing seal for drawing rooms and dining clubs. He evolved into a major writer who was admired by Byron and André Gide, and has influenced Scottish writers from Robert Louis Stevenson to Muriel Spark. In 1824 he wrote one of the masterpieces of Scottish literature: *The Private Memoirs and Confessions of a Justified Sinner.*

Hogg was born the second of four sons in 1770 in the parish of Ettrick in the Scottish Borders. When he was six years old, his father, an impoverished farmer, became bankrupt, and he was forced to leave school. Most of his childhood was spent working on farms, and in his mid-teens he became a shepherd and taught himself to write and play the fiddle. From his mother he had learned the oral tradition of ballads and folklore of the Borders. She in turn had learned them from her father, the legendary Will O'Phaup, reputed to have been the last man to converse with the fairies. Soon Hogg was composing his own songs and verses, publishing his first poem in the *Scots Magazine* in 1793, and in 1801 he published *Scottish Pastorals*, a small volume of poems. The locals dubbed him 'Jamie the Poeter'. In the summer of 1802 he first met Walter Scott while working as a shepherd for Scott's friend William Laidlaw. Scott, the newly appointed sheriff-depute of Selkirk, was scouring the countryside for the disappearing ballads of the Borders. Hogg aided Scott in his search, and the two contemporaries began a lifelong, if sometimes traumatic, friendship.

In 1810, after his attempts at farming failed, Hogg moved to Edinburgh to try to earn his living as a writer. Scott's assistance to his friend was invaluable, but he eventually achieved fame with the publication of his long poem *The Queen's Wake*, completed in Deanhaugh Street in 1813, and in 1815 *The Pilgrims of the Sun* was published. He edited the short-lived literary magazine *The Spy*, and many of his stories and poems were published in *Blackwood's (Edinburgh) Magazine*, in which he first used his now famous sobriquet, the Ettrick Shepherd. He was often caricatured by *Blackwood's* in John Wilson's (Christopher North) *Noctes Ambrosianae* as an unsophisticated 'boozing buffoon', a portrayal often accentuated and exploited by Hogg, who played up his celebrity image.

He is best remembered today for his novel *The Private Memoirs and Confessions of a Justified Sinner,* originally published anonymously because, Hogg explained, 'it being a story replete with horrors, after I had written it I durst not venture to put my name to it'. A more likely explanation may be that he didn't want to cause offence to Calvinist Edinburgh.

He lived for five years in Edinburgh at various addresses, including The Harrow Inn, Teviot Row and Ann Street, since demolished to make way for the Waverley Bridge. In 1815 the Duke of Buccleuch granted him a rent-free farm at Altrive (now Edinhope) in Yarrow, where he lived for the rest of his life. In 1820 he married Margaret Phillips, a pious woman from a Nithsdale farming family, with whom he had five children. He died on 21 November 1835 from 'what the country folks call black jaundice' (probably liver failure) and is buried in Ettrick Kirkyard. At his funeral most of the Edinburgh literati were conspicuous by their absence, except for the towering figure of John Wilson, who wept for his departed friend.

SEE ALSO: Sir Walter Scott, Tibbie Shiel's Inn, Gordon Arms, Sir Walter Scott's Courtroom.

FURTHER INFORMATION: The cottage in which Hogg was born collapsed around 1830. His grave can be seen in Ettrick Kirkyard about ten yards from the south-west corner of the church. Relics connected to Hogg can be seen in Sir Walter Scott's Courtroom in Selkirk. Overlooking Tibbie Shiel's Inn (up the hill off the A708) by St Mary's Loch is a statue of James Hogg. About four miles up the Ettrick valley from Selkirk on the B7009 stands Aikwood Tower, home of Lord and Lady Steel, which now houses a permanent James Hogg exhibition. Open Tuesday, Thursday and Sunday, May to September, 2 p.m.–5 p.m. Tel: 01750 52253. Email: enquiries@aikwoodscottishborders.com

The James Hogg Society, c/o Dr Robin MacLachlan, 8 Tybenham Road, London, SW19 3LA.

FURTHER READING: Walter Elliot, *The Hogg Trail* (Scottish Borders Tourist Board, 2001); Karl Miller, *Electric Shepherd* (Faber & Faber, 2003); David Groves, *James Hogg: The Growth of a Writer* (Scottish Academic Press Ltd, 1988); Norah Parr, *James Hogg at Home* (D.S. Mack, 1980); Mary Garden (Hogg's daughter), *Memorials of James Hogg the Ettrick Shepherd* (1885).

St Mary's Loch

Tibbie Shiel's Inn
Gathering place and watering hole for literary society in the nineteenth century

> Oft in my mind such thoughts awake
> By lone St Mary's silent lake.
> Thou know'st it well, – nor fen, nor sedge,
> Pollute the pure lake's crystal edge;
> Abrupt and sheer, the mountains sink
> At once upon the level brink;
> And just a trace of silver sand
> Marks where the water meets the land.
>   Sir Walter Scott, introduction to Canto II of *Marmion* (1808)

In 1823 Isabella (Tibbie) Shiel (1781–1878) moved with her husband Robert Richardson, a mole catcher, into St Mary's Cottage on Lord Napier's estate. Following the death of her husband in 1824, she resumed her maiden name and began supporting herself and her six children by taking in gentlemen lodgers. Said to have been a wonderful hostess with a great sense of humour, Tibbie lived to the ripe old age of 96. For over 50 years her inn, added to considerably over the years, became a gathering place for poets and writers of the time, including Sir Walter Scott, James Hogg, John Wilson, Thomas Carlyle (1795–1881), Thomas Stoddart (angler and angling poet), Mark Twain and Robert Louis Stevenson, many of whom wrote lyrics in her praise.

James Hogg, the Ettrick Shepherd, was a regular visitor to the 'wren's nest', as he called the inn. As a young girl Tibbie had worked for Hogg's mother but was no great fan of his writing, commenting, 'He wrote a deal o' trash but was a gey sensible man for a' that.' Every autumn John Wilson (Christopher North) would reside at Tibbie's with his family, and many an alcohol-fuelled evening around the fireside in the company of Hogg would have inspired their fictional dialogues in *Noctes Ambrosianae* for *Blackwood's Magazine*. The morning after one such night of feasting and philosophising, Hogg was heard to call out, 'Tibbie, bring me the Loch!'

Scott and Hogg introduced William Wordsworth to the beauties

Statue of James Hogg overlooking Tibbie Shiel's Inn and St Mary's Loch.

of St Mary's Loch, and although there is no evidence that he visited Tibbie Shiel's Inn, it's unlikely they would not have acquainted him with the wren's nest.

SEE ALSO: Sir Walter Scott, James Hogg, Robert Louis Stevenson, Thomas Carlyle.

FURTHER INFORMATION: Tibbie Shiel's Inn, St Mary's Loch, Selkirkshire, TD7 5LH. Tel: 01750 42231.
Email: info@tibbieshielsinn.com
Website: www.tibbieshielsinn.com

Tibbie Shiel's Inn is situated overlooking St Mary's Loch, on the isthmus between St Mary's Loch and Loch of the Lowes in the Scottish Borders. St Mary's Loch is situated in the Central Southern Uplands of the Scottish Borders. It lies on the A708 approximately halfway between Selkirk and Moffat. Open throughout the year but closed Monday, Tuesday and Wednesday from November to Easter. Tibbie and her husband are buried in Ettrick Kirkyard.

Overlooking Tibbie Shiel's Inn (up the hill off the A708) is a statue of James Hogg. His right hand grasps a shepherd's crook, and in his left is a scroll with the last line of *The Queen's Wake*: 'He taught the wandering winds to sing.'

Clovenfords

Clovenfords Hotel
Lodging of Sir Walter Scott

When Scott began his sheriffship in the Borders, he was still living in Edinburgh and Lasswade, and for the first four years, until he leased Ashestiel in 1804, he lodged periodically at the Clovenfords inn.

> On such occasions he took up his lodgings in the little inn at Clovenfords, a favourite fishing station on the road from Edinburgh to Selkirk. From this place he could ride to the county town when ever business required his presence, and he was also within a few miles of the vales of Yarrow and Ettrick, where he obtained large accessions to his store of ballads.
>
> J.G. Lockhart

The Border poet John Leyden (1775–1811) was a schoolmaster at

Clovenfords in 1792, and Wordsworth and his sister Dorothy spent a night at the inn on 18 September 1803, en route to a meeting with Scott in Melrose. A statue of Scott stands at the hotel entrance.

SEE ALSO: John Leyden, William and Dorothy Wordsworth, Dryburgh Abbey, Abbotsford, Ashestiel, County Hotel, Gordon Arms, Dryburgh Abbey, Scott's View, Smailholm Tower, Scott's Courtroom and Statue, Traquair House, Minchmoor, Waverley Lodge, Newark Castle, Tibbie Shiel's Inn, St Ronan's Well, Melrose Abbey, College Wynd, George Square, North Castle Street, Scott Monument.

FURTHER INFORMATION: Clovenfords Hotel, 1 Vine Street, Clovenfords, Galashiels, TD1 3LU. Tel: 01896 850203.
Website: www.clovenfordshotel.co.uk
Clovenfords is situated on the A72, three miles west of Galashiels.

Ashestiel
Former home of Sir Walter Scott

When Scott became sheriff-depute of the Borders, he was bound by statute to reside there for part of the year, and in the spring of 1804 he began looking for a house. He decided to take the lease of Ashestiel, the property of a cousin on his mother's side, who was then in India. John Buchan describes its setting in his 1932 biography of Scott as 'half-farm, half-manor, and very ancient in parts, stood on a steep bank which a strip of meadow-land separated from the Tweed. There was a little farm attached, with fields of old pasture; the garden was a beautiful old-world place with green terraces and tall holly hedges.' It was at Ashestiel that Scott composed *The Lay of the Last Minstrel*, *The Lady of the Lake, Marmion* and about a third of *Waverley*. In 1811 Scott vacated Ashestiel and moved to Abbotsford.

SEE ALSO: Dryburgh Abbey, Abbotsford, County Hotel, Clovenfords Hotel, Gordon Arms, Dryburgh Abbey, Scott's View, Scott's Courtroom and Statue, Traquair House, Minchmoor, Waverley Lodge, Newark Castle, Tibbie Shiel's Inn, St Ronan's Well, Melrose Abbey, College Wynd, George Square, North Castle Street, Scott Monument, Loch Katrine.

FURTHER INFORMATION: Ashestiel is not open to the public. The best place to view the house is at the junction of the A707 and the A72 Galashiels to Peebles road. Ashestiel can be seen on a high bank on the other side of the River Tweed.

Innerleithen

Wells Brae
St Ronan's Well
Setting for Sir Walter Scott's 1824 novel *St Ronan's Well*

> An abortive and contemptible sixth-rate novel . . . one of the weakest and most trashy productions that we have ever seen.
>
> Extract from a review of *St Ronan's Well*,
> in the *New European Magazine* (1824)

Scott was a great admirer of Jane Austen, and in 1823 he attempted a novel which he hoped would compare favourably with her style and appeal to her readers. The result was his now largely forgotten romance *St Ronan's Well*, his only novel with a nineteenth-century setting. The novel was set in the fashionable society of the spa town of St Ronan's, which not only contains elements of Innerleithen, but also nearby Melrose. Its failure, however, didn't deter droves of literary pilgrims descending on Innerleithen at the time to sample the celebrated saline waters of the well, which can still be seen today.

SEE ALSO: Dryburgh Abbey, Abbotsford, Ashestiel, County Hotel, Clovenfords Hotel, Gordon Arms, Dryburgh Abbey, Scott's View, Scott's Courtroom and Statue, Traquair House, Minchmoor, Waverley Lodge, Newark Castle, Tibbie Shiel's Inn, Melrose Abbey, College Wynd, George Square, North Castle Street, Scott Monument, Loch Katrine.

FURTHER INFORMATION: Innerleithen lies on the A72, Galashiels to Peebles road. St Ronan's Well is open from April to October, admission free. Tel: 01896 833583.

James Hogg and Sir Walter Scott were instrumental in reviving St Ronan's Games, at which Hogg was a regular competitor.

Traquair House
Inspiration for Tully-Veolan in *Waverley*

> About a bow-shot from the end of the village appeared the enclosures, proudly denominated the Parks of Tully-Veolan, being certain square fields, surrounded and divided by stone walls five feet in height. In the centre of the exterior barrier was the upper gate of the avenue, opening under an archway, battlemented on the top, and adorned with two large weather-beaten mutilated masses of upright stone, which, if the tradition of the hamlet could be trusted, had once represented, at least had been once designed to represent, two rampant Bears, the supporters of the family of Bradwardine.
>
> Sir Walter Scott, from *Waverley* (1814), chapter eight

One and a half miles south of Innerleithen stands the village of Traquair, near the right bank of Quair Water in a valley once occupied by the vast ancient woodlands of Ettrick Forest. The mansion-house of Traquair, which claims the title of the oldest inhabited house in Scotland, and which has been in the hands of the same family for over 500 years, stands in the Quair valley close to the River Tweed. The old gateway, flanked by the figures of two stone bears, is said to have suggested to Sir Walter Scott the description of Tully-Veolan in *Waverley*, but in reality the description of the house and gardens was adopted by Scott from several estates, including Craighall in Perthshire. Legend has it that the Fifth Earl of Traquair closed the Bear Gates in 1745 for the last time after the departure of his guest Prince Charles Edward Stuart, vowing never to reopen them until the Stuarts were restored to the throne. Needless to say, the gates are still locked.

SEE ALSO: Dryburgh Abbey, Abbotsford, Ashestiel, County Hotel, Clovenfords Hotel, Gordon Arms, Dryburgh Abbey, Scott's View, Smailholm Tower, Scott's Courtroom and Statue, Traquair House, Minchmoor, Waverley Lodge, Newark Castle, Tibbie Shiel's Inn, St Ronan's Well, Melrose Abbey, College Wynd, George Square, North Castle Street, Scott Monument.

FURTHER INFORMATION: From Innerleithen take the B709, St

Mary's Loch road. Open daily from April to October (weekends only in November). Tel: 01896 830323.
Website: www.traquair.co.uk

Minchmoor
Where Sir Walter Scott parted from Mungo Park

Will ye gang wi' me and fare
To the bush aboon Traquair?
Owre the high Minchmuir we'll up and awa',
This bonny simmer noon,
While the sun shines fair aboon,
And the licht sklents saftly doun on holm and ha'.
        John Campbell Shairp, 'The Bush Aboon Traquair',
        from *Kilmahoe, a Highland Pastoral, with other Poems* (1864)

Immortalised by Dr John Brown (1810–82) in his essay 'Minchmoor' in *Horae Subsecivae* (*Leisure Hours*; 1858–82), this heather-clad mountain lies a couple of miles south-east of Traquair village, rising to a height of 1,856 feet above sea level and forming part of the watershed between the Tweed and the Yarrow. The old road from Selkirk to Peebles once crossed it. Mail coaches used the route, Montrose and his cavaliers fled over it from Philiphaugh, and Sir Walter Scott's mother remembered crossing it as a young girl in a coach-and-six on her way to a ball. On the Tweed side lies the famous Cheese Well, where travellers would stop to rest, dropping bits of their provisions down the well as offerings to the fairies who lived on the mountain. It was on William-Hope ridge, to the north-east, that Sir Walter Scott bade farewell to his friend Mungo Park (1771–1806) in 1805. John Brown recalls the scene in 'Minchmoor':

> Well, it was on that ridge that the two friends – each romantic, but in such different ways – parted never to meet again. There is the ditch Park's horse stumbled over and all but fell. 'I am afraid, Mungo, that's a bad omen,' said the Sheriff; to which he answered, with a bright smile on his handsome, fearless face – 'Freits (omens) follow those who look to them.' With this expression, he struck the spurs into his horse, and Scott never saw him again . . . Scott used to say, when speaking of this parting, 'I stood and looked back, but he did not.' A more memorable place for two such men to part in would not easily be found.

Scott's premonition came true when Mungo Park set sail shortly afterwards on a doomed expedition to chart the course of the Niger where he was attacked by natives and drowned.
SEE ALSO: Mungo Park, Sir Walter Scott.
FURTHER INFORMATION: The Minchmoor road forms part of the Southern Upland Way and is signposted from Traquair village, near Innerleithen. Simply follow the marked route uphill from Traquair, continuing through the forested areas. The Cheese Well is on the south side of the footpath level with Minchmoor.

Broughton

Calzeat
The John Buchan Centre

> You are the hills that my hert kens weel,
> Hame for the weary, rest for the auld,
> Braid and high as the April sky,
> Blue on the taps and green i' the fauld:
> At ilka turn a bit wanderin' burn,
> And a canty biggin' on ilka lea
> There's nocht sae braw in the wide world's schaw
> As the heughs and holms o' the South Countrie.
>
> John Buchan, from 'The South Countrie'

Set in the beautiful Border countryside of Upper Tweeddale, this museum celebrates the life of John Buchan (1875–1940) – poet, lawyer, soldier, politician, statesman, writer, governor general of Canada and one of Scotland's most distinguished sons. John Buchan's links with Broughton hark back to his earliest childhood. In 1851 his grandfather John Masterton became tenant of the farmhouse at Broughton Green. At the age of 17, his daughter, Helen Masterton, married the Rev. John Buchan from Peebles, who had been in charge of Broughton Free Church while the regular minister was abroad for his health. After their wedding at The Green, the young couple left for Perth, where Mr Buchan had been called to the Knox Church, and it was there in 1875 that their son John was born. The family subsequently lived in Fife and later in Glasgow, but their great delight was to come to Broughton for summer holidays.

The museum is housed in a former church, where Buchan's family regularly worshipped, and features displays of photographs, books and artefacts relating to his life, including the moosehide map made for him by Native Americans, his kilt and fishing flies. A stained-glass window in the church is 'gifted by W.H. Hannay of Parkside', a name that was no doubt observed and noted by the young Buchan for future reference. There is a section in the centre on the film adaptations of Buchan's works, including the 1927 version of *Huntingtower,* starring Harry Lauder, which sadly appears to have

Deborah Buchan.

been lost without trace, although some photographs do still exist. Buchan became best known for his espionage thrillers, notably *The Thirty-Nine Steps* (1915), which Alfred Hitchcock adapted for the screen in 1935, starring Robert Donat and Madeleine Carroll. When John Buchan attended the film's premiere at the New Gallery Cinema in Regent Street, Hitchcock approached him during the interval and said, 'Tell me, my Lord, how are you enjoying the film?' to which Buchan replied, 'Well, it's very good, Mr Hitchcock, but can you tell me how it ends?'

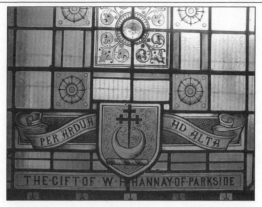

The church window viewed regularly by Buchan as a young boy, which was no doubt the inspiration for the name of his gentleman hero.

SEE ALSO: John Buchan, O. Douglas.

FURTHER INFORMATION: The John Buchan Centre is situated at Calzeat, at the south end of Broughton village, on the A701, five miles from Biggar. Open Easter weekend and from 1 May to 15 October annually or apply to Deborah Buchan, Lady Stewartby, on 01899 830362. The museum also has a section relating to his sister Anna, who wrote under the pen name 'O. Douglas'. New and second-hand books by John Buchan and O. Douglas are for sale at the centre.

'The John Buchan Way', opened in spring 2003, is a waymarked path from Peebles to Broughton, a distance of approximately 22 kilometres (13 miles), and follows long-established hill tracks and sites through the Peeblesshire countryside that were so close to Buchan's heart. The walk can be completed in one day by strong walkers, or can conveniently be split at the halfway point at Stobo by catching a bus. For further information contact Scottish Borders Tourist Board on 01870 608 0404.

Email info@scot-borders.co.uk

Website: www.scot-borders.co.uk

FURTHER READING: Vivid descriptions of Buchan's beloved Tweeddale can be found in *A Lost Lady of Old Years* (1899), *John Burnet of Barns* (1898) and *Witchwood* (1927), in which Broughton features as the village of Woodilee.

Peebles

Biggiesknowe
Birthplace of William Chambers (1800–83)

The brothers William and Robert Chambers (1802–71) were born into a mill-owning family in Peebles who hit hard times after their charitable father reputedly issued cloth on credit to French prisoners of war to make themselves clothes during the war with Napoleon. After the war, they returned to France promising to repay their benefactor but never did, and the family was ruined. William became apprenticed to an Edinburgh bookseller, and shortly afterwards his younger brother Robert set up as a bookseller on Leith Walk. When William's apprenticeship came to an end, he went into partnership with his brother. They purchased a small hand-press, and in 1824 printed and published Robert's *Traditions of Edinburgh*. In 1832 they began publishing *The Chambers' Journal*, a weekly magazine, the circulation of which reached 84,000 copies within a few years. *Chambers' Encyclopaedia* followed in 1859, published in 520 parts between 1859 and 1868. Educational publishing made both brothers extremely wealthy, and their many philanthropic gestures included funding the restoration of St Giles Cathedral. William was twice Lord Provost of Edinburgh.

Chambers was family owned until 1989 when it was purchased by Group de la Cité. In 1992 the group acquired Harrap, a London-based bilingual publisher, and the company became Chambers Harrap Ltd. The company is now part of the Vivendi University Publishing group.

FURTHER INFORMATION: Biggiesknowe runs parallel to Peebles High Street, and the birthplace of William Chambers is marked by a plaque. In 1859 he founded and endowed a museum, library and art gallery in the High Street, known as the Chambers Institution. He is buried in St Giles Cathedral in Edinburgh.

Moffat

The Sir Walter Scott Way
A cross-country walk inspired by Scott's poems and novels

The Sir Walter Scott Way is a 148-kilometre (92-mile) cross-country walk between Moffat, in Dumfries and Galloway, and Cockburnspath on the Borders coastline. It runs through lowland valleys, by lochs and reservoirs, alongside the River Tweed and its tributaries, over several corbetts (hills of height between 2,500 feet and 3,000 feet), and through Border communities steeped in history and local interest. Along the route there are numerous connections with Sir Walter Scott and the countryside that inspired many of his poems and novels.

SEE ALSO: Dryburgh Abbey, Abbotsford, Ashestiel, County Hotel, Clovenfords Hotel, Gordon Arms, Dryburgh Abbey, Scott's View, Smailholm Tower, Scott's Courtroom and Statue, Traquair House, Minchmoor, Waverley Lodge, Newark Castle, Tibbie Shiel's Inn, St Ronan's Well, Melrose Abbey, College Wynd, George Square, North Castle Street, Scott Monument, Loch Katrine.

FURTHER INFORMATION: Detailed information about the Sir Walter Scott Way, including maps required, terrains encountered, accommodation, etc., can be found at www.sirwalterscottway.fsnet.co.uk

Tel: 01896 822079.

East Lothian

Aberlady

Aberlady Bay
Memorial to Nigel Tranter (1909–2000), novelist and historian

To describe Nigel Tranter as a 'pulp novelist' would be unkind, because the quality of his writing spares him the sobriquet, but the sheer number of books he wrote during his lifetime (in excess of 130) certainly qualifies him on quantity. He wrote fact and fiction, including westerns and books for children, but he is best remembered for his historical sagas and his portrayal of Scottish history through his characters' ambitions, loves, successes and failures, popularising Scottish history more than any other author. He said he wrote 'to pay the rent' and never considered himself a writer of great talent, but his reputation as one of Scotland's most widely read and acclaimed novelists is secure. That takes talent, and no doubt he paid the rent into the bargain.

He was born in Glasgow on 23 November 1909 at 35 Brownlie Street, Mount Florida, the only child of Gilbert Tredgold Tranter, an insurance agent, and Eleanor Annie Cass, a minister's daughter. Gilbert trained as a surveyor and later became a minister of the Catholic Apostolic Church. However, his involvement with the priesthood did not prevent him speculating in diamond shares, which almost bankrupted him and lost him his licence as a minister. In 1914, in reduced circumstances, the Tranters moved to Edinburgh, where in 1917 Nigel attended George Heriot's School. He was all set to train as a restoring architect on leaving school when his father died suddenly, leaving the family once more in financial straits. An income was needed quickly, and his career in architecture was abandoned for a job as an insurance inspector.

He married gardener's daughter May Grieve in 1933 and moved into 19 McDonald

An early publicity photograph of Nigel Tranter in his mid-20s.

47

The 'Footbridge to Enchantment', Aberlady Bay.

Place in the Bellevue area of Edinburgh. He maintained that he started writing in the hope that it would help him escape the humdrum existence of the insurance business. His first book, which he also illustrated, was a work of non-fiction that chronicled his love for Scottish castles – *Fortalices and Early Mansions of Southern Scotland* (The Moray Press, 1935). Although it was a work which he later described as 'pretentious and incomplete', the book was well received. His wife, however, challenged him to write a 'real' book. In other words, a novel. The result was *In Our Arms Our Fortunes*, which, despite its snappy title, was never published. A year later in 1937 he wrote *Trespass*, which was published, but unfortunately the publisher went into liquidation, and he was never paid. Meanwhile, his first child was born, a daughter, in 1936. Two more novels, *Harsh Heritage* and *Mammon's Daughter*, were published in 1939, and in the same year a son was born. During the war, most of his army service was spent with an ack-ack unit in the Home Counties, and by this time the Tranters had moved to Aberlady on the East Lothian coast, first at Cross Cottage in the middle of the village and then Quarry House on the bay in 1951, which was his home for nearly 50 years.

After the war, he became a full-time professional writer, a process which his biographer Ray Bradfield described as follows:

> After the preliminary planning and research, he simply writes it down: he scraps a passage now and again, but by and large he does not chop and change, does not re-draft, does not re-cast. For Nigel Tranter writing a book is a bit like knitting a scarf: he starts, he goes on, he finishes, in one seamless whole.

If that's not a description of a pulp writer, I don't know what is, but that is not to diminish his craft. Nigel Tranter just went on and on and on, knitting scarf after scarf after scarf and never dropping a stitch. His best-known works were those on historical themes, notably the trilogy on the life of Robert the Bruce, *The Steps to the Empty Throne* (1969), *The Path of the Hero King* (1970) and *The Price of the King's Peace* (1971). He died aged 90 after contracting flu at his home in Gullane, and is buried in Aberlady Kirkyard.

FURTHER INFORMATION: A cairn to Tranter's memory was unveiled on 23 November 2000, the 91st anniversary of his birth. It sits at the edge of the marshes of Aberlady Bay beside the small car park just to the west of the 'Footbridge to Enchantment', the little timber bridge he crossed each day on his inspirational walks.

FURTHER READING: Ray Bradfield, *Nigel Tranter, Scotland's Storyteller* (B&W Publishing, 1999); Colin Mills, *The Nigel Tranter Bibliography* (Underhill Publications, 2003).

Haddington

Poldrate
St Mary's Church
Grave of Jane Carlyle (1801–66), wife of historian and essayist Thomas Carlyle, and one of the best and most prolific letter writers in the English language

> It was very good of God to let Carlyle and Mrs Carlyle marry one another and so make only two people miserable instead of four.
> Samuel Butler, letter to Miss Savage, 21 November 1884

Although Thomas Carlyle's reputation as one of the great historians is secure, his wife Jane's epistolary talents were nonetheless also formidable. Had she written in the novel form she may well have achieved the fame of George Eliot, George Sand or Charlotte Brontë. After her death, Thomas dated and annotated her letters, which he thought 'among the cleverest ever written'. Much has been made of Thomas Carlyle's melancholy and Jane Carlyle's frustration in the role of the 'Lion's wife' during their tempestuous 45-year relationship, but had they not met, the world would have been denied the bounteous correspondence of this high Victorian thinker and his ingenious, caustic wife. Between them they wrote thousands of letters, of which over 9,000 still survive, describing everything from revolutionary Europe to dinner parties at Charles Dickens's house, which Jane recounted in 1849:

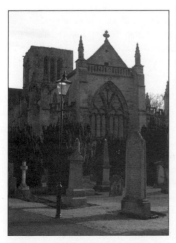

'The Lamp of Lothian', St Mary's Collegiate Church.

The dinner was served up in the new fashion – not placed on the table at all – but handed round – only the des[s]ert on the table and quantities of artificial flowers, but such an overloaded des[s]ert! – pyramids of figs raisins oranges – ach!

Thomas Carlyle first met 19-year-old Jane Welsh, the only child of Dr John Welsh and his wife Grace, at her parents' home in Haddington in 1821. After a frenetic courtship, they married in October 1826. He was 31, without a career, possibly impotent and would not achieve fame until middle age. Their first home was in Edinburgh at 21 Comely Bank. In May 1828 they went to live at Jane's family farm at Craigenputtoch in Dumfriesshire, moving in 1834 to London, where they were to spend the rest of their lives. They settled in Chelsea at 5 Cheyne Row (now renumbered 24) in June 1834, where they lived together for 32 years until Jane's death on 23 April 1866. She is buried with her father in the nave of St Mary's Collegiate Church. Thomas survived Jane by nearly 15 years, dying on 4 February 1881, aged 85, and is buried beside his parents in Ecclefechan Churchyard.

SEE ALSO: Thomas Carlyle, National Library of Scotland.

FURTHER INFORMATION: Known as 'the Lamp of Lothian', St Mary's Collegiate Church dates from the fourteenth century and is the largest parish church in Scotland. Jane Carlyle's grave is inside the church at the choir end. The birthplace of Jane, and where she entertained Thomas Carlyle prior to their marriage, is located at 1A Lodge Street, Haddington. Formerly the Jane Welsh Carlyle Museum, it is now a private house and is not open to the public.

FURTHER READING: Rosemary Ashton, *Thomas and Jane Carlyle: Portrait of a Marriage* (Pimlico, 2003). Collections of Jane's letters have been published by J.A. Froude (1883), Leonard Huxley (1924) and T. Scudder (1931). The largest collection of letters, journals and related material is in the National Library of Scotland, George IV Bridge, Edinburgh. The second-largest collection is in the Houghton Library, Harvard University.

Dunbar

128 High Street
Birthplace of John Muir (1838–1914), writer and father of the modern environmentalist movement

> Why should man value himself as more than a small part of the one great unit of creation? And what creature of all that the Lord has taken the pains to make is not essential to the completeness of that unit – the cosmos? The universe would be incomplete without man; but it would also be incomplete without the smallest transmicroscopic creature that dwells beyond our conceitful eyes and knowledge.
>
> John Muir

Several years ago the lady who lived at 128 High Street, Dunbar, opened her front door. To her amazement a Japanese gentleman was kneeling on the pavement in prayer on a square of white silk. This man had travelled from the other side of the world to pay homage outside the birthplace of the 'Great Soul', and although this gentleman was displaying overwhelming respect for a Dunbar native, very few Scots had ever heard of him. Dunbar library and the county library did not stock any of his books, and his birthplace was almost converted into a fish and chip shop. As recently as 1978 the National Library of Scotland did not possess a single copy of his works. Eventually, a plaque was erected in 1969 with the electrifying inscription, 'Birthplace of John Muir, American Naturalist, 1838–1914'.

To millions of Americans, however, this Scots genius was worth

A late portrait of John Muir by W. Dassenville (c. 1912).

more than just a plaque, and he is revered and remembered across the American landscape with over 200 sites named in his honour, including Muir Glacier and Mount Muir in Alaska, Muir Woods and Muir Beach near San Francisco, and the John Muir Wilderness and John Muir Trail in the High Sierra. In 1988 the Senate and House of Representatives of the United States of America passed a proclamation stating that '21 April 1988 is designated as "John Muir Day", and the President is authorized and requested to issue a proclamation calling upon the people of the United States to observe such day with appropriate ceremonies and activities'.

He was born on 21 April 1838, the third of eight children, to Ann Gilrye and Daniel Muir, a grain merchant, who was a strict disciplinarian and a religious fanatic, belonging to a fundamentalist sect called the 'Disciples of Christ'. Beatings from his father were commonplace and something he learned to live with throughout his childhood. School began at the age of three, and he entered Dunbar Grammar School when he was seven. Muir gives us a golden glimpse of his childhood days in Dunbar in his autobiography *The Story of My Boyhood and Youth*, written when he was over 70 in 1912:

> [I was] fond of everything that was wild, and all my life I've been growing fonder and fonder of wild places and wild creatures. Fortunately, around my native town of Dunbar, by the stormy North Sea, there was no lack of wildness . . . with red blooded playmates, wild as myself, I loved to wander in the fields, to hear the birds sing, and along the seashore to gaze and wonder at the shells and seaweeds, eels and crabs in the pools among the rocks when the tide was low.

In February 1849 all this was left behind when Daniel Muir decided to emigrate with his family to America, where he started a farm in Marquette County, Wisconsin. Here young John worked as an unpaid 'ploughboy, well-digger and lumberjack'. He attended the University at Madison, Wisconsin, where he was inspired by his very first botany lesson, which sent him 'flying to the woods and meadows in wild enthusiasm'.

He became fascinated by natural history and began exploring the western United States. In 1867 he walked a thousand miles from Indiana to the Gulf. He was captivated by the Yosemite area, where he worked as a sheepherder, all the time developing theories on its geological history and ecosystem. He successfully fought plans to annex the area as a vast sheep ranch, and so began his dedication to the conservation of the unspoiled beauty of America. In the late nineteenth century, railroads and mining companies were sweeping across the continent ravaging the forests of timber and the land of its mineral deposits. Nothing stood in the way of this flood, which was stripping much of the country's irreplaceable wilderness. Muir knew this plundering was unsustainable and confronted these powerful and dangerous cartels, who were often backed by interested parties in the Congress and Senate. Muir was completely self-taught and was often branded an interfering amateur, but most of the time, usually against overwhelming odds, his knowledge and vision won the day. His writings and speechmaking alerted the American people to the fact that their country was not boundless and inexhaustible, and if something wasn't done quickly, their great wilderness would disappear. Single-handedly, Muir transformed the consciousness of the American people, became a pioneer of the national park system, and was described by President Roosevelt as 'what few nature-lovers are – a man able to influence contemporary thought and action on the subjects to which he had devoted his life'.

Muir wrote a number of books, including *The Mountains of California* (1894), *Our National Parks* (1901), *My First Summer in the Sierra* (1911) and *The Yosemite* (1912). He married Louie Strentzel in 1880, with whom he had two daughters. John Muir died in Los Angeles on 24 December 1914, an American icon.

FURTHER INFORMATION: Scotland eventually woke up and recognised Muir's enormous contribution to the world's natural heritage. In 1976 the John Muir Country Park was inaugurated along the East Lothian coastline, stretching from the castle ruins in Dunbar to the Peffer Burn, some six kilometres to the north-west. In 1981 the local council opened the John Muir Birthplace Museum at 128 High Street (01368 865899). The National Library of Scotland now has a John Muir Archive. In 1983 the John Muir Trust in Scotland was established to conserve wild land and protect it for future generations. In 1994 a group of locals founded Dunbar's John Muir Association to further knowledge of Muir.

FURTHER READING: John Muir, *The Story of My Boyhood and Youth* (Canongate, 1987); John Muir, *The Wilderness Journeys* (Canongate, 1996); F. Turner, *From Scotland to the Sierra* (a biography of Muir; Canongate, 1997); L.M. Wolfe, *Son of the Wilderness: The Life of John Muir* (University of Wisconsin Press, 1978).

Midlothian

Roslin

Rosslyn Chapel
Featured in *The Da Vinci Code*

> When fiction is this popular, it tells us lies that we desperately want to believe.
>
> Peter Conrad, *The Observer*, 7 April 2006

When Dan Brown's bestselling novel *The Da Vinci Code* was published by Doubleday in 2003, it rivalled the sales of Harry Potter. With well over 60 million copies in print and translated into over 40 languages, it is said to be the ninth-bestselling book of all time. *The Da Vinci Code* well and truly captivated millions. Even my nineteen-year-old son read it, and the last book he read before *The Da Vinci Code* was a Ladybird about two naughty kittens called *Smoke and Fluff* when he was six. In other words, people who didn't normally read books were reading it and reading it voraciously. Almost hypnotically. Many swallowed the premise of the book, but many did not, and a stream of titles debunking *The Da Vinci Code* have surfaced in recent years, accusing Dan Brown of distorting and fabricating history. The novel is based on the contentious assumption that there is a conspiracy within the Roman Catholic Church to cover up the true facts about Jesus, especially concerning the Holy Grail and the role of Mary Magdalene. To keep itself in power, the Vatican must perpetuate the conspiracy. All clues lead the novel's two main characters, Sophie and Langdon, to Rosslyn Chapel, where they discover the location and the secret of the Holy Grail.

Rosslyn Chapel, however, didn't need *The Da Vinci Code* to make it famous. It was already famous. For centuries it has been

known for its remarkable peculiarities of architectural style, the richness of its ornaments and the conjecture over the chapel's so-called hidden 'treasure', ranging from the head of Christ to parchments revealing his bloodline. The name Rosslyn is derived from two words: 'Ross', meaning steep cliff; and 'Lyn', meaning fast-flowing water. The chapel was originally named the Collegiate Chapel of St Matthew and was built in the mid-fifteenth century by the St Clair family, a Scottish noble family descended from Norman knights who had strong connections with the Knights Templar and Scottish Freemasonry. Many foreign masons were said to be involved in its construction, a fact often used to explain some of the chapel's exuberant excesses. Built around fourteen pillars, the interior forms an arcade of twelve arches on three sides of the nave. The three pillars at the east end of the chapel are named, from north to south, the Master Pillar, the Journeyman Pillar, and the Apprentice Pillar.

The Apprentice Pillar in the south-east corner is adorned with an elaborate relief of spiralling flowers and foliage, with ornaments of Abraham offering up Isaac and dragons at its base. The story from which the pillar gets its name is a well-known Rosslyn myth. The master-mason working on the pillar's elaborate plans was said to be unable to fathom them and journeyed to Rome to view a similar pillar. On his return he discovered that his apprentice had overcome the problems and finished the work. Overcome by jealousy, he killed the apprentice with a blow from his hammer and was sentenced to death for his crime.

Sir Walter Scott mentions Rosslyn Chapel in his poem *The Lay of the Last Minstrel*, and the ceiling of the library at Abbotsford, his historic home near Melrose, is a detailed representation of Rosslyn Chapel interior. Some *Da Vinci* theorists believe Scott knew the secret of the Holy Grail, but he was just an ardent medievalist with a passion for collecting old bits of armour, and as the Grail was pre-medieval it probably would not have excited him anyway. Some early visitors to the chapel included William and Dorothy Wordsworth in 1803. Dorothy thought the architecture 'quite beautiful', and William recorded his feelings in the sonnet 'Composed in Roslin Chapel'. Visitors to Rosslyn Chapel today exceed 100,000 per year, most of them searching for associations with *The Da Vinci Code*. Their website receives around 30,000 hits a week and has an online store offering books, replicas, prints, etc., and at £7 per person for admission, one of the 'treasures' of Rosslyn must now be coffers overflowing with cash. God bless the *Code*.

SEE ALSO: Abbotsford.

FURTHER INFORMATION: Rosslyn Chapel is six miles south of Edinburgh. From the Edinburgh bypass turn off at the junction for Straiton. Follow the A701 heading towards Penicuik and Peebles. Roslin village is signposted after a short distance, and Rosslyn Chapel stands to the south-east of the village on high ground overlooking the glen of the North Esk. Open Monday to Sunday all year.

Website: www.rosslynchapel.org.uk

FURTHER READING: Father Hay, *Genealogie of the Saint Claires of Rosslyn, including the Chartellary of Rosslyn* (edited by J. Maidment; Edinburgh, 1835); T.S. Muir, *Descriptive Notices of the Ancient Churches of Scotland* (Edinburgh, 1848); S. Cox, *The Dan Brown Companion* (Mainstream, 2006); D. Burstein (ed.), *Secrets of the Code: The Unauthorized Guide to the Mysteries Behind The Da*

Vinci Code (CDS Books, 2004); A. Grant and F. Quitely, *Batman: The Scottish Connection* (DC Comics, June 1998); M. Oxbrow and I. Robertson, *Rosslyn and the Grail* (Mainstream, 2006).

Dalkeith

Newbattle Road
Newbattle Abbey College
Where poet Edwin Muir (1887–1959) held the post of warden

> I was born before the Industrial Revolution, and am now about two hundred years old. But I have skipped a hundred and fifty of them. I was really born in 1737, and till I was fourteen no time-accidents happened to me. Then in 1751 I set out from Orkney for Glasgow. When I arrived I found that it was not 1751, but 1901, and that a hundred and fifty years had been burned up in my two days' journey. But I myself was still in 1751, and remained there for a long time. All my life since I have been trying to overhaul that invisible leeway. No wonder I am obsessed with Time.
>
> Edwin Muir, diary extract (c. 1937–39)

Hugh MacDiarmid (1892–1978) once described Edwin Muir as 'not a Scottish writer at all, but an Orcadian writer', but although born in Orkney, Muir never wrote in Orcadian dialect and rarely in Scots. His finest work was always in English. Muir was a poet of quiet, almost timid emotions, whose verse often celebrates the spartan landscapes of his native Orkney. Traditional in his technique, and greatly admired by T.S. Eliot, his poetry constantly refers to the fall from Edenic innocence and a childhood long lost in the memory of a rural idyll – an idyll which was exploded when his family left Orkney for the urban nightmare of Glasgow when he was 14, an uprooting which haunted him for the rest of his life.

He was born on 15 May 1887, on a farm called the Folly in the parish of Deerness in Orkney. The family left when he was two, moving to a farm called the Bu on the island of Wyre. When he was eight, his family rented another farm called Garth, four miles from Kirkwall. Garth was not a happy time for him, which he later recalled in his autobiography:

Students at Newbattle (1951–52). George Mackay Brown front row, left.

From the start everything went wrong. The land was poor and had constantly to be drained; the dwelling house was damp; in the rooms where we slept worms writhed up between the flagstones in wet weather. My mother was always ill; my brothers and sisters, one after another, left to take up jobs in Kirkwall or Glasgow or Edinburgh; the family slowly broke up; horses and cows died; my father grew more and more discouraged, strained his heart and was unable to carry on his work. We all hated the dreary place, which gave a spiteful return for the hard work flung into it.

In 1901 the family threw in the towel and left for Glasgow, where Edwin got a job as an office boy in a law office. Within a year of his arrival two of his brothers and both his parents were dead, and he found himself in a city totally alien to him, alone and suffering from poor physical and mental health. Various menial office jobs followed, along with a conversion to socialism, and soon he began to take up writing. In 1916 he began submitting 'a series of short notes or aphorisms' to *The New Age* magazine, which was afterwards published in book form under the heading of *We Moderns*. In 1918, while working as a clerk in a Glasgow shipbuilding office, he met Willa Anderson, a college lecturer in London. They married the following year and set up house in London, where he obtained work on *The New Age* and became a drama critic for *The Scotsman*. His psychological stress at this time led him to undergo a course of Jungian analysis, which he said had an extreme effect on his writing. In 1921 the Muirs left for Prague, where they stayed for four years, and where, said Muir, 'I began to write poetry at 35 instead of at 25 or 20.' By now the Muirs were becoming interested in modernist European literature, and during their lives together they would translate over 40 novels from German, notably those of Franz Kafka. Muir's *First Poems* (1925) was published when he was 38, firmly establishing his reputation as a literary critic and a poet. Other collections followed, including *Chorus of the Newly Dead* (1926), *The Labyrinth* (1949) and *Collected Poems 1921–1951* (1952).

In 1936 Muir published a book called *Scott and Scotland*, in which he attacked the Scottish literary renaissance, a movement dedicated to using the Scots language as a serious medium of poetic expression. Muir maintained that the time had come for Scottish writers to acknowledge that they could only do their best work in English. Hugh MacDiarmid, founding father of the movement, let loose his wrath on Muir, describing him as 'a paladin in mental flight, with the presence of Larry the Lamb'. Muir never really responded to MacDiarmid's streams of invective, and though once friends, they never resolved their differences.

In 1946 he was appointed Director of the British Council, and he returned with Willa to live in Prague and later Rome. In 1950 he received an invitation to take up the post of warden of Newbattle Abbey College, a residential college for the working classes and the sole institution of its kind in Scotland, which he later recalled fondly in his autobiography:

> As soon as I returned from Rome I began work there. In October the students appeared: clerks, fitters, turners, tube-makers, railwaymen, typists, journalists, teachers, civil servants . . . they were eager and more intelligent than I had ever dreamed they could be, and to watch over them and see their minds unfolding was an experience which I am glad not to have missed . . . one of them, a miner, won a scholarship to Cambridge with a dissertation on Kant; another, a tube-maker, won a similar scholarship with an essay on *Paradise Lost*. I feel that, scattered in all sorts of odd jobs, in all parts of the country, there are countless men and women with an intellectual passion or an undeveloped gift, and that in most cases these remain lost or half-shaped, to their own misfortune and general loss.

Fellow Orcadian George Mackay Brown also studied at Newbattle, where his early writing was greatly encouraged by Muir. Brown later claimed:

> There is no doubt that the influence of Edwin Muir helped to make me a writer. If I had stayed in Orkney, I would have gone on writing, to 'be for a moment merry' in the desert of boredom and poverty. But Newbattle stimulated me and gave me a sense of purpose and direction.

Edwin Muir was made the Norton Professor of Poetry at Harvard University in 1955. Muir also wrote three novels, a collection of critical works and a memorable autobiography. He died in Cambridge in 1959 aged 71 and is buried in the churchyard of St Cyriac and St Julitta, Swaffham Prior, Cambridgeshire.

SEE ALSO: George Mackay Brown, Hugh MacDiarmid.

FURTHER INFORMATION: Newbattle Abbey College, Newbattle Road, Dalkeith, Midlothian, EH22 3LL. Tel: 0131 663 1921.

Newbattle Abbey is a sixteenth-century house which occupies the site of a twelfth-century abbey and was founded by King David I on behalf of the Cistercian order. Newbattle Abbey remained the home of the Marquesses of Lothian until being given to the nation in 1937 by Phillip Kerr, the 11th Marquess, to be used as a college of education. The public are welcome to visit the college by appointment, but its grounds are open to the public most days.

FURTHER READING: Edwin Muir, *An Autobiography* (Methuen, 1964); Willa Muir, *Belonging* (Willa Muir's memoir of Edwin Muir; The Hogarth Press,1968).

Edinburgh

Old Town

James Court
Site of the residence of James Boswell, and where he set off with Dr Johnson on their tour of Scotland and the Hebrides in 1773

> I mentioned our design to Voltaire. He looked at me as if I had talked of going to the North Pole . . .
>
> James Boswell

On Wednesday, 18 August 1773, Boswell and Johnson set out from James Court on their celebrated tour of Scotland and the Hebrides, returning to Edinburgh 83 days later on Tuesday, 9 November. Johnson was 63 and Boswell 32 years old. They each kept a journal, and while Johnson was busy cynically scrutinising Scotland, Boswell was busy scrutinising and recording Johnson. 'We came too late,' wrote Johnson, 'to see what we expected.'

Johnson's expectations of journeying through a historical time warp may not have been fully realised, but Scotland was still a pretty wild and unruly place in the late eighteenth century. It was only 28 years since the battle of Culloden and the aftermath of English repression which followed it. The Disarming Act of 1746 had made it a crime for a man to carry arms or wear a kilt. The Highlands, once a feudal and tribal place, was undergoing great change, and though cattle rustling and blood feuds were still very much a part of Highland life, the old ways were rapidly disappearing. Johnson was saddened by this and lamented the loss in his journal:

> The clans retain little now of their original character, their ferocity of temper is softened, their military ardour is extinguished, their dignity of independence is depressed, their contempt of government subdued, and their reverence for their chiefs abated . . . Such is the effect of the late regulations, that a longer journey than to the Highlands must be taken by him whose curiosity pants for the savage virtues and barbarous grandeur.

Dr Johnson in the Highlands.

Although Highland society was crumbling and would soon disappear forever, when Johnson left Edinburgh in 1773 he was still venturing into an unknown world. Even to Boswell, a lowland Scot, it was very much a strange and alien land. They travelled by post-chaise to Inverness, where the roads ended. On the way they called at the ruins of St Andrews Cathedral, visited the seat of Lord Monboddo near Montrose, were entertained by academics in Aberdeen, where Johnson was made a freeman of the city, were wined and dined at Slains Castle near Peterhead, and visited Cawdor Castle, famous for its association with *Macbeth*. At Inverness they continued on horseback with Boswell's servant and two Highland guides, and via the shores of Loch Ness they headed for the Hebrides.

They crossed over to Skye, then to Raasay, back again to Skye, across to Coll, then to Mull, Ulva, Inch Kenneth, Iona and back to Mull, reaching the mainland again at Oban on 22 October. They had trudged over mountains and through bogs, crossed lochs and sea, slept in castles and barns, and met and conversed with every part of society from crofter to laird. Later that month at the Saracen's Head in Glasgow Johnson seemed relieved and thankful to be back in the civilised world, or at least the lowlands of Scotland. Relaxing in front of a roaring fire, he remarked to Boswell, 'Here I am, an Englishman, sitting by a coal fire!'

SEE ALSO: James Boswell, Cruden Bay, Balloch, Gallowgate, Cawdor Castle, James MacPherson, Saracen's Head.

FURTHER INFORMATION: Boswell's town house was at number 501 on the western half of James Court. Unfortunately, it was destroyed by fire in 1857.

FURTHER READING: Samuel Johnson and James Boswell, *A Journey to the Western Islands of Scotland and the Journal of a Tour to the Hebrides* (Penguin, 1984); G.B. Hill, *Footsteps of Dr Johnson* (Sampson, Low, Marston, Searle & Rivington, 1890).

Lady Stair's Close
The Writers' Museum
Dedicated to the life and works of Robert Burns, Sir Walter Scott and Robert Louis Stevenson

> There's muckle lyin yont the Tay that's mair to me nor life.
> Violet Jacob (1863–1946). Quotation
> inscribed in stone in the Makars' Court

Lady Stair's Close was the chief thoroughfare for foot passengers from the Old Town to the New Town prior to the opening of Bank Street. Today it is a spacious square, but in the eighteenth century this area was packed cheek by jowl with tenements, including the adjacent Baxter's Close, where Robert Burns lodged in the winter of 1786–87. Outside the museum is the Makars' Court, where Scottish writers, from the fourteenth-century poet John Barbour to Sorley MacLean, are celebrated with inscriptions carved into stones. The house, which has had many owners, was built in 1622 for local merchant Sir William Grey, but its most memorable occupant was the Dowager Countess of Stair, who presided over Edinburgh's fashionable society and as the Viscountess Primrose inspired Scott's story 'My Aunt Margaret's Mirror'.

The museum is on three floors and is dedicated to Robert Burns, Sir Walter Scott and Robert Louis Stevenson. Artefacts connected to them on display include: a first edition of Stevenson's *A Child's Garden of Verse* (1885) and a cabinet made by the infamous Deacon Brodie that sat in young Louis's bedroom as a child; first editions of Scott's *Waverley* and a rocking horse with one foot rest higher than the other to accommodate his right leg, disabled through poliomyelitis when he was a child; and a lock of Jean Armour's (1767–1834) hair in the Burns collection, as well as a round carved oak table, made from the rafters of the Crochallan Fencibles' club rooms in Anchor Close.

SEE ALSO: Robert Burns, Sir Walter Scott, Robert Louis Stevenson, Robert Fergusson, William Smellie, the Edinburgh Book Lovers' Tour.

FURTHER INFORMATION: The Writers' Museum, Lady Stair's Close, Lawnmarket, Edinburgh, EH1 2PA. Tel: 0131 529 4901. Opening hours: 10 a.m.–5 p.m. Monday to Saturday; Sundays during August, 12 noon–5 p.m. Admission free.

The Edinburgh Book Lovers' Tour, which visits literary sites and haunts in the old town and is led by the author, departs from outside the Writers' Museum. For departure times, etc., see Edinburgh Book Lovers' Tour.

Lady Stair's Close
Site of Baxter's Close (now demolished)
Lodgings of Robert Burns on his first visit to Edinburgh during the winter of 1786–87

> He could very nearly quote all of Burns' poems from memory. I have frequently heard him quote the whole of 'Tam O' Shanter' (1790), 'Holy Willie's Prayer' and a large portion of 'Cottar's Saturday Night' from memory. He had acquired the Scottish accent and could render Burns perfectly.
>
> Milton Hay, recalling Abraham Lincoln's
> lifelong passion for Burns

Following the success of the first edition of his poems in July 1786 – the famous Kilmarnock edition of *Poems, Chiefly in the Scottish Dialect* – Burns was eager to print a second edition as soon as possible, but the printer insisted on full payment in advance. Unable to pay, he was persuaded to try for a second edition in Edinburgh.

And so the Ploughman Poet set out from Ayrshire for his first visit to the metropolis on a borrowed horse, arriving on the evening of 28 November 1786. After stabling his horse in the Grassmarket, he made his way to nearby Baxter's Close, off the Lawnmarket, where he shared lodgings with his old friend John Richmond from Mauchline, employed at that time as a clerk in a law office. Richmond's room, which he rented for three shillings a week, consisted of 'a deal table, a sanded floor and a chaff bed' and was conveniently situated below a brothel.

One of the first things he did after his arrival was to search

out poet Robert Fergusson's (1750–74) neglected grave in Canongate Kirkyard and set the wheels in motion for a simple memorial stone to be erected over his unmarked grave. He also visited the castle and the palace, stood in reverence outside Allan Ramsay's house and climbed up Arthur's Seat with all the ardour of a typical tourist; but Burns was here for much more than sightseeing.

In his pocket he carried a sheaf of introductory letters from his Masonic brothers back in Ayrshire, and within a week doors opened and his star began to rise. The Earl of Glencairn was particularly helpful, and Professor Dugald Stewart was instrumental in getting the Kilmarnock edition favourably reviewed by Henry Mackenzie in *The Lounger*, a magazine published by William Creech, who was to become the publisher of the second edition of Burns's poems – the Edinburgh edition – in April 1787. Glencairn took out a subscription of 24 copies and persuaded the Caledonian Hunt to take up a hundred copies, which earned them the book's dedication. The Edinburgh edition was heavily oversubscribed, and, after a second and third print-run, 3,000 copies were eventually printed. This edition had 22 new poems, including the 'Address to a Haggis', and the copyright was sold to Creech for 100 guineas.

Burns was twenty-eight years old, just under six foot tall, well built with a slight stoop from years at the plough, and with the twinkle in his eyes of a Don Juan. Dressed in his famous blue coat, buff waistcoat, buckskin breeches, high boots, with neck and cuffs trimmed with lace, Robert Burns the Ploughman Poet had arrived.

Everybody who was anybody made a point of meeting this latest vogue of the city's salons and drawing rooms, and Burns initially enjoyed being the focus of so much fame and attention. It wasn't long, however, before he began to feel like a prize pig brought from his pen for the amusement of the party guests. He wrote to a friend:

> I am willing to believe that my abilities deserved a better
> fate than the veriest shades of life; but to be dragged forth,
> with all my imperfections on my head, to the full glare of
> learned and polite observations is what, I am afraid, I shall
> have bitter reason to repent.

Eventually, the novelty of the Ploughman Poet wore off for the city's literati, and Burns became something of an embarrassment, with Dugald Stewart commenting, 'his conduct and manners had become so degraded that decent persons could hardly take any notice of him'. To be fair to Burns, he had probably had enough of the airs and graces of genteel Edinburgh and was reaching out for what he enjoyed best – drinking wine, wooing lassies and singing a bawdy song.

Although Burns had become disillusioned with the trappings of fame, he did achieve what he came to Edinburgh for: a second edition of his poems. He also befriended the printer of his book, William Smellie, who in turn introduced him to his famous drinking club, the Crochallan Fencibles. James Johnson approached Burns to help him with the lyrics of the second volume of his book the *Scots Musical Museum*, a collection of songs, many of which were eventually written by Burns and occupied him until the end of his life.

On 5 May 1787 Burns left Edinburgh on horseback for a tour of the Scottish Borders with his law-student friend and fellow Mason Bob Ainslie. One person Burns didn't meet in Edinburgh was James Boswell, but it's no coincidence that these two giants of Scottish literature never met. They may have both had a passion for the lassies, but political allegiances and class divided them, and Boswell kept his distance on purpose. Burns was a peasant and a supporter of the French Revolution. Boswell was a high Tory and a social climber. Burns did intimate that he would like to meet Boswell, but what could Burns do for Boswell? We could speculate on that, but what Boswell, with his photographic memory for conversation, could have done for Burns doesn't require much imagination. The failure of our greatest poet and our greatest biographer to meet must be deemed one of history's great literary tragedies.

SEE ALSO: James Boswell, The Writers' Museum, Anchor Close, Robert Fergusson, Brow Well, Ellisland Farm, Mossgiel Farm, National Burns Memorial Tower, Burns House Museum (Mauchline), Poosie Nansie's Inn, Mauchline Kirkyard, John Wilson's Printing Shop, Vennel Gallery, Burns National Heritage Park, Burns Cottage, Alloway Old Kirk, Alloway Burns Monument, Brig o' Doon, Souter Johnnie's Cottage, Bachelors' Club, Burns Trail (Dumfries), Globe Inn, Robert Burns Centre (Dumfries), St Michael's Kirkyard.

FURTHER INFORMATION: Baxter's Close, which was demolished in 1798 during the construction of Bank Street, would have been on the east side of Lady Stair's Close.

FURTHER READING: David Daiches, *Robert Burns, the Poet* (Saltire Society, 1994); James A. Mackay, *Burns: A Biography of Robert Burns* (Alloway Publishing, 2004); Ian Grimble, *Robert Burns* (Hamlyn, 1986); George Gilfillan, *Life and Works* (Edinburgh, 1856).

Anchor Close
High Street
Site of William Smellie's printing house and Dawney Douglas's Tavern; meeting place of the Crochallan Fencibles

> As I cam by Crochallan,
> I cannily keekit ben:
> Rattlin', roarin' Willie
> Was sitting at yon boord-en'
>> Robert Burns, from 'Rattlin', Roarin' Willie', dedicated to
>> William Dunbar, Colonel of the Crochallan corps

William Smellie printed the works of Robert Fergusson, Adam Smith, Adam Ferguson and later the second edition of Burns's poems – the Edinburgh edition – in 1787. Smellie was not your average, run-of-the-mill printer, but a talented editor and writer who was involved in producing the first edition of the *Encyclopaedia Britannica*

(1768–71). He also liked to drink, debate and sing a bawdy song or two, which led to his founding the renowned drinking club the Crochallan Fencibles at Dawney Douglas's Tavern. Dawney liked to sing Gaelic songs, and Smellie took the name of one of them, *Crodh Challein* (Colin's Cattle), for the first half of the club's name and Fencibles from the city's much-derided volunteer corps of militia. Its members included Adam Smith, Adam Ferguson, Henry Mackenzie and Robert Burns.

Smellie introduced Burns to the club during his first visit to Edinburgh in 1787, and the Ploughman Poet would have needed no excuse to join in the revelry after a hard day selling himself in the salons of Edinburgh society. It was at Dawney Douglas's Tavern that Burns delivered for the first time his 'Address to a Haggis' – 'Fair fa' your honest, sonsie face, Great chieftain o' the puddin-race!' – now an almost religious rite at every traditional Burns Supper. The Crochallan Fencibles also inspired many of the bawdy lyrics of Burns's *The Merry Muses of Caledonia*, verse far removed from the tea parties of the literati:

> There's no a lass in a' the land,
> Can fuck sae weel as I can;
> Louse down your breeks, lug out your wand,
> Hae ye nae a mind to try man
>
> From 'Ellibanks'

SEE ALSO: Baxter's Close, The Writers' Museum, Robert Fergusson, Ellisland Farm, Mossgiel Farm, National Burns Memorial Tower, Burns House Museum (Mauchline), Poosie Nansie's Inn, Mauchline Kirkyard, John Wilson's Printing Shop, Vennel Gallery, Burns National Heritage Park, Burns Cottage, Alloway Old Kirk, Alloway Burns Monument, Brig o' Doon, Souter Johnnie's Cottage, Tam O' Shanter Inn, Bachelors' Club, Burns Trail (Dumfries), Globe Inn, Robert Burns Centre (Dumfries), St Michael's Kirkyard, Brow Well.

FURTHER INFORMATION: The site of Smellie's printing house, including the room where Burns used to sit and correct his proofs, was at one time occupied by the machine room of *The Scotsman* newspaper. The stools from Smellie's printing house can be seen at The Writers' Museum, Lady Stair's Close.

Guthrie Street (formerly College Wynd)
Birthplace of Sir Walter Scott

Walter Scott (or 'Wattie' as he was known) was born on 15 August 1771, the ninth child of Anne Rutherford, daughter of a former professor of medicine at Edinburgh University, and Walter Scott, a solicitor and writer to the Signet. The house of his birth, along with others, was demolished to make room for the northern frontage of Old College (then known as the new college). It was situated at the top of College Wynd, near Chambers Street, and stood in the corner of a small courtyard. It was a typical dark, overcrowded and airless Old Town tenement; a warren of flats where people lived amid the stink of refuse and bad sanitation; a place where sunlight and fresh air rarely ventured. Six of the Scotts' children had died in infancy behind the walls of this cramped slum, and shortly after Wattie's birth, in 1772, the Scotts wisely moved to the clean air and leafy outlook of newly built George Square.

SEE ALSO: George Square, Scott Monument, The Writers' Museum, Dryburgh Abbey, Abbotsford, Ashestiel, County Hotel, Clovenfords Hotel, Gordon Arms, Scott's View, Smailholm Tower, Scott's Courtroom, Traquair House, Minchmoor, Newark Castle, Tibbie Shiel's Inn, St Ronan's Well, Melrose Abbey, College Wynd, North Castle Street.

FURTHER INFORMATION: A plaque high up on the eastern wall where Guthrie Street meets Chambers Street, noticed only by the odd giraffe out for a stroll, commemorates Scott's

College Wynd in 1871, shortly before demolition.

birthplace. College Wynd was originally named the Wynd of the Blessed Virgin-in-the-Fields, as the tall, gabled house at the top was built on the site of Kirk-o'-Field, where Lord Darnley was murdered in 1567 when the house he was staying in was blown to bits.

Irish playwright, novelist and poet Oliver Goldsmith (1730–74) is believed to have lived in College Wynd around 1750 while studying medicine at the university; he left without taking a degree.

25 Forrest Road
Sandy Bell's
Favourite watering hole of Hamish Henderson, poet, songwriter and guardian of Scottish folk heritage

> One morning the pub cleaner found a pair o' false teeth sittin' in a yoghurt carton on top o' the bar. A wee while later the phone rings. It's Hamish. 'Did I leave ma teeth there last night?'
>
> Charlie Woolley, landlord, Sandy Bell's

Immortalised as 'Sunday Balls in Fairest Redd' in Sydney Goodsir Smith's *Carotid Cornucopius* (1947), this pub remains very much as it has always been – a no-frills, no-tat, no-nonsense, good old Scottish drinking den. Close to the university, its clientele consists of academics, students, cloth-cap locals, and folk enthusiasts and songsters wielding fiddles. Sandy Bell's was also the favourite haunt of the late Hamish Henderson (1919–2002), generally regarded as the father of the Scottish folk revival.

'At the age of seven,' he once recalled, 'I asked my mother about a song she was singing. We had a book of songs in the house. I asked her where that song was in the book. She said, "Some of the songs we sing are not in books." That started me off as a folklorist and collector.'

Born in Blairgowrie and educated at Cambridge University, where he studied languages, he served as an intelligence officer in North Africa during the Second World War. After the war, he acted as a 'native guide' to the American folklorist Alan Lomax on

Two of Sandy Bell's most imaginative and exciting traditional musicians – fiddler Jamie Ross and guitarist Cameron Robson.

Charlie Woolley, landlord, Sandy Bell's.

his visit to Scotland in 1951 and lived for long periods with the travelling people of Scotland, collecting songs, classical ballads and stories passed along 'the carrying stream'.

'I remember in 1955 in the berry fields of Blairgowrie, picking berries and recording songs,' he said. 'Collecting in the berry fields was a wee bit like holding a tin under the Niagara Falls.'

In the early 1950s he joined the newly founded School of Scottish Studies at Edinburgh University, immersing himself in the Scottish folk tradition and building up a huge archive of songs on tape. His greatest discovery, he always maintained, was the singer Jeannie Robertson, described by A.L. Lloyd as 'a singer, sweet and heroic'. His own works included his collections of verse, *Elegies for the Dead in Cyrenaica* (1948), *Ballads of World War Two* (1947), *Alias MacAlias* (1992), *The Armstrong Nose* (1996), and various translations of the modern Italian poets Eugenio Montale, Alfonso Gatto, Salvatore Quasimodo and Giuseppe Ungaretti. Many of his songs have passed into the folk tradition, but the two songs he will be best remembered for are 'The John Maclean March', a tribute to the Red Clydesider John Maclean (1879–1923), and 'Freedom Come All Ye', often referred to as Scotland's unofficial national anthem. A veteran of many Aldermaston and Faslane marches, Henderson was a tireless campaigner for CND and the anti-apartheid movement. He believed he was the target of two assassination attempts by the South African security services, and in 1983 he publicly refused an OBE award in protest at the Thatcher government's nuclear-arms policy. Asked by the media why he refused this

prestigious award, Hamish replied, 'Simply because the woman stands for everything I detest!' – a defiant act for which Radio Scotland listeners voted him 'Scot of the Year'. Hamish Henderson died on 9 March 2002 in an Edinburgh nursing home, aged 82. The friendly atmosphere of 'Sunday Balls in Fairest Redd' is a fitting memorial to this man who dedicated his life to the survival of the Scots folk tradition and believed bursting into song was an essential ingredient of life.

SEE ALSO: The Literary Pub Crawl.

FURTHER INFORMATION: Sandy Bell's is also one of the pubs visited on the author's Literary Pub Crawl, where its ales, music and repartee have been enjoyed by literary pilgrims from all over the world.

FURTHER READING: P. Orr (ed.), *The Poet Speaks* (Routledge, 1966); T. Neat, *Hamish Henderson: The Making of a Poet (1919–1953)* (Polygon, 2007).

George IV Bridge
The National Library of Scotland

This is Scotland's largest library and is the world centre for the study of Scotland and the Scots. It also ranks among the largest libraries in the UK, housing eight million printed books, one hundred and twenty thousand volumes of manuscripts, two million maps, and over twenty thousand newspaper and magazine titles. The online catalogue records three and a half million items for public access. The NLS developed from the Advocate's Library of 1682, the legal section of which is still housed in its original premises at Parliament Square. In 1925 its entire contents, apart from its legal section, were removed to the NLS. The library also has the right to receive free of charge a copy of every book published in the United Kingdom and Ireland, based on the Legal Deposit Libraries Act 2003, and before that the Copyright Act 1911. This right has enabled the library to build extensive general collections on all subjects, though it has a special responsibility for the acquisition and preservation of material of Scottish interest. NLS is one of only five libraries in the UK today with this status.

Since 1925 the NLS has also been collecting literary manuscripts, working papers and correspondence of writers such as Robert Burns, Sir Walter Scott, Edwin Muir, Sydney Goodsir Smith, A.J. Cronin, Lewis Grassic Gibbon, Neil Gunn, Muriel Spark, Hugh MacDiarmid, Naomi Mitchison, Alasdair Gray, Eric Linklater and Robert Louis Stevenson. The NLS also holds frequent public exhibitions of its collections and has a small gift shop.

FURTHER INFORMATION: Tel: 0131 226 4531.
Website: www.nls.uk

Canongate

152 Canongate
Canongate Kirkyard

The original Canongate Kirk was located at the now ruined Abbey of the Holy Rood, adjacent to the Palace of Holyroodhouse. King James VII (James II of England) appropriated the abbey church for use as a Chapel of the Order of the Thistles and built the present church for parishioners as a replacement in 1690.

Grave of Adam Smith (1723–90), philosopher and economist

> With the greater part of rich people, the chief enjoyment of riches consists in the parade of riches, which in their eyes is never so complete as when they appear to possess those decisive marks of opulence which nobody can possess but themselves.
>
> Adam Smith, *The Wealth of Nations* (1776)

Best known for his influential book *The Wealth of Nations*, Smith was one of the great eighteenth-century moral philosophers whose ideas led to modern-day theories. He is also regarded as the world's first political economist. Born in Kirkcaldy, Fife, he was sent to Oxford at the age of 17. On his return home he joined 'the brilliant circle in Edinburgh which included David Hume, John Home, Hugh Blair, Lord Hailes and Principal Robertson'. In 1751, aged 28, he became professor of logic at the University of Glasgow. In 1752 he took the chair of moral philosophy, and his *Theory of Moral Sentiments* was published in 1759.

A shy, clumsy and absent-minded man, he lived a quiet bachelor's life with his mother, who lived to be 90. Loved by his students, he had the gift of oratory and a considerable reputation as a lecturer. He was a good friend of David Hume and discussed his ideas with the great thinkers of his day, including Samuel Johnson and Benjamin Franklin. In 1760 he travelled to France, where he met Voltaire and began writing *An Inquiry into the Nature and Causes of the Wealth of Nations*, a book which transformed the economic theories of the day by analysing the results of economic freedom, and recognising the division of labour, rather than land or money, as the main ingredient of economic growth. Smith

Grave of Adam Smith.

moved to London in 1776, and the book was published that year. In 1778 he returned to Edinburgh as commissioner of Customs. He died on 17 July 1790, after an illness. From the main entrance his grave is over on the far left against the rear wall of the Old Tolbooth building.

SEE ALSO: David Hume.

FURTHER READING: I.S. Ross, *The Life of Adam Smith* (Clarendon, 1995).

Grave of Robert Fergusson, poet who was a major influence on Robert Burns

> Mr Fergusson died in the cells.
> Entry in the Superintendent's log, Edinburgh's Bedlam,
> 16 October 1774

'O thou, my elder brother in Misfortune/By far my elder brother in the Muse,' wrote Robert Burns in epitaph on Robert Fergusson. Fergusson's poetry had a deep influence on Burns; his 'The Farmer's Ingle' clearly inspired 'The Cotter's Saturday Night'.

Robert Fergusson was born in Edinburgh on 5 September 1750 in the Cap and Feather Close, near Niddry Wynd (now Niddry Street). The close was demolished with the construction of North Bridge, which provided easier access to the seaport of Leith and the land on which the New Town now stands.

Robert was a second son born into a lower-middle-class family. His father, a clerk, came from Aberdeen farming stock. Educated privately at the Royal High School in Edinburgh for four years, Robert was awarded a bursary from the Donald Fergusson Fund, enabling him to attend Dundee High School and then St Andrews University.

He enjoyed university life. He was a good singer – a voice encouraged by a glass or several – and was popular amongst his fellow students. In May 1768, following the death of his father, Robert abandoned his studies without graduating, and returned to Edinburgh to support his mother and family. In September 1778 he

David Annand's bronze figure of Robert Fergusson.

Robert Fergusson's headstone – erected by Robert Burns.

was working as a clerk copyist in the Commissary Records Office, quilling page after page of copperplate script at a penny a page. When the Tron Kirk bell chimed eight o'clock the town stopped work. Robert enjoyed life; he danced, he sang, he drank, he became a member of the Cape Club. Each member of this club was dubbed with a 'knighthood'. Robert became Sir Precenter.

His first poems were published in *Ruddiman's Weekly Magazine* in 1771 and were written in imitation of the English style. 'Daft Days' published in 1772 was his first Scots poem and a slim volume of his works appeared in 1773, inspiring Burns to emulate his artistic vigour.

Tragically, however, Fergusson suffered from manic depression and, following a fall which exacerbated this condition, he was committed to the public asylum. He died shortly afterwards in Darien House, which, originally built in 1698 as the offices and stores of the Darien Company, had degenerated in the following century into a pauper lunatic asylum. The Bedlam Asylum stood behind the building which is now the Bedlam Theatre in Forrest Road. Fergusson's body was interred in a pauper's grave two days after his death.

Robert Fergusson wrote 33 poems in Scots and 50 poems in English, and will be chiefly remembered for 'Auld Reekie' (1773), which traces a day in the life of the city. Other well-known poems include 'Elegy on the Death of Scots Music', 'Hallow Fair', 'To the Tron Kirk Bell', 'Leith Races' and 'The Rising of the Session'.

Burns was saddened to discover that Fergusson had been buried in an unmarked grave, and in February 1787 he sought permission to erect a headstone. After it was in place, Burns took five years to settle his account with the Edinburgh architect who designed the stone, commenting in a letter that 'He was two years in erecting it, after I commissioned him for it; and I have been two years paying him, after he sent me his account; so he and I are quits . . . He had the hardiesse to ask me interest on the sum; but considering that the money was due by one Poet, for putting a tomb-stone over another, he may, with grateful surprise, thank Heaven that ever he saw a farthing of it.'

Fergusson's grave is situated close to the western wall of the church, bordered by a low chain fence. Erected and commissioned by the Friends of Robert Fergusson, a bronze figure sculpted by David Annand commemorates the poet outside the gates of the kirkyard. The statue was the brainchild of George Philp and Bob Watt, and was unveiled on 17 October 2004.

SEE ALSO: Robert Burns.

FURTHER READING: A. Law, *Robert Fergusson and the Edinburgh of his Time* (Edinburgh City Libraries, 1974); D. Irving, *The Life of Robert Fergusson* (Chapman & Lang, 1799); T. Sommers, *The Life of Robert Fergusson, the Scottish Poet* (Stewart, 1803).

Fergusson destroyed his papers just before he died. There are inscribed copies of his 1773 *Poems* and some scraps among the Cape Records, MSS 2041–2044, in the National Library of Scotland, and a few manuscripts in the Laing Collection at the Edinburgh University Library. The Edinburgh Room of the Edinburgh Central Public Library maintains a folder of newspaper clippings.

Grave of Clarinda (Agnes McLehose 1758–1841), inspiration for Robert Burns's 'Ae Fond Kiss'

> I'll ne'er blame my partial fancy,
> Naething could resist my Nancy:
> But to see her was to love her;
> Love but her, and love for ever.
>
> Robert Burns, from 'Ae Fond Kiss'

Robert Burns first met Mrs Agnes (Nancy) McLehose after she engineered an invitation for him to a tea party given by Miss Erskine Nimmo at her brother's flat in Alison Square (now demolished), off Nicolson Street, on 4 December 1787. They seem to have been well and truly smitten with each other, and that night she hurriedly sent him a letter inviting him to tea at her house in Potterrow. He never kept the appointment as he dislocated his knee shortly afterwards when his coach reputedly overturned on his way home following an evening of revelry. And so the circumstances fell into place for the start of an impassioned correspondence between the two from December until mid-March, during which time around 80 letters were written, and a relationship blossomed which would eventually inspire Burns to write one of his greatest love songs.

It is doubtful whether today's postal system could have coped with their copious correspondence – sometimes six letters each a day – but since 1773 the Edinburgh penny post had been in operation offering deliveries of letters and small parcels every hour throughout the day. Burns, who was then lodging at 2 St James Square (now demolished), used the penny post, but Nancy, careful of her reputation, often used her maid, Jennie Clow, to convey her letters.

On 8 December Burns wrote to Nancy stating:

> I cannot bear the idea of leaving Edinburgh without seeing you – I know not how to account for it – I am strangely taken with some people; nor am I often mistaken. You are a stranger to me; but I am an odd being: some yet unnamed feelings; things not principles, but better than whims, carry me farther than boasted reason ever did a philosopher.

Clarinda's headstone.

Clarinda's Tea Room – a short walk away at 69 Canongate.

Nancy replied:

> These 'nameless feelings' I perfectly comprehend, tho' the
> pen of Locke could not define them . . . If I was your sister,
> I would call on you; but tis a censorious world this; and
> in this sense 'you and I are not of this world'. Adieu. Keep
> up your heart, you will soon get well, and we shall meet.
> Farewell. God bless you.

Nancy has been described by an acquaintance as 'short in stature,
her form graceful, her hands and feet small and delicate. Her features
were regular and pleasing, her eyes lustrous, her complexion fair, her
cheeks ruddy, and a well-formed mouth displayed teeth beautifully
white.' Another said she was 'of a somewhat voluptuous style of
beauty, of lively and easy manners, of a poetical cast of mind, with
some wit, and not too high a degree of refinement or delicacy'.
She was also married to, but estranged from, James McLehose, a
Glasgow lawyer whom she had married when she was eighteen and
with whom she had borne four children (two dying in infancy) by
the time she was twenty-three. McLehose ended up in a debtor's
prison and afterwards sailed to a new life in Jamaica, leaving Nancy
struggling to make ends meet as a single parent in a flat at General's
Entry (now demolished) off Potterrow on Edinburgh's Southside.
Although separated, Nancy was still in the eyes of the law a married
woman and therefore had to be careful in her letters to Burns that
she was not in any way compromised. Soon, therefore, they adopted
for discretion's sake the Arcadian noms de plume Sylvander and
Clarinda. Burns's injury made it difficult for him to have any
opportunity to consummate the relationship and some of his letters
– through frustration – got a little overheated, one stating 'had I
been so blest as to have met with you in time, it might have led me
– God of love only knows where'. To which Nancy replied, 'When
I meet you, I must chide you for writing in your romantic style. Do
you remember that she whom you address is a married woman?'

They did meet after Burns recovered, but there is no evidence
that their relationship ever became sexual. Burns eventually left
Edinburgh in February 1788, later marrying his former lover
Jean Armour. They did, however, meet once more before Nancy's
departure to join her husband in Jamaica in a failed attempt to
rebuild her marriage. Her diary entry at the time reveals she was
still in love with Burns 'till the shadow fell . . . This day I can never
forget. Parted with Robert Burns in the year 1791 never more to
meet in this world. Oh may we meet in heaven.' Before her departure
Burns sent her a card with a lyric scrawled on it from Sanquhar Post
Office in Dumfriesshire, which began 'Ae fond kiss, and then we
sever, Ae fareweel, and then – for ever . . .'

Nancy outlived Burns by 45 years, dying aged 82 in 1841 at her
flat beneath Calton Hill. Her grave is situated against the eastern
wall of Canongate Kirkyard. The site of the house where she
corresponded with Burns is marked by a plaque at the corner of
Potterrow and Marshall Street. In November 1788 Nancy's maid,
Jennie Clow, gave birth to Burns's illegitimate son, conceived while
acting as courier for Sylvander and Clarinda.

SEE ALSO: Robert Burns.

FURTHER INFORMATION: It was the Clarinda Burns Club that
    proposed that a plaque should be erected on the site of Clarinda's

house at General's Entry in Potterrow on the wall of Bristo School in 1937. Edinburgh Corporation Education Committee thought 'the idea was totally unacceptable. It is beneath the dignity of our city to sanction such a tablet in view of Clarinda's character.' Questions were raised in the House of Commons. However, the Clarinda Burns Club stood firm, and a plaque was finally erected on 22 January 1937.

Clarinda's Tea Room is at 69 Canongate (0131 557 1888), near the entrance to Canongate Kirkyard.

5 Crichton's Close
Scottish Poetry Library

> For this is the House of Poetry. Here the heart
> finds wholeness; the spirit bursts into song.
>> Stewart Conn, from 'Flight of Fancy', on the occasion of the
>> Scottish Poetry Library's 21st birthday celebration, Friday, 4
>> February 2005

With its mono-pitch roof slung over a steel frame and walls of oak and glass, the award-winning building by architect Malcolm Fraser is deceptively simple, relaxing and, most of all, welcoming. Scottish artists were commissioned to contribute pieces, including Liz Ogilvie's glass-panelled balustrade inscribed with lines from Scottish poems, a tapestry by Ian Hamilton Finlay and a 'carpet of leaves' by Mary Bourne. As if this wasn't enough pleasure, the building also houses a collection of 30,000 items, many of which are available to borrow in person or by post (returnable by Freepost). Here you will find the poetry of Scotland in three languages – English, Scots and Gaelic.

Founded in 1984, the library's former director Tessa Ransford says, 'One of the nicest comments I've heard is that the books can breathe now. The opening up of the space is symbolic of the opening up of poetry, not just physically, but psychologically as well. Poetry has always been related to music, dance, painting and the arts, but in this building I think people will appreciate it more in its own context – taking poetry into the twenty-first century.'

FURTHER INFORMATION: Scottish Poetry Library, 5 Crichton's Close, Canongate, Edinburgh, EH8 8DT. Tel: 0131 557 2876. Email: inquiries@spl.org.uk
Website: www.spl.org.uk

Southside

Infirmary Street
Site of the Old Royal Infirmary
Where W.E. Henley (1849–1903), inspiration for Long John Silver, was hospitalised from 1873 to 1875

> It was the sight of your maimed strength and masterfulness
> that begot John Silver in *Treasure Island.*
> Robert Louis Stevenson acknowledging Henley
> as his inspiration in 1883

The son of a Gloucester bookseller, William Ernest Henley (1849–1903) came to Edinburgh in 1873 to be treated by Professor Joseph Lister for tubercular arthritis, which, seven years previously, had resulted in the amputation of his left leg below the knee. Lister's skills saved Henley's other leg and probably his life, but the treatment was painful, and he was hospitalised in Edinburgh for almost two years. Henley is chiefly remembered today as a poet, notably for his 'Invictus' (1875) – 'I am the master of my fate, I am the captain of my soul' – but Henley was an imperialist and a Tory, and much of his poetry was a platform for his jingoistic patriotism. His 'Hospital Sketches', first published in *Cornhill Magazine* in 1875, grimly recall his distressing time at the infirmary. He was also a critic and an editor, and first met Robert Louis Stevenson through their mutual friend and colleague Leslie Stephen, editor of *Cornhill Magazine* and father of Virginia Woolf.

Stevenson became a close friend of Henley, taking him out for carriage rides and even carrying an easy chair on his head all the way from Heriot Row to the infirmary for Henley's use. They collaborated on a number of plays together between 1880 and 1885, none of which was successful. Henley held a series of editorships, including *Pen* (1880) and *Magazine of Art* (1881–86), and in 1889 he returned to Edinburgh to edit the *Scots Observer*. A stinging critic and a fearless editor, Henley published the works of Hardy, Barrie, Kipling, H.G. Wells, Stevenson, Yeats and Henry James. He also published the struggling Joseph Conrad's *The Nigger of the Narcissus* in *The New Review*. 'Now that I have conquered Henley,' wrote Conrad, 'I ain't afraid of the divvle himself.'

The old Royal Infirmary.

His friendship with Stevenson was all but destroyed after their playwriting escapades, but when Henley accused Stevenson's wife of being a plagiarist over a story she'd had published, the slander was too much for Stevenson, who wrote to a friend saying, 'I fear that I have come to the end with Henley.' The incident terminated their friendship, and they never communicated again. He was of course immortalised as Long John Silver in *Treasure Island*, and Jim Hawkins's last words on Silver could well be Stevenson's lament for Henley:

W.E. Henley.

Of Silver, we have heard no more. That formidable seafaring man with one leg has at last gone clean out of my life; but I dare say he met his old negress, and perhaps still lives in comfort with her and Captain Flint. It is to be hoped so, I suppose, for his chances of comfort in another world are very small.

SEE ALSO: Robert Louis Stevenson.

FURTHER INFORMATION: The old Royal Infirmary was built between 1738 and 1748 and was on the south side of Infirmary Street on the site now occupied by the buildings of the former Infirmary Street School and swimming baths. It was eventually superseded by the Royal Infirmary at Lauriston Place in 1879. The gateway of the old infirmary can still be seen at the entrance of what was the 'New Surgical Hospital' (now part of Edinburgh University) built in 1853 on nearby Drummond Street.

FURTHER READING: J.M. Flora, *W.E. Henley* (Irvington, 1970); J.H. Buckley, *William Ernest Henley – A Study in the Counter-Decadence of the Nineties* (Princeton University Press, 1945).

8 Drummond Street
Rutherford's Howff
Favourite drinking den of Robert Louis Stevenson

Last night as I lay under my blanket in the cockpit . . . There was nothing visible but the southern stars, and the steersman there out by the binnacle lamp . . . the night was as warm as milk; and all of a sudden, I had a vision of – Drummond Street. It came to me like a flash of lightning; I simply returned thither, and into the past. And when I remembered all that I hoped and feared as I pickled about Rutherford's in the rain and the east wind: how I feared I should make a mere shipwreck, and yet timidly hoped not; how I feared I should never have a friend, far less a wife, and yet passionately hoped I might; how I hoped (if I did not take to drink) I should possibly write one little book, etc. etc. And then, now – what a change! I feel somehow as if I should like the incident set upon a brass plate at the corner of that dreary thoroughfare, for all students to read, poor devils, when their hearts are down.

Robert Louis Stevenson writing to his friend Charles Baxter aboard the yacht *Casco* in the South Pacific on 6 September 1888.

San Francisco Robert Louis Stevenson fans toast the great Tusitala.

Untouched by the Brigadoon mimicry of much of city-centre Edinburgh, Rutherford's still retains the sparse decor and friendly atmosphere of the traditional Scottish howff (tavern). It first opened its doors in 1834 and became a popular watering hole for the students of Edinburgh University just around the corner in South Bridge. Electric lighting has been installed and the price of a pint has increased dramatically, but one gets the feeling that Rutherford's hasn't changed very much since the late 1860s when the young velvet-jacketed engineering student Robert Louis Stevenson sauntered through its doors to down his first pint of the day after tedious hours of note-taking on the stress factors of lighthouses.

Stevenson was no model student, regularly playing truant, dozing and doodling in class. Despite coming from a family of engineers, he eventually gave up engineering to study law, passing his Bar exams in 1875. He never, however, actually practised law. No stranger to the howffs of the Old Town and its squalid underbelly, drink, revelry and the haunches of a whore were a delight to him. 'I was the companion,' he said, 'of seamen, chimney-sweeps and thieves; my circle was being continually changed by the action of the police magistrate.'

Of all his haunts Rutherford's seemed to hold a special place in his heart, never forgotten. A few Robert Louis Stevenson portraits and memorabilia now hang on the walls. However, the pub's homage doesn't go off the deep end into sacred-shrine territory. Among the many other thirsty undergraduates and wordsmiths to have regularly entered Rutherford's portals were a young medical student named Arthur Conan Doyle and the poet Hugh MacDiarmid.

J.M. Barrie, who was ten years younger than Stevenson, also studied at Edinburgh University. The two admired each other

greatly and corresponded in later life, but never met, much to Barrie's sincere regret. Long after Stevenson's death Barrie wrote about a fictional encounter with him in the 1925 edition of Rosaline Masson's anthology of memoirs entitled *I Can Remember Robert Louis Stevenson*: 'He led me away from the Humanities to something that he assured me was more humane, a howff called Rutherford's where we sat and talked by the solid hour.'

SEE ALSO: The Edinburgh Book Lovers' Tour, The Literary Pub Crawl, Howard Place, Inverleith Terrace, Heriot Row, J.M. Barrie, Hawes Inn, W.E. Henley, The Writers' Museum, The *Kidnapped* Trail, Kinnaird, Braemar.

6a Nicolson Street
Buffet King Restaurant (formerly Nicolson's)
Where J.K. Rowling wrote parts of *Harry Potter and the Philosopher's Stone*

> We won't be selling any Harry Potter books . . . It teaches people how to cast spells on people. Ordinary people can't cast spells, but you can by the power of Satan. It's not a laughing matter, it's quite serious. If you educate children to witchcraft, you don't know where it's going to end. It could even end with children dying.
>
> Theodore Danson-Smith, Edinburgh bookseller,
> *The Scotsman*, 10 June 2003

J.K. Rowling first appeared at the Edinburgh International Book Festival in 1997, an unknown writer promoting her first book about a boy wizard. Her audience totalled just 20 people. At the same festival in 2004 the event was closed off to everyone but herself and her fans. She was given her own purpose-built signing tent, and her queue of devotees stretched into the street. Signed copies of first editions of the Harry Potter books now sell for colossal prices at auction, and her books are sold in every corner of the planet. When *Harry Potter and the Order of the Phoenix* went on sale in China in 2003, a huge balloon in the shape of a Chinese lantern was suspended in Beijing above the Avenue of Eternal Peace. 'Harry Potter is here,' it said, 'Are you?'

J.K. Rowling (© Richard Young).

Bob Watt proudly standing beneath his 2006 plaque marking the site where J.K. Rowling wrote the early chapters of *Harry Potter and the Philosopher's Stone*.

Born and bred in the West Country, Rowling attended Exeter University, where she studied French. After various secretarial jobs, she went to Portugal when she was 26 to teach English as a foreign language, and it was while she was there that she began writing stories about Harry Potter. She met and married a Portuguese television journalist, and in 1993 their daughter Jessica was born. Four months later, however, their marriage collapsed, and Rowling decamped with her daughter to Edinburgh, where her younger sister lived. By this time she was living on benefits and experiencing the plight of many single mothers: poverty, loneliness, poor housing and inadequate or expensive childcare. She lived in Leith, in a flat at South Lorne Place, for a few years (cashing her benefits from Leith Walk Post Office), before moving to Hazelbank Terrace in Shandon, off Slateford Road, in 1997.

She enjoyed writing in cafés, particularly Nicolson's on the Southside:

> I would go to Nicolson's café, because the staff were so nice and so patient there and allowed me to order one espresso and sit there for hours, writing until Jessica woke up. You can get a hell of a lot of writing done in two hours if you know that's the only chance you are going to get.

She trained as a teacher at Moray House Teacher Training College in Holyrood Road, studying by day and writing at night, and it was while working as a French teacher that her first book, *Harry Potter and the Philosopher's Stone*, was accepted for publication. A few months later the American rights were sold, and she was able to give up teaching and write full time. She still lives in Edinburgh, and has a country retreat in Perthshire, but is rarely seen in cafés these days.

After her first book was published, she visited some pupils at Leith Academy, where she used to teach. 'They avoided the issue for half of the class,' she said, 'then someone said, "Miss! You're rich now, eh?"'

FURTHER INFORMATION: Buffet King, 1st Floor, 6a Nicolson Street, Edinburgh (opposite Festival Theatre). Open seven days, 12 noon–11 p.m. Tel: 0131 557 4567.
Website: www.buffetkingedinburgh.com

25 George Square
Childhood home of Sir Walter Scott

> Born for nae better than a gangrel scrape-gut . . .
> The teenage Walter Scott described by his father

George Square was designed by the architect James Brown and pre-dates the New Town by 20 years. It wasn't named after royalty or a worthy man of letters, but James's brother George. It was a fashionable place to live, but more importantly it was a healthy place to live, especially if you'd just arrived in 1772, like the Scotts had, from a tenement ghetto in the Old Town, where six of their children had died in infancy.

Young Wattie, however, did not spend his early childhood at George Square. In 1773, when he was about 18 months old, he contracted poliomyelitis, which left him with a limp for the rest of his life. Doctors could do nothing for him, and on the advice of his grandfather, Dr Rutherford, he was sent to live with his paternal grandfather at Sandyknowe Farm in the Scottish Borders, where it was hoped fresh air and exercise would improve his health.

25 George Square.

Thus began Wattie's lifelong love affair with the Border country. Border life didn't mend his leg, but his general health improved, and when he was four years old, the family decided to try another remedy. They returned to Sandyknowe the following summer, and two years later, between the ages of seven and eight, he returned to George Square.

His mother, Anne, was a small, plain woman, who was sagacious, friendly and lived to the ripe old age of 87. She had a head full of ballads and stories, which she passed on to Wattie, and was the first person to introduce him to the world of poetry. Her husband Walter was a solicitor and a staunch Calvinist. Almost teetotal, he possessed no hobbies but had an intense interest in theology, doling out long sermons from the family Bible on the Sabbath. Anne and Walter's marriage was a happy one, apart from the day he threw out of the window a cup in which his wife had thoughtlessly given tea to the traitor Murray of Broughton, who betrayed his fellow Jacobites after Culloden. History does not record if any passers-by or any of the Scotts' illustrious neighbours were injured. These neighbours included the Lord Advocate Lord Melville, writer Henry Mackenzie and the 'hanging judge' Lord Braxfield, the inspiration for Robert Louis Stevenson's *Weir of Hermiston*.

Scott's siblings consisted of four brothers and one sister. Robert, the eldest, joined the navy and later the East India Company, and died of malaria aged 41. John became a soldier and died aged 47. Thomas (his favourite brother), a couple of years younger than Wattie, died a regimental paymaster in Canada, aged 50. Daniel, the youngest, ended up being employed on a plantation in Jamaica, where he was accused of cowardice during a slave uprising, indelibly staining the family name. Wattie shunned him on his return and did not attend his funeral or wear mourning for him. His only sister, Anne, a year younger than him, was a highly strung and sickly girl who was terribly accident-prone. Her perilous escapades included crushing her hand in an iron door, almost drowning in a pond and seriously burning her head after her cap caught fire. She died in her late 20s.

In 1779, when he was eight, Wattie attended the High School in Infirmary Street, and in 1783, aged thirteen, he entered Edinburgh University. His studies were frequently interrupted by ill health, and in 1784–85 he was forced to convalesce once again in the Borders at his Aunt Janet's house in Kelso. By this time he was a voracious reader, reading ten times the average quota for a boy his age. He had mastered French, and by the time he was 15 he was proficient enough in Italian to read Dante and Ariosto in the original.

In 1786 he signed up for a five-year apprenticeship in his father's legal firm, where the laborious task of copying legal documents (he once wrote 10,000 words without rest or food) was invaluable training for his future career as a novelist, and in 1792 he qualified as an advocate.

As a teenager his lameness didn't seem to be any great impediment. Long walks and horse-riding did not daunt him. He could lift a blacksmith's anvil by the horn, and James Hogg once described him as the strongest man of his acquaintance. He became involved in the city's social life and was accustomed to the hard drinking and revelry of gentlemen's clubs, often not returning home until the early hours, prompting his father to complain once that he was 'born for nae better than a gangrel scrape-gut'. One of these clubs was the famous Speculative Society, a hub of literary and legal talent.

As an advocate he walked the floor of Parliament Hall waiting to be hired. He defended destitute prisoners for no fee, and on his Border circuits his clients included sheep stealers, poachers and drunkards. It was his exploration of the Borders which drew him deeper into its ancient traditions and inspired him to collect their ballads and tales before they vanished for ever. A Tory, who valued tradition and the monarchy, Scott was prompted by the country's fear of rising republicanism and the threat of a French invasion to join the newly formed Royal Edinburgh Volunteer Light Dragoons in 1797. In July of the same year he met French émigré Charlotte Charpentier while holidaying in the Lake District, and after a whirlwind romance they were married on Christmas Eve in St Mary's Church, Carlisle. Shortly afterwards the couple moved into rented accommodation on the second floor of 108 George Street, then to 10 South Castle Street and finally to 39 North Castle Street, his town house for the next 28 years.

SEE ALSO: The Writers' Museum, Dryburgh Abbey, Abbotsford, Ashestiel, County Hotel, Clovenfords Hotel, Gordon Arms, Scott's View, Smailholm Tower, Scott's Courtroom and Statue, Traquair House, Minchmoor, Newark Castle, Tibbie Shiel's Inn, St Ronan's Well, Melrose Abbey, College Wynd, North Castle Street, Scott Monument, Sir Walter Scott Way.

FURTHER READING: W. Elliot, *Sir Walter Scott Trail* (Scottish Borders Tourist Board, 2001); John Buchan, *Sir Walter Scott* (House of Stratus, 2001); Arthur Melville.Clark, *Sir Walter Scott: The Formative Years* (W. Blackwood, 1969); J.G. Lockhart, *The Life of Sir Walter Scott* (University Press of the Pacific, 2002).

Marchmont

Arden Street
Former home of Ian Rankin (1960–) and home of the fictional Inspector Rebus

> Once I caught a train to Cardenden by mistake . . . When we reached Cardenden, we got off and waited for the next train back to Edinburgh. I was very tired and if Cardenden had looked more promising, I think I would have simply stayed there. And if you've ever been to Cardenden you'll know how bad things must have been.
> Kate Atkinson, *Behind the Scenes at the Museum* (1995)

Arden Street.

Described by crime-fiction writer James Ellroy as the 'king of tartan noir', Ian Rankin was born in 1960 in the village of Cardenden in Fife. He now lives and works in Edinburgh, where most of his novels are set, graphically contrasting the picturesque 'Athens of the North' with its concrete housing schemes and criminal underclass.

Rankin writes in his introduction to *Rebus: The Early Years* (1999):

> I was living in a room in a ground-floor flat in Arden Street, so my hero, John Rebus, had to live across the road. When the book was published, I found to my astonishment that everyone was saying I'd written a whodunit, a crime novel. I think I'm still the only crime writer I know who hadn't a clue about the genre before setting out . . .

'Before setting out' Rankin had a variety of jobs: chicken-factory worker, alcohol researcher, swineherd, grape-picker, punk musician, tax collector, assistant at the National Folktale Centre in London and journalist with the monthly magazine *Hi-Fi Review*. Writing prose, poetry and pop lyrics for as long as he can remember, his influences ranged from *The Beano* to Muriel Spark. 'My dad saw himself in most of my characters,' he remarked in *Rebus: The Early Years*, 'even if that character was a nun. "Yes," he'd say, "but she speaks just like me."'

Rankin attended Edinburgh University, where he won several literary prizes. One of his short stories evolved into a novel called *The Flood*, but in the mid-1980s he started writing a book that updated *Dr Jekyll and Mr Hyde* to present-day Edinburgh. *Knots & Crosses* was published in 1987 and appropriately introduced Detective Sergeant John Rebus with 'water seeping into his shoes' standing before the grave of his father. Rebus was intended as a one-off, but the public's appetite for this sardonic, obstinate, world-weary cop has ensured his immortality with each successive bestseller. In 1988 Rankin was elected a Hawthornden Fellow, and in 1991–92 he won the Chandler-Fulbright Award, one of the world's most prestigious detective-fiction prizes.

Rebus is now on a par with the legends of the detective genre, from Marlowe to Morse, but one of the great allures of Rebus is the way Rankin weaves real places and events into his stories: Arthur's Seat in *The Falls*, the new Scottish Parliament building in *Set in Darkness*, the Mull of Kintyre helicopter crash in *A Question of Blood*, and Rebus and Rankin's local pub, the Oxford Bar.

In an interview on 17 November 2000, Ian Rankin explained the origins of Rebus's unusual name:

I was a student of English Literature when I wrote the first Rebus book, *Knots & Crosses*, and I was studying deconstruction, semiotics, etc. A rebus is a picture puzzle, and it seemed to click. After all, we already had Inspector Morse (a type of code), and in the first book, Rebus was being sent picture puzzles to solve . . . so I made him Rebus, thinking it was only for one book (I never intended turning him into a series) so it didn't matter if I gave him a strange name. Recently, I bumped into a guy called Rebus in my local pub. He lives in Rankin Drive in Edinburgh. Truth is always stranger than fiction . . .

SEE ALSO: Oxford Bar.

FURTHER INFORMATION: Since its launch in 2000, Rebus Tours, the walking tours based on Rankin's Inspector Rebus books, have attracted thousands of Rebus fans from all over the world. The tour route starts at the Royal Oak pub on Infirmary Street, just off South Bridge near to the Royal Mile.
Website: www.rebustours.com

Bruntsfield

160 Bruntsfield Place
Birthplace of Muriel Spark (1918–2006), novelist, short-story writer, biographer and poet

> But Edinburgh, said the man, was a beautiful city, more beautiful then than it is now. Of course the slums have been cleared. The Old Town was always my favourite. We used to love to explore the Grassmarket and so on. Architecturally speaking, there is no finer sight in Europe.
>
> Muriel Spark, from *The Prime of Miss Jean Brodie* (1961)

Although Muriel Spark wrote over 20 novels, it is her sixth novel, *The Prime of Miss Jean Brodie*, published in 1961 and adapted for stage and screen, which is her best-known and most discussed

Muriel Spark in 1947.

work. In fact, she could probably have written another 20 novels, but all roads would still have led back to this one, which, although easy to read and written in a relaxed style, is more complex in its theme and composition than it at first appears. And this is the reason why readers and critics keep returning to this novel, which can be read on many different levels. *The Prime of Miss Jean Brodie*, like all great classics, refuses to fade into obscurity.

Muriel Spark was born in 1918 to Sarah and Bernard Camberg, the latter an engineer. She was enrolled at James Gillespie's School in 1922, where she became known as the school's 'poet and dreamer'. Her work regularly

81

The former James Gillespie's School on Bruntsfield Links, now part of Edinburgh University.

appeared in the school magazine, and in 1932 she was crowned 'Queen of Poetry'. When she was 11, the young Muriel encountered Miss Kay, whose eccentric teaching and idealism formed the basis for the fictional character in her 1961 novel, *The Prime of Miss Jean Brodie*. After leaving school, she attended Heriot Watt College in Chambers Street, and at 18 took a job in the office of Small's department store at 106 Princes Street. In 1937, aged 19, she married Sydney Spark in Salisbury, Southern Rhodesia, and their son Robin was born in Bulawayo a year later. Her husband became increasingly mentally unstable, and, following her return to Britain in 1944, the couple were divorced. She joined the political department of the Foreign Office secret intelligence service, MI6, during the Second World War. After the war, she remained in London, where she became general secretary of the Poetry Society and editor of the *Poetry Review* (1947–49). She started writing seriously after the war, and in 1951 she won *The Observer*'s short-story competition with 'Seraph and the Zambesi'. Her first collection of poems, *The Fanfario and Other Verse*, was published in 1952, and in 1954 she was converted to Roman Catholicism, an event which influenced her later writing. Her first novel, *The Comforters* (1957), was praised by Evelyn Waugh as 'brilliantly original and fascinating', and during the next four years she penned a further five novels: *Robinson* (1958), *Memento Mori* (1959), *The Bachelors* (1960), *The Ballad of Peckham Rye* (1960) and *The Prime of Miss Jean Brodie* (1961).

The Prime of Miss Jean Brodie was first published in *The New Yorker* magazine to great acclaim, prompting her move to New York in the early 1960s, where she worked for the magazine with fellow contributors J.D. Salinger, John Updike and Vladimir Nabokov. During this period she wrote two further novels, *The Girls of Slender Means* (1963) and the prize-winning *The Mandelbaum Gate* (1965). In the late 1960s she moved to Rome and in 1979 settled in Tuscany. Her later works include *The Abbess of Crewe* (1974), *Loitering with Intent* (1981) and *A Far Cry from Kensington* (1988). The first volume of her autobiography, *Curriculum Vitae*, was published in 1992.

FURTHER INFORMATION: The building that was James Gillespie's School (the model for the Marcia Blaine School in the novel *The Prime of Miss Jean Brodie*) is on nearby Bruntsfield Links and is now Edinburgh University student accommodation. Today James Gillespie's School is situated in Lauderdale Street, Bruntsfield.

The Muriel Spark Society can be contacted through Gail

Wylie, 13 Bangholm Bower Avenue, Edinburgh EH5 3NS.
Email: gewylie@btinternet.com
FURTHER READING: A. Bold, *Muriel Spark* (Routledge, 1986).

7 Leamington Terrace
Former home of Norman MacCaig (1910–96), poet

Hugh MacDiarmid: After I am gone my poetry will be remembered and read for hundreds of years, but after you have gone, your poetry will soon be forgotten.
Norman MacCaig: Ah, but I am not planning to go!

Norman MacCaig was one of the great Scottish poets, who wrote not in Scots or Gaelic, but in English in a simple way, observing nature, people and especially his friends. From rhyme to free verse, MacCaig produced unique poetry which, despite MacDiarmid's tongue-in-cheek prediction, will not be forgotten.

He was born on 14 November 1910 to Robert MacCaig and Joan MacLeod. His father, who came from Haugh of Urr in Dumfriesshire, was a chemist who had a shop at 9 Dundas Street, and the family lived in a tenement flat at 11 Dundas Street. His mother, who had never been taught to read or write, was from Scalpay, off Harris. Norman was the youngest of four children and was educated at the Royal High School and studied classics at Edinburgh University. He became a primary-school teacher and remained in teaching until 1967, when he was appointed as fellow in creative writing at Edinburgh University. In 1970 he joined the Department of English Studies at the University of Stirling and became a reader in poetry, retiring in 1978.

His first volumes of poetry, *Far Cry* (1943) and *The Inward Eye* (1946), earmarked him as a devotee of the 'anti-cerebral' New Apocalypse, a group of writers who, for a brief time in the 1940s, reacted against the 'classicism' of Auden with savage and disorderly verse. Other collections included *Riding Lights* (1955), *Measures* (1965), *Rings on a Tree* (1968), *A Man in my Position* (1969) and *Collected Poems* (1985).

He first met the poets of the Scottish Renaissance (including Hugh MacDiarmid, Sydney Goodsir Smith and Sorley MacLean) in the Southern Bar in South Clerk Street in 1946. In a radio interview with Roderick Watson he recalled his early meetings with them: 'For a while they despised and rejected me, of course, because I write in English: "Lickspittle of the English ascendancy; stabber in the back of the Scottish movement; cultural Quisling." But, of course, when they got to know me and found that I was tall, handsome, rich and could sing in tune, they decided I wasn't so bad after all and Douglas Young invented a phrase, he said, "It's a pity Norman doesn't write in Scots but he's got a Scots accent of the mind." Whatever that means.'

After the pubs had closed, the sessions of debate and flyting often continued at MacCaig's flat in Leamington Terrace, where he lived from 1943 to 1996. 'In his own house he was a generous host,' recalled George Mackay Brown. 'In this he had a good partner in Isabel, his wife. By 10 p.m., closing time in those days, the burn of lyricism and laughter was only beginning to gather head. Often a group of merry figures was to be seen at a bus stop, burdened with "cerry-oots".'

MacCaig never wrote long, continuous screeds of verse, and

critics have sometimes claimed his poetry is lightweight and without political clout. Once, when asked how long it takes him to write a poem, he replied, 'Two fags. Sometimes, it's only one.' He died in the Astley Ainslie Hospital on 23 January 1996, aged 85.

SEE ALSO: Hugh MacDiarmid.

Greenside

Picardy Place
Site of the birthplace of Sir Arthur Conan Doyle (1859–1930)

> The strain was something I could not endure any longer. Of course had I continued [to write Sherlock Holmes] I could have coined money, for the stories were the most remunerative I have written; but as regards literature, they would have been mere trash.
>
> Conan Doyle, quoted in Stashower, *Teller of Tales* (1999)

Arthur Ignatius Conan Doyle, creator of the world's greatest fictional detective, was born on 22 May 1859, in a small flat at 11 Picardy Place (demolished in 1969). A bronze sculpture of Sherlock Holmes clutching his famous pipe, but minus his hypodermic syringe, now marks the site. Situated beside one of the city's busiest and noisiest road junctions, the gaslit streets, Hansom cabs and grubby street urchins of Conan Doyle's era seem as remote as Mars.

Doyle is chiefly remembered today for his stories about the great sleuth, which, although they made him a fortune, also became a millstone round his neck. Few people today read his historical romances, the works he most wanted to be remembered for, and his obsession in later life with the occult greatly diminished his reputation and credibility.

Born of Irish-Catholic parentage, he was the second of ten children of Mary Foley and Charles Doyle, an assistant surveyor. Charles came from an artistic family and was himself a talented artist. All three of his brothers prospered in the art world, but Charles, who was an alcoholic and an epileptic, did not. He was involved in designing a fountain at Holyrood Palace and a window at Glasgow Cathedral, and did occasional book illustration and sketching, but his career came to nothing. He was eventually institutionalised.

Conan Doyle described his mother in his autobiographical novel *The Stark Munro Letters* as having a 'sweet face' and being suggestive of 'a plump little hen'. She was known as 'the Ma'am', and was a voracious reader and storyteller. Conan Doyle recalled in his autobiography that 'as far back as I can remember anything at all, the vivid stories which she would tell me stand out so clearly that they obscure the real facts of life'.

Arthur Conan Doyle as a young doctor in Southsea, around 1886, when he wrote 'A Study in Scarlet'.

The real 'facts of life' were that he had an alcoholic father to contend with, and life at home was a strain for all. In 1868, when he was nine years old, his wealthy uncles sent him to a Jesuit boarding school in England – a move which may have lifted the stress of home life, but ended up destroying his Catholic faith. He went on to study medicine at Edinburgh, where the uncanny observational powers of his teacher Dr Joseph Bell made him the model for Sherlock Holmes. He received his Bachelor of Medicine and Master of Surgery qualifications in 1881, and after a short stint as a ship's medical officer, he set up as a GP in Southsea in 1882.

While still at university, he had his first short story published – 'The Mystery of Sasassa Valley' – in Edinburgh's *Chambers' Journal*, for which he was paid three guineas. Many other stories followed, usually resulting in a rejection slip. Doyle's income after his first year practising in Southsea was a mere £150. Patients were thin on the ground to begin with, and his consulting room was more a place in which to write stories than to consult.

The detective genre in 1886 had only been around for 40 years, and among the role models which were the inspiration for the Holmes character were Poe's Auguste Dupin and Emile Gaboriau's Monsieur Lecoq. On 8 March 1886 he began writing a story called 'A Tangled Skein', which introduced the characters Sherringford Holmes and Ormond Slacker. By April the title had changed to 'A Study in Scarlet', and the characters had evolved into Sherlock Holmes and Dr Watson. After three rejections, it was accepted by Ward Lock & Co. Doyle reluctantly sold the copyright for £25, and it was published as the main story in the November 1887 issue of *Beeton's Christmas Annual*. Shortly afterwards, it appeared in book form, with pen and ink drawings by Doyle's father. 'The Sign of Four' followed in 1890, but it wasn't until *The Strand* magazine published 'A Scandal in Bohemia', and subsequent monthly short stories, that the public developed an insatiable appetite for Sherlock Holmes. And so the legend was born, adding 100,000 copies to *The Strand*'s monthly circulation.

While churning out Holmes stories, Doyle was also busy working on his real love – historical fiction: *Micah Clarke* (1889), *The White Company* (1891), *Brigadier Gerard* (1896), *Rodney Stone* (1896) and *Sir Nigel* (1906). Later came *The Lost World* (1912) and the Professor Challenger stories. Although all these books were extremely competent literary efforts, they never eclipsed the popularity of Sherlock Holmes, much to the dismay of Doyle, who wanted so much to be remembered as a writer of 'quality' fiction.

Eighteen months after the appearance in *The Strand* of his first piece, Doyle was so fed up with his creation that he pitched Holmes over the Reichenbach Falls in 'The Final Problem'. This caused a tremendous public outcry. Doyle may have buried Holmes, but he also buried his bank account along with him. Eight years later, in 1902, he revived them both with *The Hound of the Baskervilles*. Shortly afterwards, the American magazine *Collier's Weekly* offered him a staggering $45,000 for thirteen stories. Holmes was back, and he was here to stay.

Doyle stated in his 1924 autobiography *Memories and Adventures* that he was giving up his 'congenial and lucrative' writings for the psychic crusade, 'which will occupy, either by voice or pen, the remainder of my life'.

In the *Journal of the Society for Psychical Research*, he claimed he had been contacted by Charles Dickens and asked if he would finish off his unfinished novel, *The Mystery of Edwin Drood*. 'I shall be honoured, Mr Dickens,' Doyle replied to his spirit. 'Charles, if you please,' replied the spirit. 'We like friends to be friends.' As far as we know, Doyle never did carry out this project.

After his first wife's death from tuberculosis in 1906, he married Jean Leckie. Doyle died in 1930 and the couple are buried together beneath an oak tree in All Saints' Churchyard, Minstead, Hampshire.

SEE ALSO: Rutherford's Howff.

FURTHER INFORMATION: Conan Doyle stayed at various addresses in the city as a young medical student, including 2 Argyle Park Terrace and 32 George Square. Picardy Place is so called because it was the site of the village of Picardy formed by French refugees from the province of that name who came to Edinburgh after the revocation of the Edict of Nantes in 1685. The Franco Midland Hardware Company is an international Sherlock Holmes study group run by Holmesian scholar Phillip Weller, 6 Bramham Moor, Hill Head, Fareham, Hampshire, PO14 3RU. Tel: 01329 667325.

FURTHER READING: A.C. Doyle, *Memories and Adventures* (Oxford, 1989); J.D. Carr, *Life of Sir Arthur Conan Doyle* (Carroll & Graf, 2003); M. Booth, *The Doctor and the Detective* (Thomas Dunne Books, 2000); D. Stashower, *Teller of Tales* (Penguin, 2001); R.L. Green and J.M. Gibson, *A Bibliography of A. Conan Doyle* (Clarendon, 1983); J. Cooper, *The Case of the Cottingley Fairies* (Pocket Books, 1998).

New Town

East Princes Street Gardens
The Scott Monument
A memorial to Sir Walter Scott, inventor of the historical and romantic novel

> I am sorry to report the Scott Monument a failure. It is like the spire of a Gothic church taken off and stuck in the ground.
> Charles Dickens voicing his dislike
> of the monument in 1847

Following his death in 1832, there was a growing desire that something should be built in the city to commemorate Scott's enormous contribution to Scottish literature. J.G. Lockhart, Scott's biographer and son-in-law, proposed the erection of 'a huge Homeric Cairn on Arthur's Seat – a land and sea mark'. Many other suggestions were mooted, and eventually a competition was organised for the best-designed monument. Fifty-four plans were submitted, and included twenty-two Gothic structures, fourteen Grecian temples, five pillars, eleven statues, an obelisk and a fountain.

The winning design was submitted by Biggar-born draughtsman and self-taught architect George Meikle Kemp (1795–1844), who drew up his plan in five days. Kemp probably thought his humble origins and lack of eminence might prejudice his chances of winning, and shrewdly submitted his design to the selecting committee under the pseudonym John Morvo, the medieval master-mason of Melrose Abbey. The Border abbey was also the inspiration for his design, Kemp admitting 'it was in all its details derived'. Tragically, Kemp died before the completion of the monument, when he drowned in mysterious circumstances in the Union Canal at Fountainbridge on the evening of 6 March 1844.

The two-hundred-feet-high monument, with two hundred and eighty-seven steps to its pinnacle, incorporating three Scottish monarchs, sixteen poets and sixty-four of Scott's characters into its design, was officially inaugurated fourteen years after Scott's death on 15 August 1846. The twice-life-size statue of Scott at its base was sculpted by Sir John Steell (1804–1901) in white Carrara marble and is one of the cleverest innovations of the whole structure, skilfully camouflaging the seagull guano deposited daily on his noble brow.

SEE ALSO: Dryburgh Abbey, Abbotsford, Ashestiel, County Hotel, Clovenfords Hotel, Gordon Arms, Dryburgh Abbey, Scott's View, Smailholm Tower, Scott's Courtroom and Statue, Traquair House, Minchmoor, Waverley Lodge, Newark Castle, Tibbie Shiel's Inn, St Ronan's Well, Melrose Abbey, College Wynd, George Square, North Castle Street, Sir Walter Scott Way.

8 Young Street
The Oxford Bar

Wullie Roose's Coxfork in Bung Strait
Sydney Goodsir Smith, *Carotid Cornucopius* (1947)

Today this pub is synonymous with Ian Rankin and Inspector Rebus, who both regularly drink here. You may, therefore, catch a glimpse of Ian Rankin, but the closest you'll get to Rebus is by ordering a beetroot-filled 'Rebus Roll'. The Oxford Bar has always been a popular watering hole for Scottish writers and artists, especially of the Scottish Renaissance, who frequented it when it was run by the late and legendary Willie Ross. Ian Rankin gave a colourful description of Ross in *Guardian Unlimited* in October 2002:

> He left in 1979, just before I started drinking there . . .
> You weren't allowed to hit on women because no women
> were allowed in. There was no women's toilet. If you were
> English, you weren't allowed in. If you were a student,
> you weren't allowed in. If you asked for food, like a
> packet of crisps, he dragged you outside, pointed at the
> sign and said, 'Does that say bar or fucking restaurant?'

> Some people have got great stories about him. He sounds like a terrible man to me, but a character, and you need characters.

Although Willie Ross is now part of the pub's history, there is no shortage of colourful characters at the Oxford Bar, and, as one local commented, 'It's the only pub I know with an emergency entrance.'

SEE ALSO: Ian Rankin, Sandy Bell's.

FURTHER INFORMATION: The Oxford Bar, 8 Young Street, Edinburgh, EH2 4JB. Tel: 0131 539 7119.
Website: www.oxfordbar.com

39 North Castle Street
Town house of Sir Walter Scott

Walter Scott married French émigré Charlotte Charpentier on Christmas Eve 1797, and the couple took temporary lodgings on the second floor of 108 George Street for a few weeks before moving into 10 South Castle Street, which was soon exchanged for 39 North Castle Street, where they lived until 1826. Scott, now in his late 20s, was beginning to settle down in life. The income from his Bar earnings, his wife's allowances, his father's estate (his father died in 1799) and his newly appointed post as sheriff-depute of Selkirkshire was bringing in around £1,000 a year. In February 1799 he published his translation of Gottfried Burger's *The Chase* and *William and Helen*, the first publication to bear his name. His writing hobby was now absorbing him more and more, and law was becoming a chore, but there was never any question of devoting his life to the Muses. His father's advice – that literature was a good staff but a bad crutch – was wise counsel not forgotten.

Between 1799 and 1805 Charlotte gave birth to two sons and two daughters. In the autumn of 1804 the family moved to Ashestiel, near Clovenfords, the sheriff being bound by statute to reside for part of the year in the Borders. North Castle Street was kept on as a winter residence. In 1806 he became principal clerk to the Court of Session in Edinburgh, which meant he no longer needed to

39 North Castle Street.

An engraving of Walter Scott from a painting by T. Lawrence.

practise as an advocate. In 1809 he became a secret partner in James Ballantyne's printing business, a rash move for which he would later pay dearly.

Byron was beginning to eclipse Scott as a poet, and, wisely, Scott turned his talents to novel-writing. *Waverley*, his first novel, was published by Constable anonymously on 7 July 1814 and was staggeringly successful, much to Scott's surprise. The impact the novel had on the literary world at that time is difficult to take in today, but it was a literary phenomenon which caused a sensation around the world. With one book, Scott had established the form of the historical novel, a genre that did not exist before, and, perhaps more importantly, he gave the novel prestige. In the early nineteenth century the novel was an extremely questionable form of literature, and far beneath the dignity of a clerk of the Court of Session. Scott knew the legal establishment would not have approved, so rather than jeopardise his career, he published anonymously.

After the success of *Waverley*, Scott turned into a virtual novel-writing machine, producing some of his best work over the next five years, all without giving up the day job and all published anonymously, including *Guy Mannering* (written in six weeks in 1815), *The Antiquary* (1816), *Old Mortality* (1816), *Rob Roy* (1818), *The Heart of Midlothian* (1818), *The Bride of Lammermoor* (1819) and *Ivanhoe* (1820).

Scott was created a baronet in 1820 and did not publicly admit authorship of his novels until 1827. In 1826 disaster struck when he became insolvent after the failure of his printer, James Ballantyne, and his publisher Archibald Constable. As a partner of Ballantyne's, he was liable for debts of over £100,000. His wife Charlotte died the same year.

Most men would have buckled under this enormous burden, but all Scott asked of his creditors was time to write his way out of debt. After his death six years later in 1832, his creditors were paid in full; the novel-writing machine had ground to a halt, leaving Scottish literature more riches than it had ever known. He died at Abbotsford, and his remains were laid by the side of those of his wife in the sepulchre of his ancestors in the ruins of Dryburgh Abbey. Lockhart quotes a fitting epitaph from the *Iliad*: 'There lay he, mighty and mightily fallen, having done with his chivalry.'

SEE ALSO: The Writers' Museum, Dryburgh Abbey, Abbotsford, Ashestiel, County Hotel, Clovenfords Hotel, Gordon Arms, Scott's View, Smailholm Tower, Scott's Courtroom and Statue, Traquair House, Minchmoor, Newark Castle, Tibbie Shiel's Inn, St Ronan's Well, Melrose Abbey, College Wynd, Scott Monument, Sir Walter Scott Way, James Hogg.

FURTHER INFORMATION: 39 North Castle Street is not open to the public. James Ballantyne's printing office – Old Paul's Work – was in old Leith Wynd, now the lower end of Cranston Street, off the Canongate.

FURTHER READING: Walter Elliot, *The Walter Scott Trail* (Scottish Borders Tourist Board, 2001); Jane Millgate, *Walter Scott: The Making of the Novelist* (University of Toronto Press, 1984); Eric Quayle, *The Ruin of Sir Walter Scott* (Hart-Davis, 1968); Sir Walter Scott and W.E.K. Anderson (ed.), *The Journal of Sir Walter Scott* (Oxford University Press, 1972); Sir Walter Scott and H.J.C. Grierson (ed.), *The Letters of Sir Walter Scott* (Clarendon Press, 1979).

17 Heriot Row
Former home of Robert Louis Stevenson

> For we are very lucky with a lamp before the door,
> And Leerie stops to light it as he lights so many more;
> And O! before you hurry by with ladder and with light,
> O Leerie, see a little child and nod to him tonight!
>
> Robert Louis Stevenson, from 'The Lamplighter',
> *A Child's Garden of Verse* (1885)

Thomas Stevenson, engineer to the Northern Lighthouse Board, was prospering, and his new house reflected it. The Stevensons moved to Heriot Row in 1857, a Georgian street in Edinburgh's New Town which today still exudes affluence and pedigree. Built between 1802 and 1806, this large terraced house overlooking Queen Street Gardens is spacious enough to billet a boy-scout troop. For the three Stevensons and a couple of servants it must have seemed positively Brobdingnagian. Looking at number 17 from the street, Louis's bedroom was situated on the top floor on the far right, overlooking the gardens. These were the windows from which the sickly Louis would have observed Leerie, 'The Lamplighter', and heard the coarse cries of the carters as they wound their way up from Stockbridge to the town.

Thomas Stevenson had hoped that his son would follow in his footsteps and become an engineer, but Louis gave up his engineering studies in favour of law, passing his Bar exams in 1875. Louis the advocate, however, was never a serious proposition. What he really wanted to be was a writer, an artist and a free spirit. In appearance and lifestyle he was already halfway there, wandering around the Old Town in his famous velvet jacket, carousing with the city's underbelly and sowing his wild oats. And, like all good bohemians, he doubted the existence of God (which infuriated his father), became seriously depressed, wrote and abandoned novels, fell in love with an older woman and yearned to travel.

In France in 1876 he met his future wife, Fanny Osbourne, and in the same year he canoed through Belgium and France with his friend Walter Simpson, a journey which inspired the creation of his first book, *An Inland Voyage* (1878). In 1878 he tramped across the Cévennes with his obstreperous donkey Modestine, which resulted in *Travels with a Donkey* (1879). He travelled to California in pursuit of Fanny in 1879, a trip which nearly killed him. The literary outcome of this was *The Silverado Squatters* (1883). After marrying Fanny, who was ten years his senior, Stevenson and his new wife returned to Britain in 1884 and settled in Bournemouth for three years. His short stories, essays and travel writings were now appearing regularly in magazines, and in 1883 he published *Treasure Island*, his first full-length work of fiction. *The Strange Case of Dr Jekyll and Mr Hyde* (1886) and *Kidnapped* (1886) followed, establishing his reputation as a master storyteller.

Following his father's death in

A youthful Louis.

May 1887, he returned home for the funeral. However, he was too ill on the day of the service to attend. This was to be his last visit to Heriot Row before departing for the South Seas in 1888.

Flora Masson recalled his departure from Edinburgh in *I Can Remember Robert Louis Stevenson* (1922):

> An open cab, with a man and a woman in it, seated side by side, and leaning back – the rest of the cab piled high with rather untidy luggage – came slowly towards us . . . As it passed us, out on the broad roadway . . . a slender, loose garbed figure stood up in the cab and waved a wide-brimmed hat.
>
> 'Good-bye!' he called to us. 'Good-bye!'

Searching for the climate that he hoped would prolong his life, Stevenson eventually settled in Samoa. In his exile he still wrote prodigiously, notably *Island Nights' Entertainments* (1893) and his unfinished masterpiece *Weir of Hermiston* (1896). Not even an island paradise, however, could prolong his life. He died of a brain haemorrhage shortly after 8 p.m. on 3 December 1894 and is buried on the summit of Mount Vea in Samoa.

SEE ALSO: The Edinburgh Book Lovers' Tour, The Literary Pub Crawl, Howard Place, Inverleith Terrace, Rutherford's Howff, Hawes Inn, W.E. Henley, The Writers' Museum, The *Kidnapped* Trail, Kinnaird, Braemar.

FURTHER INFORMATION: 17 Heriot Row is not open to the public, but it does operate as a bed and breakfast, and is available to hire for dinners, weddings or any other special occasions. Accommodation consists of one double bedroom and one twin bedroom at the rear of the house with a view of Fife. The double bedroom used to be the bedroom of Robert Louis Stevenson's parents, with the en suite bathroom being the original Stevenson installation. Contact John and Felicitas Macfie on 0131 556 1896.
Email: mail@stevenson-house.co.uk
Website: www.stevenson-house.co.uk
An information panel, erected by the Robert Louis Stevenson Club, can be seen opposite on the railings of Queen Street Gardens.

FURTHER READING: Robert Louis Stevenson, *Edinburgh: Picturesque Notes* (Pallas Athene, 2003); R. Masson (ed.), *I Can Remember Robert Louis Stevenson* (1922); E.B. Simpson, *Robert Louis Stevenson's Edinburgh Days* (Kessinger, 2005); J. Calder, *Stevenson and Victorian Scotland* (Edinburgh University Press, 1984).

Scotland Street
Fictional setting for Alexander McCall Smith's 'daily novel', *44 Scotland Street*

> We hear that Irvine Welsh might be buying a flat in Scotland Street for the next series and will his arrival alter the tone of the place?
>
> A question from the audience at a special charity reading of *44 Scotland Street*, June 2004

Scotland Street is an unassuming New Town street which does not quite possess the class of Heriot Row or Abercromby Place.

Nevertheless, it is the setting for one of Edinburgh's most famous fictional addresses: 44 Scotland Street. This celebrity status is due to Alexander McCall Smith's daily novel of the same name which appeared in *The Scotsman* during 2004. To write weekly instalments of a novel for the press is a daunting enough prospect, but to write daily ones is a feat only a novel-writing machine like McCall Smith – who can polish off 3,000 words before lunch – can tackle. 'In the last three weeks,' he told *The Scotsman* in May 2004, 'I've written episodes at Palm Springs in the Californian desert, in Hollywood and New York, and on the plane between Las Vegas and Virginia. I wrote two the other day, coming up on the train from London . . .'

McCall Smith – Sandy to his friends – grew up in Zimbabwe (then Rhodesia) and was educated there and in Scotland. He became a law professor and is currently professor of medical law at Edinburgh University. He also helped set up a new law school at the University of Botswana, is an international authority on genetics, and an adviser to UNESCO and the UK government on bioethics. How he has found the time to write more than 50 books over the past 20 years is anybody's guess.

Alexander McCall Smith
(© Graham Clark).

Although he's written specialist academic titles, children's books and short-story collections, it was his 1998 detective novel, *The No.1 Ladies' Detective Agency*, that introduced his heroine Mma Ramotswe, Botswana's finest – and only – female detective, and that shot him to literary super-stardom. More than four million copies of the books in the series have been sold in the English-speaking world, and they have been translated into twenty-six other languages from Catalan to Estonian. He also created Isabel Dalhousie, a respectable lady detective who inhabits genteel Merchiston, in *The Sunday Philosophy Club*, in which a young man plunges to his death from the gods in Edinburgh's Usher Hall.

When not on gruelling American book tours, McCall Smith lives in Edinburgh with his wife and two daughters. He plays the bassoon with 'The Really Terrible Orchestra', but dislikes 'the very high notes'. And by the way, not only is number 44 Scotland Street fictional, but its residents are too, so if you're after the blood of Bruce, the vain surveyor, you'll have to vent your wrath on someone else.

Canonmills

8 Howard Place
Birthplace of Robert Louis Stevenson

A fractious little fellow . . . though decidedly pretty.
A description of the baby Robert Louis Stevenson
by one of his mother's bridesmaids

Robert Lewis Balfour Stevenson was born on 13 November 1850 and was named after his grandfathers, Robert Stevenson and Rev. Lewis Balfour. His parents, Thomas Stevenson and Margaret Balfour, married in 1848 and set up their first home at 8 Howard Place, a relatively new Georgian Terrace situated just beyond the northern rim of the New Town. Their only child was christened by his grandfather at Howard Place, and the family nicknamed him 'Smout', after the Scots word for salmon fry.

The universal image of Stevenson is synonymous with that of chronic ill health, but for the first two of years of his life Smout was a healthy child, with no signs of the purgatory to come. Like many Victorians, his parents worried about the family's health, perhaps overly so, but for the time being Smout was in no danger. When he was 18 months old, his nurse, Alison Cunningham, entered his life. 'Cummy' was from Torryburn, in Fife, and her zealous devotion to her young charge, coupled with her strict Calvinism and 'blood-curdling tales of the Covenanters', had a profound and lasting influence on Stevenson for the rest of his life. It was Cummy to whom he dedicated *A Child's Garden of Verse* in 1885.

Howard Place was small, and a little too close to the dampness of the Water of Leith for comfort, which in those days conveyed sewage and secretions, and their hovering stench, from local mills towards the sea. Hence the move in 1853 to a house at 1 Inverleith Terrace, which, although just across the street, was a larger and, it was hoped, a healthier one.

SEE ALSO: Inverleith Terrace, Heriot Row, Rutherford's Howff, Hawes Inn, W.E. Henley, The Writers' Museum, Kinnaird, Braemar, The *Kidnapped* Trail.

FURTHER INFORMATION: From 1926 until 1963, 8 Howard Place was an RLS museum and headquarters of the RLS Club (www.

8 Howard Place.

robertlouisstevensonclub.org.uk). It was sold in 1964 and its exhibits can now be seen in The Writers' Museum, Lady Stair's Close. Poet and critic W.E. Henley, friend, collaborator and ultimately antagonist of Robert Louis Stevenson, lived at 11 Howard Place between 1889 and 1891, when he was editor of the *Scots Observer*.

FURTHER READING: J.C. Furnas, *Voyage to Windward* (Faber and Faber, 1952); I. Bell, *Dreams of Exile: Robert Louis Stevenson – A Biography* (Mainstream, 1992); J. Calder, *RLS: A Life Study* (Hamish Hamilton, 1980); C. Harman, *Robert Louis Stevenson: A Biography* (HarperCollins, 2005).

Inverleith

9 Inverleith Terrace
Childhood home of Robert Louis Stevenson

> Whenever the moon and stars are set,
> Whenever the wind is high,
> All night long in the dark and wet,
> A man goes riding by.
> Late in the night when the fires are out,
> Why does he gallop and gallop about?
>> Robert Louis Stevenson recalling his fear of stormy nights at
>> Inverleith Terrace, from 'Windy Nights',
>> *A Child's Garden of Verse* (1885)

On 27 June 1853, when Robert Louis Stevenson was two years six months old, the Stevenson family moved from 8 Howard Place to 1 (now number 9) Inverleith Terrace, conveniently situated just across the road. This larger three-storey house was, at first glance, more salubrious, but in reality it proved to be the opposite and was draughty, damp and mildewed. Whether Inverleith Terrace was a catalyst for Stevenson's decline in health around this time is debatable, but it sounds likely. Both his parents had bronchial complaints, so his respiratory problems would probably have been inherited anyway, but a combination of 'one of the vilest climates under heaven', dampness, air pollution and chronic chest trouble doesn't bode well. Tuberculosis of the lungs is a diagnosis which is often put forward but cannot be confirmed, as there were no blood tests or X-rays available in the nineteenth century.

Stevenson wrote of Inverleith Terrace in *Notes of Childhood* (1873):

> All this time, be it borne in mind, my health was of the most precarious description. Many winters I never crossed the threshold, but used to lie on my face on the nursery floor, chalking or painting in water-colours the pictures in

9 Inverleith Terrace.

Louis and his father, Thomas Stevenson.

the illustrated newspapers; or sit up in bed, with a little shawl pinned about my shoulders, to play with bricks or whatnot.

When he was well, his devoted nurse Cummy took him for walks to the Royal Botanic Gardens and nearby Warriston Cemetery. 'Do you remember, at Warriston, one autumn Sunday,' he wrote to Cummy in 1883, 'when the beech-nuts were on the ground, seeing Heaven open? I would like to make a rhyme of that, but cannot.' His spirits were lifted in October 1856 when cousin Bob, his uncle Alan's son, came to spend the winter. Stevenson wrote in *Memoirs of Himself* (1880):

> This visit of Bob's was altogether a great holiday in my life. We lived together in a purely visionary state. We had countries; his was Nosingtonia, mine Encyclopaedia; where we ruled and made wars and inventions . . . We were never weary of dressing up. We drew, we coloured our pictures; we painted and cut out figures for a pasteboard theatre; this last one of the dearest pleasures of my childhood.

In 1856 the Stevensons moved to their new south-facing home at 17 Heriot Row in the middle of the New Town – a move that reflected Thomas Stevenson's thriving career and would, it was hoped, improve little Lou's health.

SEE ALSO: Howard Place, Heriot Row, Rutherford's Howff, Hawes Inn, W.E. Henley, The Writers' Museum, The *Kidnapped* Trail, Kinnaird, Braemar.

FURTHER READING: R. Woodhead, *The Strange Case of R.L. Stevenson* (Luath Press, 2001).

Leith

2 Wellington Place
Former home of Irvine Welsh (1958–), Hibs supporter and author of *Trainspotting*

> Somebody said, 'There's too many f***s and too many c***s in the book.' I says, 'Well, how many is enough and how much is too many?'
>
> Irvine Welsh

Born in Leith and brought up in Muirhouse, Irvine Welsh became a household name in 1993 when his novel *Trainspotting*, about a group of heroin addicts living in Leith, exploded with the shock and impact of a thunderbolt and saw Welsh acknowledged as the voice of 1990s British youth culture. Danny Boyle's 1996 film reached an even wider audience, securing Welsh's place in Scotland's literary hall of fame – or infamy, depending on your taste. Today the controversy and outrage has all but evaporated, and *Trainspotting* sits comfortably on bookshop shelves beside the Waverley novels, where Leith meets the Heart of Midlothian (why did Scott never write a book about the Hibs?).

A controversial figure, who has a love-hate relationship with his native city, Welsh is never afraid of expressing his opinions in

Irvine Welsh (© Rankin).

PARCEL OF ROGUES

FROM
NEW NOVELS BY
JAMES KELMAN
AND
JANICE GALLOWAY

TO
STORIES BY
JANET PAISLEY
AND
GORDON LEGGE

AND MORE ROGUISH NEW WRITING

vernacular expletives. There have been many media 'claims' about Welsh's background. The word 'shrouded', for example, is often used when referring to his roots, but there's nothing sinister about a man who wants to keep his past from the muck-rakers. Personally, I would respect his privacy and enquire no further, mainly because Welsh himself would probably tell me to 'F**k off, ya plukey-faced wee hing-oot.'

We both went to the same secondary school – Ainslie Park in Pilton Avenue (now flats) – but we never met. Our council estates were virtually next door to each other, and my Auntie Lizzie lived in sunny Leith, where her window looked directly onto the bleak stone wall of Leith Central Station, from which Welsh derived his title for *Trainspotting*, an ironic reference to the fact that trains no longer stop there, Leith now being a community ignored and forgotten.

Welsh was reputedly born in 1958 and left school aged 16 to serve his time as an apprentice TV repair man. He later moved to London, where he had various jobs, got involved in the punk scene and ended up working in the offices of Hackney Council. He returned to Scotland and was employed as a training officer with Edinburgh City Council from 1986 to 1994, during which time he took computer studies at Heriot Watt University.

REBEL inc.

New Writing From:
Irvine Welsh
Graham Fulton
Brent Hodgson
Brian Whittingham
Alison Kermack
Rab Fulton
Kim Oliver
David Millar
Tom Kone
Hazel Carmichael
David Scott
Shug Hanlan
Ruth Thomas
Keith Mackie
James Walker
Marina Blake
Alan Warner
Jack Fuller
Chrissy O'Brien
Alan Warner

ISSUE 3

2 Wellington Place (second floor, left).

Trainspotting began appearing in 1991 in the London-based low-budget magazine *DOG* and also in Glasgow's *West Coast Magazine* and *Scream, If You Want to Go Faster: New Writing Scotland No. 9*, edited by Hamish Whyte and Janice Galloway. Early drafts of *Trainspotting* also appeared in the first edition of the Edinburgh-based *Rebel Inc.* in April 1992 and in Duncan McLean's *Clocktower Booklet: A Parcel of Rogues*. It was McLean who recommended Welsh to Robin Robertson, editorial director of Secker & Warburg, who decided to publish *Trainspotting*.

Following the book's success, Welsh gave up his day job and turned to full-time writing. Stories proliferate that he peaked with his debut and begot the craze for lad-lit, but he did reach a vast audience who understood where he was coming from and recognised a language they could tune into. Welsh continues to produce some startling work. *Porno* (2002) continues the story of the principal characters of *Trainspotting* ten years on, where Sick Boy is now a director of porno movies and Spud is writing a history of Leith, though still an addict. Other works include *The Acid House* (1994), *Marabou Stork Nightmares* (1995), *Ecstasy* (1996), *Filth* (1998) and *Glue* (2001).

Literary travellers searching out the sites of *Trainspotting* will need to move fast, as the city's landscape is forever changing. The bookmaker's in Muirhouse's Pennywell Road where Renton searched for drugs in the 'worst toilet in the world' is now no more, and the 'jigsaw' flats off West Granton Road where Tommy died of AIDS have been demolished. Deacon Brodie's pub in the Royal Mile, visited by Renton and his pals, and Begbie's regular boozer, the Central Bar at the foot of Leith Walk, are still going strong. Welsh's favourite Leith bar, the Boundary Bar at 379 Leith Walk, is now called City Limits.

According to Ron McKay of *The Observer* (4 February 1996), not everyone in Muirhouse is a fan:

> 'Ah ken that Irvine Welsh,' said the scarfaced barman in the Penny Farthing pub. 'He's a sad f**king case, he is. He's a f**king Hibee . . .' One woman defended him stoutly, 'Ah don't care what they say, naebody's ever written aboot Muirhouse before,' but, asked whether she'd actually read any of his books, she said, 'Ah'll get roon tae them when they're on offer at Kwik Save.'

FURTHER INFORMATION: The *Trainspotting* Tour departs from the Port o' Leith Bar, 58 Constitution Street, Leith, and lasts around two hours with a refreshment stop. For programme dates and times, contact Tim Bell on 0131 555 2500 or consult www. leithwalks.co.uk

Muirhouse can be reached by the intrepid literary pilgrim by jumping on a number 37 bus outside Fraser's department store at the west end of Princes Street or by catching a northbound number 27 bus in Hanover Street. From Leith take a westbound number 32 from Bernard Street.

South Queensferry

Newhalls Road
The Hawes Inn
Sixteenth-century inn featured in Robert Louis Stevenson's
Kidnapped

> Some day, I think, a boat shall put off from the Queen's Ferry,
> fraught with a dear cargo.
> Robert Louis Stevenson, 'A Gossip on Romance' (1882)

The romantic setting of the Hawes Inn first appealed to Sir Walter Scott, who had Lovel and Jonathan Oldbuck dining there in *The Antiquary* in 1816, but it was Robert Louis Stevenson who secured its immortality when he wove it into the plot of *Kidnapped* (1886), his tale of the Jacobite rising of 1745 and its sad aftermath. 'There it stands,' he wrote, 'apart from the town, beside the pier, in a climate of its own, half inland, half marine – in front, the ferry bubbling with the tide and the guardship swinging to her anchor; behind, the old garden with the trees.'

Although altered and extended over the years, the Hawes Inn still retains some of the backdrop, and perhaps a little of the spirit, in which old Ebenezer arranged the kidnap of his nephew David Balfour with the assistance of Captain Hoseason in 'a small room, with a bed in it, and heated like an oven by a great fire of coal'. The unsuspecting David Balfour later boards the brig *Covenant*, moored at South Queensferry, where he is kidnapped and destined to be sold as a slave in the Carolinas.

Stevenson was a regular visitor to Queensferry in his youth, rambling along the shores of Cramond and canoeing in the Forth with Walter Simpson, his companion in *An Inland Voyage*. Since 1890 the Hawes Inn has been dwarfed by the adjacent Forth Railway Bridge, a spectacular feat of Victorian engineering that Stevenson never saw. The ferry disappeared in the early 1960s with the opening of the Forth Road Bridge.

SEE ALSO: The *Kidnapped* Trail, Sir Walter Scott, Howard Place, Inverleith Terrace, Heriot Row, Rutherford's Howff, W.E. Henley, Kinnaird, Braemar.

FURTHER INFORMATION: The Hawes Inn, Newhalls Road, South Queensferry, EH30 9TA. Tel: 0131 331 1990.

In *Catriona* (1893), the sequel to *Kidnapped*, David Balfour is

imprisoned on the Bass Rock, opposite North Berwick, about 20 miles east of Edinburgh. Stevenson visited North Berwick for holidays as a young boy and set his essay 'The Lantern-Bearers' (1887) there.

FURTHER READING: Ian Nimmo, *Walking With Murder: On the Kidnapped Trail* (Birlinn, 2005).

Dumfries and Galloway

Dumfries

Then out spak mim-mou'd Meg o' Nith,
And she spak up wi' pride,
And she wad send the Soger youth,
Whatever might betide.
                    Robert Burns, from 'The Five Carlins' (1789)

The places connected with Robert Burns in Dumfries far outweigh
those of any other towns he is often associated with, namely Ayr,
Irvine, Kilmarnock, Tarbolton, Mauchline and Edinburgh. From
the time of his arrival in Dumfries on 4 June 1787 to his death in
the town on 21 July 1796, he produced a formidable body of work.
Nearly a hundred of his most popular songs, including 'Scots wha
ha'e wi' Wallace bled', 'A man's a man for a' that', 'O whistle and I'll
come to ye, my lad', 'My love is like a red, red rose', 'Ye banks and
braes o' bonnie doon', 'Cauld kail in Aberdeen', 'Willie Wastle',
'Auld Rob Morris' and 'Duncan Gray', were written by him either
in his house in Bank Street or in the house at Millbrae. Many local
characters and sites are also enshrined in his verse. The following
'Trail' follows closely in the footsteps of Scotland's national bard.

The Burns Trail

Leave the **Tourist Information Centre (1)** by crossing the
Whitesands and walking along the riverside to the truncated end
of the medieval 'Old Bridge'. Pass by the bus park, once the site of
a market for farm animals and where cattle drovers assembled and
watered their herds. With care, recross the 'Sands' and to your right
reach the foot of another medieval route, the narrow 'Friars Vennel'.
This takes you up from the watercourse of the Nith to the ridge on
which the town centre stands. Once the vennel went through an
orchard until it reached a town gate at today's Irish Street junction.
Note the Celtic cross design in the roadway. Continue up the vennel
to the crescent dominated by the **Burns Statue (2)**, erected by
public subscription in 1882. Walk along the pedestrianised High
Street. About 50 metres on your left is the **Hole in the Wa' (3)** (Hole
in the Wall) close, with an inn at the end. This is in the 'Midraw',
or Midrow, and dates from the early seventeenth century. Continue
down the High Street until you reach **Queensberry Square (4)**
on your left. Burns would have paraded here with the Dumfries
Volunteers. Pass the 1707 **Midsteeple (5)** on the 'girse hill' on your
right. Here in July 1796 Burns's body lay in state before the funeral

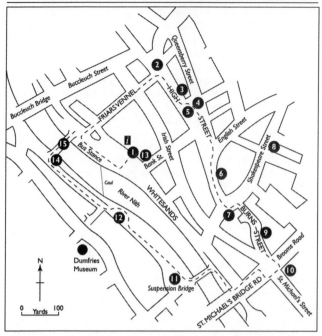

procession to St Michael's Kirkyard on 25 July. Continue past the fountain. On your left is Globe Inn Close, location of Burns's local hostelry, **The Globe Inn (6).** Continue down the High Street. At the Southergate end, cross Nith Place after passing the shopping mall on your right. In front of you is the **Georgian town house (7)** built for the town clerk around 1760 and reputedly designed by Robert Adam. Turn left, and before turning first right down Burns Street, glance up Shakespeare Street, where 200 metres ahead is the **Theatre Royal (8),** which was regularly patronised by Burns. On the crest of the cobbled roadway named Burns Street is **Robert Burns House (9),** where Burns and his family lived from May 1793 and where he died on 21 July 1796. Leaving the house, continue along Burns Street, where you can see the statue to Jean Armour. Cross over Brooms Road. Ascend the steps of **St Michael's Kirkyard (10)**. Go round the front of the church, and near its southeast corner is a useful indicator pinpointing numerous friends and colleagues of Burns who are buried in the kirkyard. Turn right then left for a striking view of the Grecian Mausoleum in which Burns and his family lie. As you return to the kirk, note the grey painted stone. This marks the grave of Burns's great friend, Rev. William Inglis, a minister of radical inclination whose Loreburn Kirk Burns often attended. Burns had a family pew in St Michael's, and for a further 30 years after his death Jean Armour regularly attended the church. A plaque on a pillar inside the church marks where the Burns family worshipped.

Return to the kirkyard gate and cross St Michael's Street, towards the Moorhead's Hospital building (1742). Walk down towards the river, turning right along the 'Dockhead', and cross the suspension bridge built in 1875 to allow mill workers to cross to work, saving a considerable walk to the old bridge upstream. You are now in the parish of Troqueer and the former burgh of Maxwelltown, amalgamated with Dumfries in 1929. The union was cemented by the construction of the St Michael's bridge on your left. Turn right along the small terrace of houses, **number 1 (11)** being the former home of the veteran actor John Laurie, best known for his role in *Dad's Army* but also remembered for his recitations of Burns. Continue upstream through the appropriately named 'Mill Green'. Soon you will reach the old burgh mill designed by engineer Thomas Smeaton and now converted into the **Robert Burns Centre (12)**. The centre has displays of Burns artefacts and a model of the burgh in 1794, depicting Dumfries in the time of Burns.

As you leave the Robert Burns Centre stand on the elevated platform and look over the river to Dumfries, chiefly on the higher ground above the Nith watercourse. Note the Midsteeple and Bank Street coming down from the High Street. At the foot of Bank Street, on your left-hand side, is another hostelry from Burns's day – the Coach and Horses. Above and beyond this you will see the white gable of the **tenement (13)** where Burns lived when he first came to Dumfries in November 1791, having given up the farm of Ellisland a few miles north of the burgh. The tenement is in Bank Street, but in Burns's day it was known as the Wee or Stinking Vennel. His was the first-floor flat, which is now privately owned. The flat has been referred to as the 'Sanghoose o' Scotland', since during his brief stay there Burns collected, improved or composed numerous songs, including 'Ae Fond Kiss', 'The Deil's Awa wi' the Exiseman' and 'Lea Rig'.

Walk down the steps then left along the riverside, noting the distinctive old weir – the 'caul' – and continue to the **Old Bridge House (14)** at the end of the bridge, which is now a museum. Appropriately, this was the chief entrance into the 'Brig End o' Dumfries' in the days before this part of Galloway had become the sophisticated burgh of Maxwelltown (1810) and then part of Dumfries. The Brig End was reputedly a fairly lawless place, not held in the highest regard by its neighbours over the Nith.

Cross **Devorguilla Bridge (15)**, built in 1431 and which Burns knew well. Come down the steep steps back onto the Sands and turn right back to your starting point **(1)**.

SEE ALSO: Baxter's Close, The Writers' Museum, Robert Fergusson, Brow Well, Ellisland Farm, Mossgiel Farm, National Burns Memorial Tower, Burns House Museum (Mauchline), Poosie Nansie's Inn, Mauchline Kirkyard, John Wilson's Printing Shop, Vennel Gallery, Burns National Heritage Park, Burns Cottage, Alloway Old Kirk, Alloway Burns Monument, Brig o' Doon, Souter Johnnie's Cottage, Tam O' Shanter Inn, Bachelors' Club, Robert Burns Centre, Robert Burns House (Dumfries), Globe Inn, Murray Arms, Tomb of Robert Burns.

FURTHER INFORMATION: Two excellent local reference sources for those wishing to dig deeper into the life of Burns are the Ewart Library on Catherine Street (01387 253820) and the Dumfries Archives Centre on Burns Street (01387 269254). Broughton House at 12 High Street, Kirkcudbright (01557 330437), also holds a comprehensive library on Burns collected by the artist E.A. Hornel.

24 Burns Street
Robert Burns House
Where Burns stayed from 1793 until his death in 1796

> Burns was not an early riser excepting when he had anything particular to do in the way of his profession. Even tho' he had dined out, he never lay after nine o'clock. The family breakfasted at nine. If he lay long in bed awake he was always reading. At all meals he had a book beside him on the table. He did his work in the forenoon and was seldom engaged professionally in the evening. He was fond of plain things and hated tarts, pies and puddings. When at home in the evening he employed his time in writing and reading with the children playing around him. Their prattle never distracted him in the least.
>
> Jean Armour

Burns and his family moved into this small, two-storey sandstone house in May 1793. The street was then called Millbrae, or Millbrae-Hole, but after Burns's death it was renamed Burns Street. It was in the smaller of the two bedrooms where he died of endocarditis on 21 July 1796. His widow Jean Armour occupied the house until her death in 1834, and in 1850 it was purchased by Burns's son, William Nicol Burns. Numerous artefacts connected to Burns can be viewed at the house, including his desk and chair, the Kilmarnock and Edinburgh editions of his poems, original manuscripts, and personal belongings. Many famous writers have called here to pay homage to Burns, among them Wordsworth, Keats and Coleridge.

SEE ALSO: Baxter's Close, The Writers' Museum, Robert Fergusson, Brow Well, Ellisland Farm, Mossgiel Farm, National Burns Memorial Tower, Burns House Museum (Mauchline), Poosie Nansie's Inn, Mauchline Kirkyard, John Wilson's Printing Shop, Vennel Gallery, Burns National Heritage Park, Burns Cottage, Alloway Old Kirk, Alloway Burns Monument, Brig o' Doon, Souter Johnnie's Cottage, Tam O' Shanter Inn, Bachelors' Club, Robert Burns Centre, Burns Trail (Dumfries), Globe Inn, Murray Arms, Tomb of Robert Burns.

FURTHER INFORMATION: Open all year, but closed Sunday and Monday from October to March. Admission free. Tel: 01387 255297.

16 Globe Inn Close
The Globe Inn
Favourite hostelry of Robert Burns

> O lovely Polly Stewart
> O Charming Polly Stewart
> There's not a flower that blooms in May
> That's half so fair as thou art.
> > Etched on a bedroom window at the Globe by
> > Robert Burns using a diamond ring. The
> > inscription survives to this day

Burns lived in Dumfries from 11 November 1791 until his death on 21 July 1796. He wrote many of his finest songs in Dumfries, and his local pub, the Globe Inn, off the High Street, was a source of both inspiration and pleasure. He had a daughter by the Globe's barmaid Anna Park. Jean Armour, Burns's wife, took the child into her own home to care for with the apparently nonchalant remark that 'Our Robbie should have had twa wives.'

Established in 1610, the Globe Inn has long been associated with Robert Burns. In 1796, Burns wrote, 'the Globe Tavern here, which these many years has been my Howff'. Some fine eighteenth-century panelling and the bedroom he used have been preserved. His favourite seat still survives, and some of his poetry may still be seen inscribed by Burns with a diamond ring on his bedroom windows. It was during landlord William Hyslop's time that the Mausoleum Committee met within the Globe Inn on 25 January 1819. This was effectively the first Burns Supper, when steps were taken to arrange an annual celebration. On one occasion Robert Burns forgot to order dinner for Nicol, Masterton and himself. Meg Hyslop produced a sheep's heid which she and Jock had intended for themselves. Nicol 'fined' Burns for his neglect by ordering him to compose grace. These stanzas were the result:

> O Lord when hunger pinches sore,
> Do Thou stand us in stead,
> And send us, from Thy bounteous store,
> A tup or wether head!
>
> O, Lord since we have feasted thus,
> Which we so little merit,
> Let Meg take away the flesh,
> And Jock bring in the spirit!

The Burns Room displays poems, pictures, gauger (exciseman) sticks, glasses, books, busts, jugs and, of course, the famous Burns Chair, which was gifted to the poet and used by him on his many visits to the Globe. If you sit in the chair, you must recite a line of Burns or your penalty is to buy all the customers in the bar a drink!

SEE ALSO: Baxter's Close, The Writers' Museum, Robert Fergusson, Brow Well, Ellisland Farm, Mossgiel Farm, National Burns Memorial Tower, Burns House Museum (Mauchline), Poosie Nansie's Inn, Mauchline Kirkyard, John Wilson's Printing Shop, Vennel Gallery, Burns National Heritage Park, Burns Cottage, Alloway Old Kirk, Alloway Burns Monument, Brig o' Doon, Souter Johnnie's Cottage, Tam O' Shanter Inn, Bachelors' Club,

Robert Burns Centre, Burns Trail (Dumfries), Robert Burns House (Dumfries), Murray Arms, Tomb of Robert Burns.

FURTHER INFORMATION: The Globe Inn, 16 Globe Inn Close, Dumfries. Tel: 01387 255297.

Email: mail@globeinndumfries.co.uk

Website: www.globeinndumfries.co.uk

The Burns Howff Club (01387 261033) was formed in the Globe Inn in 1889 and meets on 25 January each year to celebrate the anniversary of the birth of Robert Burns in 1759 with a Burns Supper. The club takes its name from a reference by Robert Burns to the Globe Inn being his favourite 'howff', an old Scottish term for a much-frequented tavern.

Mill Road
Robert Burns Centre

Dedicated to Robert Burns, this award-winning visitor centre tells the story of the Ploughman Poet's relationship with Dumfries through original documents, Rabbie's relics and audio-visual presentations. The centre also houses a bookshop and a café–gallery.

SEE ALSO: Baxter's Close, The Writers' Museum, Robert Fergusson, Brow Well, Ellisland Farm, Mossgiel Farm, National Burns Memorial Tower, Burns House Museum (Mauchline), Poosie Nansie's Inn, Mauchline Kirkyard, John Wilson's Printing Shop, Vennel Gallery, Burns National Heritage Park, Burns Cottage, Alloway Old Kirk, Alloway Burns Monument, Brig o' Doon, Souter Johnnie's Cottage, Tam O' Shanter Inn, Bachelors' Club, Burns Trail (Dumfries), Robert Burns House (Dumfries), Globe Inn, Murray Arms, Tomb of Robert Burns.

FURTHER INFORMATION: Situated off the A756 on Mill Road in Dumfries town centre. Opening hours: 10 a.m.–8 p.m. Monday to Saturday and 2 p.m.–5 p.m. Sunday, April to September; 10 a.m.–1 p.m. and 2 p.m.–5 p.m. Tuesday to Saturday, October to March. Admission free. Tel: 01387 264808.

St Michael Street
St Michael's Kirkyard
Tomb of Robert Burns

Men and women quite suddenly realised that here lay one who was the poet of the country – perhaps of mankind – as none had been before, because none before had combined so many human weaknesses with so great an ardour of living and so generous a warmth of admission. Certainly none had ever possessed a racier gift of expression for his own people.

Catherine Carswell, on the death of Burns
in *The Life of Robert Burns* (1930)

Robert Burns died of endocarditis induced by rheumatism at five in the morning on 21 July 1796 at home in the smaller of the two bedrooms in what is now Burns House in Burns Street. His coffin was removed to the Town Hall on the east side of the High Street opposite the Mid Steeple, where 'a vast concourse of persons' were gathering, and it was from here that his funeral cortège departed on Monday, 25 July. Burns was given a military funeral because he was a member of the Royal Dumfries Volunteers and was 'interred with military honours and every suitable respect'. As well as Burns's beloved volunteers, the half-mile of streets between the Town Hall and his grave were lined by regiments of the Angus-shire Fencible Infantry and the Cinque Ports Cavalry, who were also stationed in the town. The toll of church bells and the 'Dead March' from Handel's *Saul* accompanied the coffin to its final resting place in the north-east corner of St Michael's Kirkyard. Three volleys by the 'awkward squad' (Royal Dumfries Volunteers) were fired over his grave.

On the day of the funeral, Jean Armour (1767–1834) gave birth to his son Maxwell, their ninth child. In 1815 Burns's remains were transferred to a vault on the south-east border of the kirkyard, where a mausoleum, in the form of

Colonel William Nicol Burns, third son of Robert Burns, at his father's tomb.

a Grecian temple, was erected by subscription from his admirers at a cost of £1,500. It houses a mural sculpture by Peter Turnerelli, depicting the Muse of Poetry finding Burns in rustic dress at the plough. His widow Jean and their five sons are also interred there.

SEE ALSO: Baxter's Close, The Writers' Museum, Robert Fergusson, Brow Well, Ellisland Farm, Mossgiel Farm, National Burns Memorial Tower, Burns House Museum (Mauchline), Poosie Nansie's Inn, Mauchline Kirkyard, John Wilson's Printing Shop, Vennel Gallery, Burns National Heritage Park, Burns Cottage, Alloway Old Kirk, Alloway Burns Monument, Brig o' Doon, Souter Johnnie's Cottage, Tam O' Shanter Inn, Bachelors' Club, Burns Trail (Dumfries), Robert Burns House (Dumfries), Robert Burns Centre, Globe Inn, Murray Arms.

FURTHER INFORMATION: St Michael's Kirkyard is situated off the A756 on the corner of St Michael's Street and Brooms Road. Up until 1869 a pew that was regularly occupied by Burns, and on which he carved his initials with a knife, could be seen inside the church. During church renovations in 1869, the pew was sold for £5.

FURTHER READING: William McDowall, *Burns in Dumfriesshire* (Edinburgh, 1870); Julia Muir Watt, *Dumfries and Galloway: A Literary Guide* (Dumfries and Galloway Libraries, Information and Archives, 2000).

Ellisland Farm
Home of Robert Burns
Where he wrote 'Tam O' Shanter'

Burns rented Ellisland Farm from 11 June 1788 to 10 September 1791, and like all his previous farming ventures it would end in despondency and debt. It's not that he was a bad farmer, just an extremely unlucky one. When he took over the tenancy, the soil was exhausted, stony and badly drained. There was no farmhouse, and while one was being built he lived in a damp bothy on the farm, his wife Jean remaining behind in Mauchline with their son Robert until the house was made ready. The farm consisted of one

hundred and seventy acres, with an orchard, around ten cows, four horses and some sheep. His sons Francis Wallace and William Nicol were born at Ellisland, and their half-sister (fathered by Burns with Anna Park, barmaid of the Globe Inn, Dumfries) spent the first months of her life there.

Meanwhile, Burns was looking for a steady job that would give him a regular income, and he applied for an Excise post. On 14 July 1788 he obtained his commission and embarked on a new career as an officer of His Majesty's Excise as a 'gauger', or measurer. Excise was a tax levied on locally produced goods such as candles, salt, soap, tobacco, whisky, etc., and the Exciseman travelled his area measuring productivity and calculating the tax payable on these goods. Burns's territory encompassed ten parishes in Dumfriesshire, and sometimes he covered over two hundred miles a week. To cope with the two jobs of farmer and gauger, he converted Ellisland from an arable to a dairy farm, with Jean overseeing the milking and cheese-making.

Although he was mentally and physically exhausted, often sinking into deep depressions with the shadow of poverty continually hanging over his head, Burns's time at Ellisland was a particularly creative period in his life, and he composed 130 poems and songs there. These include 'Of a' the airts the wind can blaw', 'O were I on Parnassus hill', 'I hae a wife o' my ain', and 'Willie brewed a peck o' maut'. He is supposed to have penned 'Tam O' Shanter' one day during 1790 while walking a path overlooking the Nith, now called Shanter Walk.

The 'ruinous business' of Ellisland was eventually abandoned on 25 August 1791, when his crops were auctioned, and on 10 September he surrendered the lease. With all their worldly possessions crammed on carts, the family made their way to a new home at 11 Bank Street in Dumfries. On reaching town, Burns remembered he had etched the windows of Ellisland with much of his verse, and bid his brother-in-law to return and smash them, loath to leave his poetry on 'this accursed farm'.

SEE ALSO: Baxter's Close, The Writers' Museum, Robert Fergusson, Brow Well, Mossgiel Farm, National Burns Memorial Tower, Burns House Museum (Mauchline), Poosie Nansie's Inn, Mauchline Kirkyard, John Wilson's Printing Shop, Vennel Gallery, Burns National Heritage Park, Burns Cottage, Alloway Old Kirk, Alloway Burns Monument, Brig o' Doon, Souter Johnnie's Cottage, Tam O' Shanter Inn, Bachelors' Club, Burns Trail (Dumfries), Globe Inn, Robert Burns Centre (Dumfries), Murray Arms, Tomb of Robert Burns.

FURTHER INFORMATION: Ellisland Farm, now a museum, was gifted to the nation in 1929, and lies six miles north-west of Dumfries on the west bank of the River Nith, just off the A76. Opening times: 10 a.m.–1 p.m. and 2 p.m.–5 p.m Monday to Friday, and 2 p.m.–4 p.m. Sunday, April to September; 10 a.m.–4 p.m. Tuesday to Saturday, October to March. Tel: 01387 740426.

Website: www.ellislandfarm.co.uk

Gatehouse of Fleet

High Street
Murray Arms Hotel
The inn where Robert Burns reputedly wrote 'Scots wha ha'e wi' Wallace bled'

> Lay the proud usurpers low!
> Tyrants fall in every foe!
> Liberty's in every blow!
> Let us do – or die!
> Robert Burns, from 'Scots wha ha'e wi' Wallace bled'

Nine miles north-west of Kirkcudbright on the Water of Fleet lies the town of Gatehouse of Fleet, where in 1642 an old posting inn was established. During a tour of Galloway in the summer of 1793, Robert Burns and his friend John Syme spent the night there. Local legend has it that he wrote the song 'Scots wha ha'e wi' Wallace bled' during his stay, but John Syme said he composed it on the way to Kenmure and on returning from St Mary's Isle. Whatever the precise facts are, it seems fairly certain that he wrote it sometime during his Galloway tour.

Burns was inspired to write the song after hearing of the harsh sentence given to a group of men (including most notably Glasgow lawyer Thomas Muir) who became known as the 'Scottish Martyrs' and who were transported to Botany Bay for supporting parliamentary reform. Muir was tried for sedition and sentenced to 14 years' transportation by Lord Braxfield. In court Braxfield was reminded that Jesus Christ was a reformer too, to which he replied, 'Muckle he made o' that. He was hanget.'

SEE ALSO: Baxter's Close, The Writers' Museum, Robert Fergusson, Brow Well, Ellisland Farm, Mossgiel Farm, National Burns Memorial Tower, Burns House Museum (Mauchline), Poosie Nansie's Inn, Mauchline Kirkyard, John Wilson's Printing Shop, Vennel Gallery, Burns National Heritage Park, Burns Cottage, Alloway Old Kirk, Alloway Burns Monument, Brig o' Doon, Souter Johnnie's Cottage, Tam O' Shanter Inn, Bachelors' Club, Burns Trail (Dumfries), Robert Burns House (Dumfries), Robert Burns Centre, Globe Inn, Tomb of Robert Burns.

FURTHER INFORMATION: Murray Arms Hotel, High Street, Gatehouse of Fleet, Dumfries and Galloway, DG7 2HY. Tel: 01557 814207.

Website: www.murrayarms.com

The Martyrs' Monument, a 90-feet-high obelisk, was erected in 1844 to the memory of the political martyrs of 1793 in the Old Calton Burial Ground, Waterloo Place, Edinburgh.

Ruthwell

Brow Well
Where Robert Burns attempted to restore his failing constitution during the summer of 1796

With hindsight, it seems almost like a suicidal act for a dying man to stand up to his armpits in the freezing water of the Solway Firth in the hope of gaining a cure, but this was what Burns's friend and physician, Dr Robert Maxwell, advised him to do if he wished to restore his health. And so with his body 'reduced nearly to the last stage' by 'an excruciating rheumatism', Burns dutifully immersed himself in the waters around the village of Brow, bathing in the sea and in the chalybeate spring of Brow Well for the last three weeks of his life in July 1796. The village of Brow was described by Burns's biographer Catherine Carswell as 'a mean, dilapidated, dismal little clachan, consisting of a dozen cottages and an inn that was no more than a cottage itself. For the spa some rickety benches in a broken shed did duty, and a twenty-yard "esplanade" of tufted sea grass.'

Burns's friend Maria Riddel was convalescing nearby at the time and was quite shocked at his appearance, commenting that 'the stamp of death was imprinted on his features. He seemed already touching the brink of eternity. His first salutation was "Well, madam, have you any commands for the other world?"'

The treatment was to no avail, and on 21 July Robert Burns, the jewel of Scotland, died of endocarditis.

SEE ALSO: Baxter's Close, The Writers' Museum, Robert Fergusson, Ellisland Farm, Mossgiel Farm, National Burns Memorial Tower, Burns House Museum (Mauchline), Poosie Nansie's Inn, Mauchline Kirkyard, John Wilson's Printing Shop, Vennel Gallery, Burns National Heritage Park, Burns Cottage, Alloway Old Kirk, Alloway Burns Monument, Brig o' Doon, Souter Johnnie's Cottage, Tam O' Shanter Inn, Bachelors' Club, Burns Trail (Dumfries), Globe Inn, Robert Burns Centre (Dumfries), St Michael's Kirkyard.

FURTHER INFORMATION: Brow Well is signposted on the edge of the village of Ruthwell, nine miles south-east of Dumfries on the B724/B725. The inscription reads 'The Brow Well, visited by the poet Burns, July 1796'. Take care on the sands here as the unpredictable tides are said to ebb with the 'speed of a galloping horse'.

Ecclefechan

Main Street
The Arched House
Birthplace of Thomas Carlyle, historian and essayist

The village of Ecclefechan, situated midway between Lockerbie and the Solway Firth, has been generally identified as the 'Entepfuhl' of Carlyle's *Sartor Resartus*. There it is, little altered from what it was when Carlyle knew it in his early days, lying in a hollow, surrounded by wooded slopes, with its little 'Kuhbach' still gushing kindly by . . . There are the beechrows; and here by the side of the road, is the field where the annual cattle fair is held – 'undoubtedly the grand summary of Entepfuhl child's culture, whither, assembling from all the four winds, come the elements of an unspeakable hurly-burly'.

The Scotsman, 11 February 1881

Carlyle's birthplace is a plain two-storey building that stands on the west side of the main street, near the south end of the village.

It's undergone many changes over the years, but he was reputedly born in a room above the keyed archway on 4 December 1795. He was the eldest of nine children of James Carlyle (1758–1832), a stonemason, and Margaret Aitken (1771–1853), a local girl, thirteen years her husband's junior. 'He was irascible, choleric, and we all dreaded his wrath . . . I was ever more or less awed and chilled before him,' wrote Thomas Carlyle of his father in later years, and although 'an atmosphere of fear' distanced the man from his children, Carlyle

Thomas Carlyle, by Robert Tait, 1856.

also wrote that he had 'a sacred pride in [his] Peasant Father, and would not exchange him even now for any King known to me'.

He attended secondary school in nearby Annan, and in 1809, barely 14 years of age, he left for Edinburgh (covering the 80 miles on foot) to study at the university for a general arts degree. He left in 1813 without taking his degree and took up teaching at his old school in Annan. He returned to Edinburgh again in 1817 to begin theological training, but religious doubts and disaffection with the Church put an end to his intended career in divinity. He first met 19-year-old Jane Welsh, the only child of Dr John Welsh and his wife Grace, at her parents' home in Haddington in 1821, and they married in October 1826 and settled in Edinburgh.

Carlyle's early efforts at trying to make a living from his pen included writing entries for Brewster's encyclopaedia. He also tutored and began penning articles for *The Edinburgh Review*. As a writer and historian he became influenced by German philosophy and literature, and in 1824 he published a translation of Goethe's *Wilhelm Meister's Apprenticeship*. In 1833–34 *Sartor Resartus*, his first major work on social philosophy, was published in

The Arched House, Ecclefechan.

instalments in *Fraser's Magazine*. His best-known work remains his *History of the French Revolution* (1837), published in three volumes, the first of which had to be rewritten after a servant accidentally burnt the draft. Described by Dickens as 'that wonderful book', which he claimed in a letter in 1851 to be reading 'for the 500th time', it was no doubt a major influence on his own *A Tale of Two Cities* (1859).

In 1848 William Thackeray told his mother that 'Tom Carlyle lives in perfect dignity' in a little house in Chelsea 'with a snuffy Scotch maid to open the door, and the best company in England ringing at it'. The Sage of Chelsea, as he became known, died on 4 February 1881, aged 85. Westminster Abbey, however, did not claim him, as his will requested that he be buried beside his parents in Ecclefechan.

SEE ALSO: Jane Carlyle, National Library of Scotland, Tibbie Shiel's Inn.

FURTHER INFORMATION: Thomas Carlyle's birthplace is now a museum run by the National Trust for Scotland, furnished to reflect domestic life in his time, and contains a collection of portraits and Carlyle's belongings. The Arched House, Ecclefechan, Dumfries and Galloway, DG11 3DG. Off the M74, five miles south-east of Lockerbie. Open June to September. Tel: 01576 300666.

FURTHER READING: J.A. Froude, *Thomas Carlyle: A History of his Life* (1884); Rosemary Ashton, *Thomas and Jane Carlyle: Portrait of a Marriage* (Pimlico, 2003).

Moniave

Ardnacloich
Former home of Rumer Godden (1907–98), novelist, poet and children's author

> I think nuns are irresistibly dramatic. Theirs is the greatest love story on earth.
>
> Rumer Godden

Rumer Godden will be best remembered for her 1938 bestseller  *Black Narcissus*, which tells the story of a group of nuns and their struggle to establish a convent in a disused Indian palace in the Himalayas, where their beliefs are challenged and consumed amid its ancient pagan atmosphere. The book has never been out of print, and she was inspired to write it while on a picnic in Assam, where she saw the grave of a nun. Michael Powell successfully adapted the book for the cinema in 1947, but Godden hated the film, commenting that 'everything about it was phoney. The outside shots were done in a Surrey garden, and the Himalayas were just muslin mounted on poles . . . the whole thing was an abomination.' She converted

Rumer Godden at 90.

On the set of *Black Narcissus*, 1946.

to Catholicism in 1968, commenting, 'I like the way everything is clear and concise. You'll always be forgiven, but you must know the rules.'

She was born in Eastbourne and spent her childhood in Narayanganj, India, where her father controlled the traffic on the town's inland waterways. The second-eldest of four daughters, she was sent to England after the First World War to be educated and did not return to India until she was 17. She published her first novel, a children's book, when she was 28. After the Second World War, she returned to England, where she wrote a successful series of novels and children's books. Altogether she published 24 novels, including *Kingfishers Catch Fire* (1953), *An Episode of Sparrows* (1955), *Two Under the Indian Sun* (1966), *Shiva's Pigeons* (1972), *The Peacock Spring* (1975) and *Coromandel Sea Change* (1991). Her 1946 autobiographical novel *The River* was successfully adapted for the screen by Jean Renoir in 1951. Rumer Godden also published poetry, translations, a biography of Hans Christian Andersen and two volumes of autobiography: *A Time to Dance, No Time To Weep* (1987) and *A House with Four Rooms* (1989).

FURTHER INFORMATION: Rumer Godden moved from Rye (where she lived in Henry James's old house) to Moniave in the early 1980s to be closer to her family. Her favourite walks in and around the conservation village of Moniave included Dalwhat Glen and the grounds of Maxwelton House Chapel. She may have thought Michael Powell's film adaptation of *Black Narcissus* an 'abomination', but cameraman Jack Cardiff won an Oscar and a Golden Globe for his cinematography. The film was shot in the exotic gardens of Leonardslee House, Lower Beeding, in West Sussex.

FURTHER READING: Anne Chisolm, *Rumer Godden: A Storyteller's Life* (Macmillan, 1998); Michael Powell, *A Life in Movies* (Faber and Faber, 2000).

North Ayrshire

Irvine

Glasgow Vennel
The Vennel Gallery and Heckling Shed
Where Robert Burns encountered the trade of flax-dressing

My twenty-third year was to me an important era. Partly through whim, and partly that I wished to set about doing something in life, I joined with a flax-dresser in a neighbouring town, to learn his trade and carry on the business of manufacturing and retailing flax. This turned out a sadly unlucky affair. My partner was a scoundrel of the first water who made money by the mystery of thieving; and to finish the whole, while we were giving a welcome carousal to the new year, our shop, by the drunken carelessness of my partner's wife, took fire and was burnt to ashes, and left me like a true Poet, not worth sixpence. (O why the deuce should I repine, and be an ill-forboder? I'm twenty-three, and five-feet-nine, – I'll go and be a sodger!) I was obliged to give up business: the clouds of misfortune were gathering thick round my father's head, the darkest of which was, he was visibly far gone in a consumption; and to crown all, a belle-fille whom I adored [probably Ellison Begbie], and who had pledged her soul to meet me in the field of matrimony, jilted me with peculiar circumstances of mortification. The finishing evil that brought up the rear of this infernal file, was my hypochondriac complaint being irritated to such a degree that, for three months, I was in diseased state of body and mind, scarcely to be envied by the hopeless wretches who have got their mittimus – 'Depart from me, ye cursed'.

Robert Burns, autobiographical
letter to Dr John Moore, 1787

In 1781 23-year-old Robert Burns arrived in the then major seaport of Irvine to learn the trade of flax-dressing. His father's farm at Lochlie, near Tarbolton, was growing flax, whose fibres are transformed into linen, and Burns wanted to learn the processes involved in its manufacturing and retailing. His partner was his mother's half-brother, a rogue named Alexander Peacock, who plied his trade in Glasgow Vennel. Flax-heckling, however, proved to be a monotonous and dusty occupation in cramped and airless conditions – a stark contrast to the open-air farm life Burns was accustomed to. He spent seven months in Irvine, before returning to Lochlie with his plans for a career in flax well and truly buried, but he did gain first-hand experience of town life and gained some interesting friends.

SEE ALSO: Baxter's Close, The Writers' Museum, Robert Fergusson, Brow Well, Ellisland Farm, Mossgiel Farm, National Burns Memorial Tower, Burns House Museum (Mauchline), Poosie Nansie's Inn, Mauchline Kirkyard, John Wilson's Printing Shop, Burns National Heritage Park, Burns Cottage, Alloway Old Kirk, Alloway Burns Monument, Brig o' Doon, Souter Johnnie's Cottage, Tam O' Shanter Inn, Bachelors' Club, Burns Trail (Dumfries), Globe Inn, Murray Arms, Robert Burns Centre (Dumfries), Tomb of Robert Burns.

FURTHER INFORMATION: The Vennel Gallery and Heckling Shed (off the High Street) is open all year from Friday to Sunday. Tel: 01294 275059. The gallery, which ajoins the Heckling Shed, hosts various art exhibitions. Access to the lodging house Burns used during his stay can be arranged with staff at the gallery.

The Irvine Burns Club and Museum at 28 Eglinton Street (01294 274511) is also worth a visit. It holds the only surviving manuscript Burns had sent to the press for his first edition, several original letters, and an extensive library and art collection.

At the Old Parish Church, Kirk Vennel (off the High Street), are the graves of David Sillar (the 'Dainty Davie' of Burns's 'Second Epistle to Davie', 1789) and Helen Miller (the Nell of 'A Mauchline Wedding'). The church also has a stained-glass window to Burns by artist Susan Bradbury.

Off Bank Street, at Mackinnon Terrace, a cairn records the Drukken Steps (St Bryde's Well) in Eglinton woods, a favourite walk of Burns and Captain Richard Brown, his seafaring friend who encouraged him to publish his work and 'the only man I ever saw who was a greater fool than myself when woman was the presiding star'. A statue was unveiled to Burns on Gallows Knowe, Irvine, on 18 July 1896, and another graces the gardens of Eglinton Country Park.

Kilwinning

Main Street
Site of the childhood home of Robert Service (1874–1958), Bard of the Yukon

> A bunch of the boys were whooping it up in the Malamite saloon;
> The kid that handles the music box was hitting a ragtime tune;
> Back of the bar in a solo game, sat Dangerous Dan McGrew,
> And watching his luck was his light o' love, the lady that's known as Lou.
>
> Robert Service, from 'The Shooting of Dangerous Dan McGrew', *The Songs of a Sourdough* (1907)

Robert Service once described his role in life as 'writing verse for those who wouldn't be seen dead reading poetry'. His poetry was written for the man in the street, but he was such a master of metre, rhyme and alliteration that his storytelling powers and graphic verse captivated the imagination of millions and rocketed him to fame and fortune. His description of the desolate and sub-

arctic landscapes of the Yukon and the wild, lawless characters who inhabited it during the gold-rush years are unforgettable. It was a time recaptured in his most memorable poems, 'The Shooting of Dangerous Dan McGrew' and 'The Cremation of Sam McGee'. He became known as the 'Bard of the Yukon', and his war poetry outsold that of Wilfred Owen and Siegfried Sassoon. He became the world's first million-selling poet, and his wanderings took him all over the world, but his childhood roots were in Ayrshire.

He was born on 16 January 1874, the eldest of ten children, in Preston in Lancashire to Sarah Emily Parker and Robert Service, a bank cashier. At the age of five he was sent to live with his paternal grandparents and three maiden aunts in the Ayrshire town of Kilwinning, where his grandfather and aunts worked in the post office. He later remarked that Services in Ayrshire 'were as thick as fleas on a yellow dog'. It was a typical Scots Presbyterian household: thrifty, pious and dominated by the Kirk, where tongues wagged behind lace curtains and on the Lord's day everyone dressed in their Sunday best. In his autobiography *Ploughman of the Moon* (1945) he playfully recalls the Kilwinning logic:

> 'Please, Aunt Jeannie, can I go and look at the hens?'
> Over her spectacles my aunt gazed at me suspiciously.
> 'Whit fur Rubbert, do you want to look at the hens?'
> 'I don't know whit fur, I just want to look at them.'
> 'Ye'd be faur better lookin' at yer bonnie Bible. Don't ye like yer wee Bible?'
> 'Aye, but I like the hens better.'

His mother came from a wealthy Preston family who had made their money from cotton – money which she eventually inherited. In 1883 his family moved to Glasgow. Robert joined them in a tenement flat in Hillhead, where he attended Hillhead High School. On leaving school he entered a shipping office, but shortly afterwards became a trainee bank clerk at the Stobcross branch of the Commercial Bank of Scotland. At the age of 21 he emigrated to Canada with dreams of becoming a cowboy, first settling in Vancouver Island, then wandering through the Western States and British Columbia. In 1903 he joined the Canadian Bank of Commerce in Victoria, and the following year he was posted to the Yukon, where he began to write the verse that would make him famous.

He wrote about a territory immersed in gold fever, bar-room brawls, shoot-outs, mining camps and dance halls, peopled with unforgettable characters with names like Klondike Kate, the Lady known as Lou, Sam McGee and the Ragtime Kid. Service himself, however, was the antithesis of all this. He was no gambler, boozer or womaniser. He was what he was: a Scottish banker who was considered quite dapper and who was never seen without a stiff collar. But underneath this conservative veneer he had adventure in his veins. He was a loner and an observer who took long walks (one lasted for 2,000 miles), often on snowshoes, for exercise, but also for inspiration. In 1907 his first collection of verse was published under the title *The Songs of a Sourdough*, which brought him wealth for the first time in his life, and within two years he resigned from the bank and headed for Paris.

He travelled as a reporter for the *Toronto Star*, and during the First World War he was turned down by the army on medical grounds and so became an ambulance driver and later a war correspondent for the Canadian government. In 1913 he married Germaine Bourgoin, with whom he had twin girls. His later years were spent at his house in Lancieux, Brittany, where he died in September 1958.

He wrote copiously throughout his life, both poetry and novels, including *Ballads of a Cheecako* (1909), *The Trail of '98* (1910), *Rhymes of a Rolling Stone* (1912), *The Pretender* (1914), *Rhymes of a Red Cross Man* (1916), *Ballads of a Bohemian* (1921), *Why Not Grow Young?* (1928) and his two volumes of autobiography, *Ploughman of the Moon* (1946) and *Harper of Heaven* (1947). Robert Service will not stand comparison with Keats or Shelley, or even Kipling, whom he admired and with whom he was often compared. He never considered himself a poet, but a skilled rhymester for the man in the street. In 'A Verseman's Apology' he wrote:

> The classics! Well, most of them bore me
> The Moderns I don't understand;
> But I keep Burns, my kinsman, before me,
> And Kipling, my friend, is at hand.
> They taught me my trade as I know it,
> Yet though at their feet I have sat,
> For God-sake don't call me a poet,
> For I've never been guilty of that.
>
> And I fancy my grave-digger griping
> As he gives my last lodging a pat:
> 'This guy wrote McGrew;
> 'Twas the best he could do' . . .
> So I'll go to my maker with that.

FURTHER INFORMATION: A plaque was unveiled in 1976 by Robert Service's daughter Iris Davies at the site of his childhood home on Main Street, opposite the Clydesdale Bank. A sheltered housing complex is also a memorial to him at Robert Service Court.

Many of Service's characters were based on real people: the Ragtime Kid was Hartley Claude Myrick, who died in Seattle in 1950; the Lady known as Lou was cabaret singer Lulu Johnson, who drowned when the steamship *Princess Sofia* sank in the Lynn Canal in 1918; and Sam McGee was a Dawson prospector whose name Service found in a bank ledger.

FURTHER READING: G.W. Lockhart, *On the Trail of Robert Service* (Luath Press, 1991); Carl F. Klinck, *Robert Service: A Biography* (McGraw-Hill Ryerson, 1977); James A. Mackay, *Vagabond of Verse: Biography of Robert Service* (Mainstream Publishing, 1995).

South Ayrshire

Alloway

Burns National Heritage Park

This park links all the Burns sites and haunts in Alloway, including Burns's birthplace and museum, the Burns Monument and Memorial Gardens, The Statue House, Kirk Alloway and Brig o' Doon. And if the title 'Heritage Park' hasn't already put you off, wait till you see the Tam O' Shanter Experience . . .

Tam O' Shanter Experience

An audio-visual presentation 'where modern technology brings an old tale to life', or, depending on your taste, where modern technology transforms one of the world's greatest narrative poems into a fairground sideshow. This oasis of tartan tat comes complete with a licensed restaurant, gift shop, gardens and play area. Built on the site of the old railway yards in 1975 and extended in 1995, it was originally criticised for its 'modern' appearance. Condemnation of this Burnsian eyesore seems to have abated somewhat in recent years, as a local guidebook claims that it 'now fits comfortably into the fabric of Alloway'.

Burns Cottage and Museum
Birthplace of Robert Burns

> Burns has given voice to all the experiences of common life . . . he has made that Lowland Scotch a dialect of fame. It is the only example in history of a language made classic by the genius of a single man.
>
> Ralph Waldo Emerson, responding to the primary toast at the Celebration of the Hundredth Anniversary of the Birth of Robert Burns by the Boston Burns Club, 25 January 1859

Burns-related tourism and branding is worth almost £160 million a year to Scotland's economy, much of it spent in Ayrshire, and Dumfries and Galloway, but 'No wan in fifty kens a wurd Burns wrote' sneered Hugh MacDiarmid in *A Drunk Man Looks at the Thistle* (1926). He was probably right, but this minor detail has never hindered Burns's status as Scotland's most celebrated bard, who left for posterity a volume of work which, written in his native tongue and championing the common man, has contributed significantly to the Scottish cultural identity. Other cultures equally embrace and adore him, from Japan to Russia, not for his Scottishness or any romantic hero image, but because of his honesty, love of life and lassies, drinking bouts, sexual misdemeanours, debts, melancholy, and

The auld clay biggin, birthplace of Robert Burns.

perverse behaviour; in other words, the voice of the common man. Hugh MacDiarmid can scoff all he likes that few 'kens a wurd Burns wrote', but we all ken the spirit in which he wrote, which in the end transcends the wurd and has become immortal.

His life was brief; never reaching his 40th year, he died when he was only 37 years old, his health broken by the harsh physical labour he endured as a youth on his father's farm. He was born, the first of seven children, in an 'auld clay biggin' ('The Vision', 1786) on 25 January 1759 in the village of Alloway to William Burnes, a gardener, and Agnes Broun, a farmer's daughter from Kirkoswald. William built the two-roomed clay thatched cottage with his own hands, and the couple settled down to a future of relentless toil, debts, poor harvests and punitive Scottish winters. This, however, only strengthened William's passion for education and escape, and he made sure Robert went to school. Although poor, his ardour for education extended to engaging for Robert and his brother Gilbert a private tutor named John Murdoch, who once wrote, 'In this cottage . . . I really believe there dwelt a larger portion of content than in any Palace in Europe. "The Cotter's Saturday Night" will give some idea of the temper and manners that prevailed there.' Robert had only three years of formal education but learned to read and write and master the rudiments of grammar. This all ended when he was nine, when, through financial necessity, he was put to work on the farm. His father continued to instruct his sons in the evenings from his collection of books on grammar and theology, but Burns's education from that time was irregular and haphazard.

By 1766, when Robert was seven, William and Agnes and their brood had outgrown their little but-and-ben, and they rented a seventy-acre hilltop farm at Mount Oliphant, two miles to the south-east. However, the cottage at Mount Oliphant wasn't much bigger than Alloway, the soil was poor and William was hounded by the factor for rent arrears. It was on this farm that Robert, aged 15, fell in love with Nellie Kilpatrick at harvest time and 'first committed the sin of RHYME' when he wrote the song 'Handsome Nell' for her. In 1777 the family moved to the one hundred and thirty swampy acres of Lochlea Farm, three miles north-west of Mauchline, and continued their unyielding struggle to survive. In 1781 Robert became a Freemason and moved to Irvine for seven months to learn the trade of flax-dressing, but he knew his future did not lie there and returned to the farm, where his father died of consumption on 13 February

1784, browbeaten by disputes with landlords, rent arrears and the never-ending labour of life. Robert, now a grown man and head of the family, changed the spelling of the family name to Burns and rented Mossgiel Farm, one mile north of Mauchline.

Today Burns's birthplace is a place of pilgrimage for the literary tourist. It was sold in 1781 for £14 to the Incorporation of Shoemakers, a charitable organisation who turned the cottage into a public house to raise funds for retired shoemakers and their families. John Keats had a dram there in 1818 and recalled that 'we drank toddy to Burns' memory with an old man who knew Burns – damn him and damn his anecdotes – he was a great bore . . . a mahogany-faced jackass . . . he ought to have been kicked for having spoken to him'. One hundred years later, in 1881, the property was acquired by the Trustees of the Burns Monument for £4,000. A museum was added next door in 1900. Today it is run by the National Trust for Scotland. Who would Keats kick today, I wonder?

Alloway Old Kirk

> While glowring round wi' prudent cares,
> Lest bogles catch him unawares:
> Kirk-Alloway was drawing nigh,
> Whare ghaists and houlets nightly cry.
>
> Robert Burns, from 'Tam O' Shanter'

The roofless ruin of 'Alloway's auld haunted kirk' stands just below the 'Auld Brig' of Doon and was the scene of the witches' orgy in one of the greatest narrative poems ever written: 'Tam O' Shanter'. And if you ever visit it after sunset, you will not need a lot of convincing. Dating back to the sixteenth century, the kirk remains very much as Burns knew it. The gables are still standing, one with a double lancet window and a seventeenth-century bellcote. At the entrance to the kirkyard gate is the grave of William Burnes (1721–84), the poet's father, marked by a modest stone. The original stone disappeared years ago, a piecemeal victim of souvenir hunters, but unlike the present marker, it probably did not use the standardised spelling of his surname Robert adopted after his death. When William Burnes

Grave of William Burnes, the poet's father, with Alloway Old Kirk in the background.

Scotia's darling son.

119

was buried there, his famous son was still an unknown. It struck me as strange, therefore, that the first stone facing you as you enter the gates is his. My guess is that the stone was moved from its original location in the kirkyard to its present, and more imposing, spot when his son's star was ascending.

FURTHER INFORMATION: After Robert died, his brother Gilbert became factor to Lord Blantyre at Lennoxlove, near Bolton in East Lothian. He took up residence at Grant's Braes, about one mile north of the village, and his mother Agnes and sister Annabel came to live with him. All three are buried in Bolton Parish Churchyard. A roadside memorial, called Burns's Mother's Well, marks the site of their home.

Burns Monument and Memorial Gardens

> Ah, Robbie, ye asked them for bread and they hae gi'en ye a stane.
>> Burns's mother Agnes commenting on a stately monument to her son's memory

The Burns Monument.

Situated between Brig o' Doon and Alloway Kirk, about half a mile from Burns's birthplace, the Burns Monument was completed on 4 July 1823 at a cost of £3,350, a sum which would have kept Burns and his family's descendants in 'bread' for generations. It was built in the Greek Revival style by Edinburgh architect Thomas Hamilton, who designed a similar memorial to Burns in 1830 on the south side of Edinburgh's Calton Hill. As well as a monument to Burns, Alloway's memorial is also a monument to Masonic pride. Its ornate cupola and surmounting tripod was escorted with great ceremony from Ayr amid the banners and bands of 15 Masonic lodges. Each of the Corinthian columns represents one of the nine Muses, and a spiral staircase leads to a viewing platform. The triangular base represents Cunninghame, Kyle and Carrick, the three districts of Ayrshire. In the grounds can also be seen James Thom's statues of Tam O' Shanter, Souter Johnnie and Nanse Tinnock, a landlady from Mauchline whose inn was frequented by Burns.

Brig o' Doon

> Ae spring brought off her master hale,
> But left behind her ain grey tail:
> The carlin claught her by the rump,
> And left poor Maggie scarce a stump.
>> Robert Burns, from 'Tam O' Shanter'

This is the bridge in 'Tam O' Shanter' over which Tam and his grey

Brig o' Doon.

mare Maggie 'left behind her ain grey tail' and narrowly escaped the carlins (old witches), because 'A running stream they dare na cross'. The bridge probably dates from the fifteenth century and narrowly escaped demolition when the New Bridge of Doon was built downstream in 1816. Plans to tear down this shrine of literary tourism were mooted, but later wisely abandoned.

SEE ALSO: Baxter's Close, The Writers' Museum, Robert Fergusson, Brow Well, Ellisland Farm, Mossgiel Farm, National Burns Memorial Tower, Burns House Museum (Mauchline), Poosie Nansie's Inn, Mauchline Kirkyard, John Wilson's Printing Shop, Vennel Gallery, Souter Johnnie's Cottage, Tam O' Shanter Inn, Bachelors' Club, Burns Trail (Dumfries), Globe Inn, Murray Arms, Robert Burns Centre (Dumfries), Tomb of Robert Burns, Robert Tannahill.

FURTHER INFORMATION: Burns National Heritage Park, Murdoch's Lone, Alloway, Ayr. Open seven days, year round: 10 a.m.–5.30 p.m. April to September; 10 a.m.–5 p.m. October to March. Tel: 01292 443700 for group rates and special bookings or email info@burnsheritagepark.com

Website: www.burnsheritagepark.com

If you are driving there, park in the Tam O' Shanter Experience car park. A nice place to eat is the Brig o' Doon Hotel, situated on the narrow road beneath the Burns Monument, leading down to the Brig o' Doon. At the time of writing, signposting to the Burns National Heritage Park was poor; in fact, Burns Country as a whole feels fragmented and lacking any kind of national strategy.

Failford

Monument commemorating the parting of Robert Burns and Highland Mary

How sweetly bloomed the gay green birk,
How rich the hawthorn's blossom,
As underneath the fragrant shade,
I clasped her to my bosom!
The golden hours, on angel wings,
Flew o'er me and my dearie:
For dear to me as light and life,
Was my sweet Highland Mary.

Wi' mony a vow, and lock'd embrace,
Our parting was fu' tender;
And, pledging aft to meet again,
We tore ourselves asunder;
But, oh! fell death's untimely frost,
That nipt my flower sae early!
Now green's the sod and cauld's the clay,
That wraps my Highland Mary!

Robert Burns, from 'Highland Mary' (1792)

In 1786 Robert Burns became smitten with his friend Gavin Hamilton's new nursemaid, a blonde beauty named Mary Hamilton (1763–86), known as Highland Mary. The two of them secretly courted each other and made plans to marry and settle in Jamaica, but tragically Mary died shortly after leaving Hamilton's employ in Mauchline. The lovers' last meeting, and where they pledged themselves to each other, was at Failford on 'the second Sunday of May, 1786', a parting described by Archibald R. Adamson in his classic 1879 travelogue, *Rambles Through the Land of Burns*:

> After fifty yards from Coilsfield House I paused before an aged but shattered and decayed thorn which grows by the side of the drive leading to the Tarbolton entrance of the domain. The stately trees by which it is guarded overlook a steep bank clothed with verdure and dense masses of shrubs which screen the rippling Fail as it gurgles on to mingle its water with the winding Ayr. There is nothing remarkable about the appearance of the thorn, nothing to attract attention, yet curiously enough its rotten moss-grown trunk is chipped and hacked, and its remaining limb disfigured with rude initials and gashes which wanton relic-hunters have inflicted with pocket knives. What is the cause of all this? and why is the grass round about it trampled and bare? Well, tradition states that it is the identical tree beneath which Robert Burns took the last farewell of his sweet Highland Mary.
>
> In all likelihood the tradition is correct, for the position of the thorn and its nearness to the mansion makes it more

A popular painting of the lovers pledging themselves to one other.

The Highland Mary Monument, Failford.

than probable that the parting took place beneath its shade – in fact, Burns was by far too great a gallant to part from his mistress at any great distance from her home. The lovers stood on each side of a purling brook . . . they layed their hands in the limpid stream – and holding a Bible between them pronounced their vows to be faithful to each other. As already stated, they exchanged Bibles, but what became of that which Burns received was never known; the half-Bibles presented to Mary are preserved in the monument on the banks of Doon.

SEE ALSO: Highland Mary (Dunoon).

FURTHER INFORMATION: A monument commemorating the last farewell of Burns and Mary can be seen in Failford with an inscription from Burns's 'Thou Lingering Star':

> That sacred hour can I forget,
> Can I forget the hallowed grove,
> Where by the winding Ayr we met,
> To live one day of parting love.

The monument is located at the top of a track accessed from the village bridge on the main road.

Kirkoswald

Main Road
Souter Johnnie's Cottage
Former home of John Davidson, Souter Johnnie in Robert Burns's 'Tam O' Shanter'

> And at his elbow, Souter Johnny,
> His ancient, trusty, drouthy crony;
> Tam lo'ed him like a vera brither –
> They had been fou for weeks thegither!
> Robert Burns, from 'Tam O' Shanter'

This cottage was the home of John Davidson (1728–1806), the village souter (shoemaker), inspiration for Souter Johnnie in 'Tam O' Shanter', Burns's narrative poem about a drunken farmer's meeting with witches, warlocks and Auld Nick in the Kirk of Alloway. Davidson lived there from 1785 until his death in 1806 and is buried in the local kirkyard. He married Anne

Souter Johnnie's Cottage.

Gillespie in 1763, who had been in service to Burns's maternal grandfather Gilbert Broun. He was a man known for his humour and wit and originally lived at Glenfoot of Ardlochan, near a farm called Shanter. It was while visiting Davidson there that Burns met Douglas Graham (1739–1811), who leased the farm of Shanter, between the Maidens Rock in Carrick, and who would become his inspiration for 'Tam O' Shanter'. Graham was supposedly fond of the drink and had a boat named *Tam o' Shanter*, believed to be used for smuggling contraband. Legend also has it that one market day his drunken friends clipped his horse's tail, which he explained away to his superstitious wife as having been done by witches.

Burns, aged 17, was sent to study and lodge at Kirkoswald in the summer of 1775 under the auspices of a local schoolmaster. Although he made 'pretty good progress' at his studies, they were always a grind to him until one day he met 'a charming Fillette, who lived next door to the school':

> [Who] overset my Trigonometry and set me off in a tangent from the sphere of my studies. I struggled on with my Sines and Co-sines for a few days more; but stepping out to the garden one charming noon, to take the sun's altitude, I met with my Angel . . . It was vain to think of doing any more good at school. The remaining week I staid, I did nothing but craze the faculties of my soul about her, or steal out to meet with her; and the two last nights of my stay in the country, had sleep been a mortal sin, I was innocent. I returned home very considerably improved . . .'

The 'charming Fillette' was Peggy Thomson, said to have inspired his poem 'Composed in August'.

SEE ALSO: Baxter's Close, The Writers' Museum, Robert Fergusson, Brow Well, Ellisland Farm, Mossgiel Farm, National Burns Memorial Tower, Burns House Museum (Mauchline), Poosie Nansie's Inn, Mauchline Kirkyard, John Wilson's Printing Shop, Vennel Gallery, Burns National Heritage Park, Burns Cottage, Alloway Old Kirk, Alloway Burns Monument, Brig o' Doon, Tam O' Shanter Inn, Bachelors' Club, Burns Trail (Dumfries), Globe Inn, Murray Arms, Robert Burns Centre (Dumfries), Tomb of Robert Burns.

FURTHER INFORMATION: Souter Johnnie's Cottage, Main Road, Kirkoswald, South Ayrshire, KA19 8HY. Tel: 01655 760603. Open April to September.

The cottage has been completely refurbished in period style with a souter's workshop and comical statues of the characters in 'Tam O' Shanter'. Burns's grand- and great-grandparents, the Brouns, are also buried in the local kirkyard. John Davidson's mull (snuff container) is preserved in the Burns Monument in Edinburgh. The Shanter Hotel at 47 Main Street, Kirkoswald (01506 832121), carries a plaque showing that its southern end formed the school at which Burns studied while in the village and that the central part of the inn was home to Peggy Thomson.

Ayr

230 High Street
The Tam O' Shanter Inn

> Auld Ayr, whaur ne'er a town surpasses,
> for honest men and bonie lassies
> > Robert Burns, from 'Tam O' Shanter'

Built around the mid-1700s, and originally named The Plough, this inn was once said to have been supplied with ale by Douglas Graham, the original Tam. The hostelry shrewdly changed its name during the nineteenth century to the Tam O' Shanter Inn and promoted itself as 'the house where Tam O' Shanter and Souter Johnnie held their meetings'. It was all a sham, but the pub still rides today on the publicity, and folk hae been fou here for years thegither, wi sangs and clatter, and been nane the wiser.

SEE ALSO: Baxter's Close, The Writers' Museum, Robert Fergusson, Brow Well, Ellisland Farm, Mossgiel Farm, National Burns Memorial Tower, Burns House Museum (Mauchline), Poosie Nansie's Inn, Mauchline Kirkyard, John Wilson's Printing Shop, Vennel Gallery, Burns National Heritage Park, Burns Cottage, Alloway Old Kirk, Alloway Burns Monument, Brig o' Doon, Souter Johnnie's Cottage, Bachelors' Club, Burns Trail (Dumfries), Globe Inn, Murray Arms, Robert Burns Centre (Dumfries), Tomb of Robert Burns.

FURTHER INFORMATION: The Tam O' Shanter Inn, 230 High Street, Ayr, KA7 1RQ. Tel: 01292 611684.

Ayr is also the home of Ayrshire's annual Burns Festival, 'Burns an' a' That!', which takes place every May with live events across Burns country celebrating the life of the Bard and contemporary Scottish culture. Contact Burns Festival, County Buildings, Wellington Square, Ayr, KA7 1DR. Tel: 01292 290300.

Website: www.burnsfestival.com

A statue to Burns, erected in 1891, stands in the square outside the railway station. William Burnes (1721–84), the poet's father, was an elder in the Auld Kirk of Ayr (off the High Street, up Kirk Close), and Burns composed 'The Brigs of Ayr' in the autumn of 1786, in which he compares the fifteenth-century 'Auld Brig' with Robert Adams's 'New Brig', completed in 1788.

Further Burns references can be found at the Carnegie Library on Main Street (01292 286385); Ayrshire Archives Centre, Craigie Estate (01292 287584); North Ayrshire Museum, Manse Street, Saltcoats (01294 464174); and the local history department of North Ayrshire Libraries Headquarters, Princes Street, Ardrossan (01294 469137).

Tarbolton

Sandgate
The Bachelors' Club

In 1780 Burns helped found the Bachelors' Club, a debating society for unmarried men on the upper room of this two-storey seventeenth-century cottage and former inn. He became its first president, and at one time this meeting place was the largest room in the village. Burns also took dancing lessons here in 1777, and on 4 July 1781 he was inaugurated as a Freemason at St David's Lodge, number 174, Tarbolton, who also used the room for their meetings. The lower level was once the living quarters of John Richard, and period furnishings recreate what his house may have looked like when a byre and an alehouse adjoined it.

SEE ALSO: Baxter's Close, The Writers' Museum, Robert Fergusson, Brow Well, Ellisland Farm, Mossgiel Farm, National Burns Memorial Tower, Burns House Museum (Mauchline), Poosie Nansie's Inn, Mauchline Kirkyard, John Wilson's Printing Shop, Vennel Gallery, Burns National Heritage Park, Burns Cottage, Alloway Old Kirk, Alloway Burns Monument, Brig o' Doon, Souter Johnnie's Cottage, Tam O' Shanter Inn, Burns Trail (Dumfries), Globe Inn, Murray Arms, Robert Burns Centre (Dumfries), Tomb of Robert Burns.

FURTHER INFORMATION: Open April to September, afternoons only. Tel: 01292 541940.

A dispute later divided the Tarbolton Freemasons into two lodges, and Burns moved to the St James's Lodge, which met at nearby James Manson's Inn, now located at 67 Montgomery Street, where items connected to his Masonic career are on display (01290 551100).

The Bachelors' Club.

East Ayrshire

Kilmarnock

Star Inn Close
Site of John Wilson's Printing Shop
Where the first edition of Burns's *Poems, Chiefly in the Scottish Dialect* was printed in 1786

On the corner of King Street and Waterloo Street is Star Inn Close, site of John Wilson's Printing Shop (now demolished but marked by a granite slab) and where Robert Burns published by subscription his first book *Poems, Chiefly in the Scottish Dialect* – the famous Kilmarnock edition – on 31 July 1786. In early April 1786, Burns drew up the following:

> PROPOSALS for publishing, by subscription,
> SCOTTISH POEMS, by Robert Burns
> The work to be elegantly printed, in one volume octavo. Price stitched, three shillings. As the author has not the most distant mercenary view in publishing, as soon as so many subscribers appear as will defray the necessary expense the work will be sent to the press.
>
> > Set out the brunt side of your shin,
> > For pride in poets is nae sin:
> > Glory's the prize for which they rin,
> > And fame their joe;
> > And whaw blaws best his horn shall win,
> > And wharefore no?

The print run totalled six hundred and twelve copies, all stitched in blue paper and costing three shillings each. Subscribers amounted to 350, but the remaining copies sold out in a month. The book was an overnight success, and Burns made a respectable profit of around £50. He then wanted to publish a second edition, but the publisher demanded money up front, which Burns didn't have, and so he decided to seek a second edition in Edinburgh, where fame but alas not fortune awaited him.

SEE ALSO: Baxter's Close, The Writers' Museum, Robert Fergusson, Brow Well, Ellisland Farm, Mossgiel Farm, National Burns Memorial Tower, Burns House Museum (Mauchline), Poosie Nansie's Inn, Mauchline Kirkyard, Vennel Gallery, Burns National Heritage Park, Burns Cottage, Alloway Old Kirk, Alloway Burns Monument, Brig o' Doon, Souter Johnnie's Cottage, Tam O' Shanter Inn, Bachelors' Club, Burns Trail (Dumfries), Globe Inn, Murray Arms, Robert Burns Centre (Dumfries), Tomb of Robert Burns.

FURTHER INFORMATION: At Kilmarnock Cross in the town centre stands a statue of Burns and the printer John Wilson, commemorating the publication of the first edition. An original copy of the Kilmarnock edition can be seen at Dean Castle, Kilmarnock (01563 554701), along with a collection of Burns's handwritten manuscripts. In the north-east part of the town, and east of the High Street, is Kay Park. Near the centre of the park stands the Burns Monument, a two-storey building in Scots Baronial style, erected in 1878–79. The building once boasted a tower rising to a height of 80 feet, containing a marble statue of Burns, but it was destroyed by fire in 2005, and only the statue now remains. The Robert Burns Foundation was formed in Kilmarnock in 1885. The group's main objectives were, and still are, to advance the education of the public about the life, poetry and works of Robert Burns. The Robert Burns World Federation Ltd, Dean Castle Country Park, Kilmarnock, Ayrshire, KA3 1XB. Tel: 01563 572469.

Website: www.worldburnsclub.com

Mauchline Parish

Mossgiel Farm
Where Robert Burns spent one of the most prolific periods of his poetic genius

> The best-laid schemes o' Mice an' Men
> Gang aft agley,
> An' lea'e us nought but grief an' pain,
> For promis'd joy!
>> Robert Burns, from 'To a Mouse, On turning her up
>> in her Nest, with the Plough, November 1785'

A month after the death of his father, Robert Burns and his brother Gilbert took over the lease of a 100-acre farm called Mossgiel in March 1784. The house was a single-storey but-and-ben of two rooms. One room was the kitchen, which housed concealed beds where the womenfolk slept, and the other was the 'spence' or parlour. Burns slept with his brother in a bedroom in the stable loft, and it was at a table in this loft that he wrote some of his greatest poetry, including 'The Vision', 'The Jolly Beggars', 'The

Mossgiel Farm.

Cotter's Saturday Night', 'Holy Willie's Prayer', 'Death and Dr Hornbrook', 'Scotch Drink' and 'The Twa Dogs'. In a nearby field, 'while holding the plough', his brother recalled him writing 'To a Mouse'.

Burns, or Rob Mossgiel as he was known, carried pen, ink and paper everywhere he went, whether at the plough or boozing at Poosie Nansie's. It was while he was tenant at Mossgiel that he met Jean Armour, learned of the death of Highland Mary and published his first book, *Poems, Chiefly in the Scottish Dialect*. It was an extremely prolific and emotionally fraught period of his life. However, Mossgiel may have produced great poetry, but great crops it did not. The brothers had purchased bad seed and, together with a late harvest, half their crops were lost – the farm was a failure. In July 1786 Burns transferred his share of the farm to Gilbert, and shortly afterwards he decided to try his luck in Edinburgh.

SEE ALSO: Baxter's Close, The Writers' Museum, Robert Fergusson, Brow Well, Ellisland Farm, National Burns Memorial Tower, Burns House Museum (Mauchline), Poosie Nansie's Inn, Mauchline Kirkyard, John Wilson's Printing Shop, Vennel Gallery, Burns National Heritage Park, Burns Cottage, Alloway Old Kirk, Alloway Burns Monument, Brig o' Doon, Souter Johnnie's Cottage, Tam O' Shanter Inn, Bachelors' Club, Burns Trail (Dumfries), Globe Inn, Murray Arms, Robert Burns Centre (Dumfries), Tomb of Robert Burns.

FURTHER INFORMATION: Mossgiel Farm is still a working farm but bears no resemblance to that which was there in Burns's day. It is not open to the public, but private visits may be arranged. To reach Mossgiel take the A76 from Mauchline heading towards Kilmarnock. After leaving Mauchline, about one mile north, take the Tarbolton road, the first turning on the left leading to the B744. Mossgiel is the first farm on your right.

Mauchline

Castle Street
Burns House Museum
First marital home of Robert Burns and Jean Armour

Robert Burns and Jean Armour probably met in the village of Mauchline in April 1784. She lived with her father, a master mason,

The Burns House, Castle Street.

Mauchline Castle – Gavin Hamilton's house.

The Bleaching Green (opposite Mauchline Castle).

at the foot of the Cowgate, at its junction with Howard Place, but she did not immediately attract his eye at the dancing upstairs at Morton's Tavern during the Mauchline Fair of that year. That night Burns's dog had managed to infiltrate its way upstairs to the dance floor and ruin a reel. Kicking it outside again, Burns remarked, 'I wish I could find a lass that would lo'e me as weel's my dog!' A few days later, while crossing the Bleaching Green where the village women bleached and dried their linen, he whistled on his dog to steer it clear of fouling any clothes. A young girl hailed him, 'Weel, Mossgiel, hae ye gotten ony lass yet to lo'e ye as weel's your dog?' Burns immediately recognised her from the dance. Jean Armour would have been 19 or 20, of darkish complexion, with a square set face, small hands and feet, shapely legs, and wide dark eyes. Their courtship led to the two lovers setting up home in February 1788 in an upstairs rented room in the house of Burns's doctor and friend Dr John Mackenzie in Backcauseway (now Castle Street). It was in this room, their first marital home, on 3 March 1788, that Jean gave birth to twins, but they both died within the month and are buried in the kirkyard opposite. This remained their home until late November 1788, when they moved to Ellisland Farm.

The statue to Jean Armour at The Cross.

Exhibits at the museum include Burns manuscripts, articles belonging to Burns and his contemporaries, and a collection of Mauchline ware, decorative boxware produced in the town during the 1930s.

SEE ALSO: Baxter's Close, The Writers' Museum, Robert Fergusson, Brow Well, Ellisland Farm, Mossgiel Farm, National Burns Memorial Tower, Poosie Nansie's Inn, Mauchline Kirkyard, John Wilson's Printing Shop, Vennel Gallery, Burns National Heritage Park, Burns Cottage, Alloway Old Kirk, Alloway Burns Monument, Brig o' Doon, Souter Johnnie's Cottage, Tam O' Shanter Inn, Bachelors' Club, Burns Trail (Dumfries), Globe Inn, Robert Burns Centre (Dumfries), Tomb of Robert Burns.

FURTHER INFORMATION: Open Tuesday to Saturday all year. Burns House Museum, 2–4 Castle Street, Mauchline, KA5 5B2. Tel: 01290 550045.

Burns and Jean Armour were married in Gavin Hamilton's house, an old relic of a former priory known as Mauchline Castle, next door to Mauchline Kirk. A bronze statue to Jean Armour was erected by Mauchline Burns Club in 2002 at The Cross. Diagonally opposite the Burns House Museum is the site of Nanse Tinnock's Inn, frequented by Burns, and mentioned by him in 'The Author's Earnest Cry and Prayer' and 'The Holy Fair'. Approximately one mile north of Mauchline on the A76 at the Tarbolton junction is the National Burns Memorial Tower, which opened in 1896. Since refurbished, it is now a Tourist Information office with an interpretation centre charting Burns's life in Mauchline. Opening hours: 9.15 a.m.–5 p.m. Monday to Saturday. Tel: 01290 551916.

Castle Street
Mauchline Kirkyard
Setting for 'The Holy Fair'

How monie hearts this day converts
O' sinners and o' lasses!
Their hearts o' stane, gin night, are gane
As saft as onie flesh is:
There's some are fou o' love divine;
There's some are fou o' brandy;
An monie jobs that day begin,
May end in houghmagandie
Some ither day.
Robert Burns, final stanza of 'The Holy Fair' (1785)

Holy Willie castigating fornicators at Mauchline's annual Holy Fair (Photo courtesy of Rab Steele).

Mauchline Kirkyard, opposite the Burns House Museum, was the setting for 'The Holy Fair', Burns's famous satire on religious hypocrisy. The Holy Fair was a common phrase in eighteenth-century Scotland for a sacramental occasion. In 1785 Mauchline had around 400 church members, but this could triple for the annual communion service. Tents were set up in the church grounds to accommodate the crowds, while rival preachers addressed the multitude. For many, though, it was more an entertainment than a religious experience. The contradictory nature of these fairs is elegantly summed up in *A Letter from a Blacksmith to the Ministers and Elders of the Church of Scotland*, a document published in 1759:

> In this sacred assembly there is an odd mixture of religion, sleep, drinking, courtship, and a confusion of sexes, ages and characters . . . in a word, there is such an absurd mixture of the serious and the comick, that were we convened for any other purpose than that of worshipping the God and Governor of Nature, the scene would exceed all power of farce.

This letter is said to have been one of the sources of Burns's poem, and many local characters were also included, notably 'Racer Jess' (Janet Gibson, the dim-witted daughter of Poosie Nansie) and several 'Auld Licht' and 'New Licht' ministers. In the poem Burns hilariously juxtaposes religious ceremony with social frolicking and 'houghmagandie' (fornication).

The kirk dates from 1829 and replaced the twelfth-century building Burns would have worshipped in and which Hew Ainslie described in his *Pilgrimage to the Land of Burns* (1820) as having been 'as ugly an old lump of consecrated stone as ever cumbered the earth'. Several of Burns's contemporaries and family are buried in Mauchline Kirkyard (all clearly marked), including the Armour burial plot (where four of Burns's children are buried), Gavin Hamilton (friend of Burns and from whom he subleased Mossgiel), Rev. William Auld (minister of Mauchline), William Fisher (inspiration for 'Holy Willie's Prayer'), Nanse Tinnock (landlady of the alehouse opposite Burns's house in Castle Street, who always maintained to the last that 'Burns never drank twa half-munchkins in her house in a' his life, and that what he stated in his poems was just a wheen 'leein' blethers'), Poosie Nansie (Agnes Gibson, landlady of Poosie Nansie's Inn) and Racer Jess.

SEE ALSO: Baxter's Close, The Writers' Museum, Robert Fergusson, Brow Well, Ellisland Farm, Mossgiel Farm, National Burns Memorial Tower, Burns House Museum (Mauchline), Poosie Nansie's Inn, John Wilson's Printing Shop, Vennel Gallery, Burns National Heritage Park, Burns Cottage, Alloway Old Kirk, Alloway Burns Monument, Brig o' Doon, Souter Johnnie's Cottage, Tam O' Shanter Inn, Bachelors' Club, Burns Trail (Dumfries), Globe Inn, Murray Arms, Robert Burns Centre (Dumfries), Tomb of Robert Burns.

FURTHER INFORMATION: The Mauchline Burns Club (01290 559304) meets regularly at Poosie Nansie's and organises the annual Holy Fair every May, which turns historic Castle Street into an eighteenth-century marketplace with 'minstrels, jugglers, circus performers and other street entertainers amusing the crowds, while screaming preachers verbally attack supposed offenders and fornicators'.

Websites: www.mauchlineburnsclub.com and www.mauchlinevillage.co.uk

Loudon Street
Poosie Nansie's Inn
Setting for Robert Burns's 'The Jolly Beggars'

> Ae night at e'en a merry core
> O' randie, gangrel bodies,
> In Poosie-Nansie's held the splore,
> To drink their orra duddies . . .
>> Robert Burns, from 'The Jolly Beggars: A Cantata' (1785)

Once the cottage or change-house of Agnes Gibson (Poosie Nansie), this inn was the setting for Burns's 'The Jolly Beggars' and said to have been the favourite hang-out of sailors, soldiers, wandering tinkers and travelling ballad singers – a place, in other words, that Burns would have felt at home in. Catherine Carswell in *The Life of Robert Burns* wrote:

> Because of her peculiar contumacy in sin Nansie had been 'excluded from the privileges of the church'. She was a drunken slut and a receiver of stolen goods. With her villainous, black-bearded husband she kept a lodging house and tavern for thieves and beggars. Her servant was a doxy off the roads, her daughter Jess a half-wit, nicknamed 'Racer' because she could run like a hare and would any day for a wager or a fee.

Archibald Adamson in his *Rambles Through the Land of Burns* (1879) describes Poosie Nansie as one 'who lodged vagrants and other questionable characters. The halt, the blind, and the lame found shelter beneath her roof, and her kitchen was not infrequently the

Poosie Nansie's Inn from Mauchline Kirkyard.

A Burns Club outing to Poosie Nansie's Inn (c.1890s).

133

scene of frantic mirth and bouts of drunkenness. Here Burns studied humanity in its lowest forms . . .' Needless to say, Poosie Nansie's is still a favourite haunt of the Mauchline Burns Club, and there is a Burns Room to the right of the entrance. Today Poosie Nansie's is no longer a 'tavern for thieves and beggars' and is a respectable public house, but Burns's legacy of poems about the characters and inns of the village lives on in the poetry of local poet and Poosie Nansie's regular Matt Welsh:

> It's Friday night an' I'm nearly ready,
> Fur doon the streets tae hae a bevy,
> two or three pints in the Loudon Bar,
> then up tae Poosies fur anither jar.

> A'll wave cheerio, tae awe a ken,
> An' stagger oot the door an' then,
> Singin' up the road fur awe a'm worth,
> This is the homeland of my birth.

> Matt Welsh, from 'The Pubs' (c. 1980)

SEE ALSO: Baxter's Close, The Writers' Museum, Robert Fergusson, Brow Well, Ellisland Farm, Mossgiel Farm, National Burns Memorial Tower, Burns House Museum (Mauchline), Mauchline Kirkyard, John Wilson's Printing Shop, Vennel Gallery, Burns National Heritage Park, Burns Cottage, Alloway Old Kirk, Alloway Burns Monument, Brig o' Doon, Souter Johnnie's Cottage, Tam O' Shanter Inn, Bachelors' Club, Burns Trail (Dumfries), Globe Inn, Murray Arms, Robert Burns Centre (Dumfries), Tomb of Robert Burns.

FURTHER INFORMATION: Poosie Nansie's Inn, 21 Loudoun Street, Mauchline, KA5 5BA. Tel: 01290 550316.

Near Poosie Nansie's is the site of the Whitefoord Arms (plaque erected in Loudon Street), which was situated in the Cowgate opposite the parish church, close to where Jean Armour's parents resided. It was the meeting place of Burns's 'Court of Equity', a bachelors' club where fornication seemed to be the chief topic of conversation. Mine host of this plain, thatched building of two storeys was John Dove, for whom Burns wrote on a pane of glass the 'Epitaph on John Dove'.

FURTHER READING: Matt Welsh, *Mauchline Village Poetry* (available from Poosie Nansie's or email matthew@welsh273.freeserve.co.uk).

Ochiltree

Main Street
Birthplace of George Douglas Brown (1869–1902)
Inspiration for *The House with the Green Shutters*

> Gourlay felt for the house of his pride even more than for himself – rather the house was himself; there was no division between them. He had built it bluff to represent him to the world. It was his character in stone and lime. He clung to it, as the dull, fierce mind, unable to live in thoughts, clings to a material source of pride.

> George Douglas Brown, from
> *The House with the Green Shutters*

George Douglas Brown's only novel *The House with the Green Shutters*, published in 1901, could be viewed as a one-hit wonder, but as Brown died the following year in 1902, aged only 33, he had no time to let us know otherwise, and Scottish literature lost a writer who could have grown into one of its greatest sons. The book is set in the rural community of Barbie, widely believed to be based on his birthplace. Up until this time rural Scotland had been portrayed by writers of the Kailyard school, which typified a sentimental and romantic image of Scottish rural life, written in the cosy vernacular. J.M. Barrie and S.R. Crockett were among its chief exponents. *The House with the Green Shutters* shattered this stereotypical image forever, bulldozing a chasm through the sentimental escapism of the Kailyard that other modernists like Hugh MacDiarmid and Lewis Grassic Gibbon (1901–35) would follow.

The novel is a study of small-town greed and selfishness. The main protagonist, John Gourlay, is a successful merchant whose profits built the house with the green shutters. Gourlay is a fearless bully, despised by his townsmen, referring to them as 'bodies' (local gossips). As industrialisation creeps up on him, he is slow to adapt and his business declines. His gifted but bullied son drifts into alcoholism, and with the arrival of the railway the family fortune evaporates. And like all great Greek tragedies, the son murders the father, and the mother and sister commit suicide. No wonder Brown described it as a 'brutal and bloody work'.

George Douglas Brown was born on 26 January 1869, the illegitimate son of farmer George Douglas Brown, who rejected him, and farm servant Sarah Gemmell. He was educated locally and at Ayr Academy, before studying classics at the University of Glasgow. In 1891 he won a scholarship to Balliol College, Oxford, and in the late 1890s moved to London, where he became a journalist writing magazine and boys' fiction. In 1899 he published the boys' adventure story *Love and a Sword* under the pen name Kennedy King, and the

George Douglas Brown's birthplace in Ochiltree in 1954.

135

following year, in the autumn of 1900, he began writing *The House with the Green Shutters*, which was published under the pen name George Douglas. J.B. Priestley described it as 'a masterpiece', and George Mackay Brown claimed it was the best Scottish novel of the twentieth century. What could have been the launch pad of a great literary career ended suddenly with Brown's death the following year. He may have died young and unfulfilled, but he left us a book that became a landmark in Scottish fiction.

FURTHER INFORMATION: The house, marked by a plaque, is situated in the main street at the top of the village.

Auchinleck

Auchinleck House
Family seat of James Boswell (1740–95), writer and biographer of Dr Johnson

> Servile and impertinent, shallow and pedantic, a bigot and a sot, bloated with family pride, and eternally blustering about the dignity of a born gentleman, yet stooping to be a talebearer, and eavesdropper, a common butt in the taverns of London . . . Everything which another man would have hidden, everything the publication of which would have made another man hang himself, was matter of exaltation to his weak and diseased mind.
>
> Lord Macaulay (1800–59) on Boswell

American literary critic Edmund Wilson once described Boswell as 'a vain and pushing artist', and he was probably right. He certainly comes across as extremely persistent and an ardent social climber. He also picked up prostitutes, contracted gonorrhoea, was the father of an illegitimate child, had prolonged bouts of drunkenness and was unfaithful to his wife. In spite of these apparent shortcomings, however, Boswell's inherently perspicacious nature and his intimate knowledge of Samuel Johnson combined to produce a biographical masterpiece that has never been equalled.

Boswell was born in Edinburgh in 1740, the eldest son of Lord Auchinleck, a lawyer who came from a family of wealthy Ayrshire landowners. He was educated at a private academy in Edinburgh and by private tutors, later studying law at Edinburgh, Glasgow and Utrecht. His ambitions began leaning towards literature, politics and the theatre, but it was as an advocate, which left him feeling 'sadly low spirited, indolent, listless and gloomy', that he practised for most of his life. While in Europe he skilfully effected meetings with Voltaire, Rousseau and the Corsican hero Pasquale de Paoli, which inspired him to write his *Account of Corsica* (1768), his first significant work. In 1769 he married his cousin, Margaret Montgomerie, a long-suffering woman who endured

his infidelities until her death, leaving Boswell with six children and a guilt complex.

He first met Dr Johnson (1709–84) on his second visit to London on 16 May 1763, at Tom Davies's bookshop in Russell Street, and from then on cemented his friendship with him on his all too infrequent visits to London. In 1773 they set out from Edinburgh together on a tour of Scotland and the Hebrides, which Boswell recounted in his *The Journal of a Tour to the Hebrides* in 1785. In 1784, when Boswell was 44, Johnson died. Two years later Boswell was called to the English Bar and moved to London with his wife and children, but his practice was unsuccessful. He was also unsuccessful in his pursuit of a political career, and he eventually began to write his *Life of Samuel Johnson*, 'perhaps now the only concern of any consequence' that he would 'ever have in this world'. While he was writing his *Life*, other biographies of Johnson were being published, and his greatest fear must have been that the public, having gorged on Johnson, would finally say enough was enough – and Boswell's was stretching to two volumes at a cost of two guineas. It was finally published in 1791 and its reception, recorded Boswell, was 'very favourable'. Forty years later, in 1831, Thomas Macaulay declared it the best biography ever written, and Thomas Carlyle, writing in *Fraser's Magazine* in 1832, wrote:

> [It is a book] beyond any other product of the eighteenth century . . . It was as if the curtains of the past were drawn aside, and we looked into a country . . . which had seemed forever hidden from our eyes . . . Wondrously given back to us, there once more it lay. There it still lies.

The 20,000-acre Auchinleck estate was owned by the Boswell family as far back as 1504. The present Auchinleck House was built between 1755 and 1760 by James Boswell's father, Alexander Boswell, the eighth Laird of Auchinleck. When court was in session, the Boswells resided in Edinburgh, but during the spring and summer they lived at their country estate. 'Auchinleck is a most sweet, romantic place,' Boswell once wrote to a friend. 'There is a vast deal of wood and water, fine retired shady walks, and everything that can render the country agreeable to contemplative minds.'

Johnson stayed at Auchinleck with Boswell at the end of their tour of Scotland in 1773, but the latter, quite rightly, feared conflict between his father and his friend. Johnson put Boswell's mind at ease, promising that he would 'not talk on subjects which I am told are disagreeable to a gentleman under whose roof I am; especially I shall not do so to your father'. Johnson tried his best, but the inevitable happened. The Presbyterian Whig and the Anglican Tory clashed when 'fatal topics of difference' surfaced. 'I cannot be certain whether it was on this day, or a former, that Dr Johnson and my father came in collision,' wrote Boswell in his journal entry for Saturday, 6 November. 'If I recollect right, the contest began while my father was shewing him his collection of medals and Oliver Cromwell's coin unfortunately introduced Charles the First and Toryism.'

Boswell inherited his father's estate, and his final years were spent in London revelling and whoring. With mounting debts and a constitution wrecked by endless venereal infections, he died from kidney failure and uraemia aged 54 at Auchinleck. A man well aware of his own talents, he wrote in his journal for 20 January 1763, 'I think there is a blossom about me of something more distinguished than the generality of mankind.' He is buried in the family vault in Auchinleck Churchyard.

SEE ALSO: James Court (Edinburgh), Robert Burns (Baxter's Close, Edinburgh), Cruden Bay, Gallowgate, Balloch, Dr Johnson.

FURTHER INFORMATION: Auchinleck House was uninhabited from the mid-1960s and fell into considerable disrepair. In 1986 the then owner sold the house to the Scottish Historic Buildings Trust, who made it watertight, and in 1999 it underwent a major programme of restoration by the Landmark Trust, who have restored it to reflect its original eighteenth-century splendour. The house is now available for holiday renting and sleeps 13 guests. Tel: 01628 825925.

Boswell is commemorated with portraits and mementoes in the Auchinleck Parish Church Museum next to the family mausoleum.

FURTHER READING: A. Sisman, *Boswell's Presumptuous Task: The Making of the Life of Dr Johnson* (Farrar, Straus & Giroux, 2001); I. Finlayson, *The Moth and the Candle: A Life of James Boswell* (Constable, 1985); G. Turnbull (ed.), *The Yale Editions of the Private Papers of James Boswell* (Edinburgh University Press, 2004); D. Hankins and J. Caudle (ed.), *The General Correspondence of James Boswell, 1757–1763* (Edinburgh University Press, 2004).

South Lanarkshire

Biggar

Brownsbank Cottage
Former home of Hugh MacDiarmid (1892–1978), Scotland's greatest twentieth-century poet

> He was there for a quarter of a century and hundreds of people from pretty well all over the world made their pilgrimage to that little home.
>
> Norman MacCaig

Regarded as the greatest of twentieth-century Scottish poets, and by many as the greatest of all poets in the Scots tradition, Hugh MacDiarmid's interpretation of the Scottish consciousness through his baiting and unsentimental verse helped Scotland recognise its true self. He became the catalyst of the Scottish literary renaissance – which strove to detach itself from the romantic and nostalgic literature of the nineteenth century and establish Scottish writing as a contemporary force – and in doing so, revitalised poetry in Scotland.

He lived for 27 years at Brownsbank Cottage, now the only A-listed farm labourer's cottage in Scotland – not because of any architectural merits, but because it was the last home of MacDiarmid and his wife Valda, who remained there until they died: MacDiarmid in 1978; Valda in 1989. In January 1951 MacDiarmid was introduced by his publisher William MacLellan to Thomas Tweedie, the owner of Brownsbank Farm near Biggar.

MacDiarmid and his wife Valda at Brownsbank (c.1950s).

Tweedie offered one of his cottages rent-free to MacDiarmid for the rest of his life. The cottage was no Xanadu, but a basic but-and-ben with no water or electricity. Friends later raised the money to install amenities and build a lean-to kitchen and bathroom. A wooden studio was also built in the back garden for him to work in, but he preferred writing by the fireside in his favourite armchair, puffing on his pipe. Today the cottage retains many of its original artefacts: portraits, books, pipes, wallie dugs and other memorabilia. MacDiarmid

139

Scots–Canadian poet Tom Bryan, writer in residence
with the Brownsbank Fellowship, at his second home
– Brownsbank Cottage.

The author sitting in MacDiarmid's favourite chair in the
living room at Brownsbank.

himself once observed, 'This place is a growing shrine to my vanity.'
Most of MacDiarmid's best work was written before he moved to
Brownsbank, but many works, including *In Memoriam James Joyce*
(1955) and his *Collected Poems* (1976), were published during his
time there. It was from Brownsbank that MacDiarmid set out on his
worldwide journeys, and it was there that many came to visit and
pay homage to the great bard, including Yevgeny Yevtushenko and
Allen Ginsberg.

MacDiarmid was born Christopher Murray Grieve on 11 August
1892 in Langholm, Dumfriesshire, 'the wonderful little border
burgh' just a few miles from England. The son of a postman, he
attended Langholm Academy, and in 1908 he became a pupil–teacher
at Broughton Higher Grade School in Edinburgh. For some years
he worked as a journalist for newspapers in Scotland and Wales.
He became active in left-wing politics, and in 1915 he joined the
Royal Army Medical Corps, serving in Salonika, Italy and France.
Invalided home with cerebral malaria, he married June Skinner in
1918. On demobilisation he joined the staff of the *Montrose Review*
and began writing poetry that soon began to be noticed.

Between 1920 and 1922 he edited three volumes of *Northern
Numbers*, and in August 1922 he founded the periodical *Scottish
Chapbook*, which became a platform for talented Scots poets, including
himself, now writing under the pseudonym Hugh MacDiarmid. The
Scottish Chapbook became dedicated to the furthering of a Scottish

Renaissance using Scots as a serious medium of poetic expression, liberating it from the Kailyard, comic verse and pseudo-Burnsian mawkishness. The 'golden lyrics' of *Sangschaw* (1925) and *Penny Wheep* (1926) were his first collections of mainly Scots poems. In 1926 he published his dramatic masterpiece *A Drunk Man Looks at the Thistle*, a meditation that defines and analyses the state of the Scottish nation. Next came *To Circumjack Cencrastus* (1930), an even longer poem-sequence.

He founded the Scottish chapter of PEN in 1927 and helped to found the National Party of Scotland in 1928. In 1934 he joined the Communist Party but was expelled in 1938 and only rejoined in 1957 after the Russians invaded Hungary – a time when others were deserting the party. Until 1929 Grieve lived in Montrose, where he served as a Labour councillor. In 1929 he left for London to edit Compton Mackenzie's doomed radio magazine *Vox*. In 1932 he divorced his first wife and married a Cornish girl, Valda Trevlyn. Shortly afterwards, they moved to the Island of Whalsay in Shetland, where they lived until 1941. During the war, he was a labourer on Clydeside and later entered the Merchant Service. In 1951 the Grieves, together with their only son, moved to Brownsbank Cottage. Towards the end of his life MacDiarmid evolved into a Scottish institution. His genius was recognised and rewarded, though never financially, and he is now rightly regarded as one of Scotland's greatest poets.

Other publications include the three *Hymns to Lenin* (1931, 1932, 1957), *Scots Unbound* (1932), *Stony Limits* (1934), *A Kist o' Whistles* (1947) and *In Memoriam James Joyce* (1956). His autobiography was published in *Lucky Poet* (1943) and *The Company I've Kept* (1966). MacDiarmid's *Complete Poems* was published in 1976.

SEE ALSO: Alexander Trocchi.

FURTHER INFORMATION: Those interested in visiting Brownsbank should contact Biggar Museum Trust, Moat Park Heritage Centre, Biggar, ML12 6DT. Tel: 01899 221050.

Hugh MacDiarmid is buried in Langholm Cemetery, Dumfries and Galloway, located about a mile south of Langholm. The Hugh MacDiarmid Memorial Sculpture was unveiled in 1985 on a hill above Langholm (OS ref: NT382857). The memorial, created by sculptor Jake Harvey, depicts an open book decorated with images from MacDiarmid's poetry. From the A7 just north of Langholm, turn left along the minor road to Newcastleton. Where the road crosses Whita Yett, a path leads from a parking place up to the memorial.

FURTHER READING: A. Bold (ed.), *The Letters of Hugh MacDiarmid* (Georgia Press, 1985); A. Bold, *MacDiarmid: A Critical Biography* (John Murray, 1988).

Blantyre

Shuttle Row
Birthplace of David Livingstone (1813–73), missionary, explorer and writer

When in the act of ramming down the bullets I heard a shout. Starting, and looking half round, I saw the lion just in the act of springing upon me. I was upon a little height; he caught my shoulder as he sprang, and we both came to the

141

> ground below together. Growling horribly close to my ear,
> he shook me as a terrier dog a rat . . . Besides crunching
> the bone into splinters, he left eleven teeth wounds on the
> upper part of my arm.
>
> David Livingstone, from *Missionary Travels and
> Researches in Southern Africa* (1857)

Best known as a Christian missionary and explorer, David Livingstone wrote an account of his travels in a book that became one of the nineteenth century's bestsellers. *Missionary Travels and Researches in Southern Africa* sold a staggering 70,000 copies and spread his fame, and ultimately legend, to the world. He was born on 18 March 1813 in a 'single end' in a tenement in Blantyre, where he shared a room with his six siblings. From the age of ten until twenty-four he worked in the local cotton mill and was inspired to become a medical missionary after reading pamphlets appealing for volunteers to go to China. He studied medicine at Anderson College in Glasgow, but the Opium Wars curtailed any dreams he had of going to China, and so, by default, the 'dark continent' beckoned.

Through the London Missionary Society he arrived in Cape Town in 1841. He worked for a decade as a missionary in Bechuanaland (now Botswana) and married fellow-missionary's daughter Mary Moffat, with whom he had four children. Between 1853 and 1856 he made his epic journeys from central Africa to the west coast and across the eastern side of the continent. He explored the Zambezi, and in 1855 discovered the falls he named after Queen Victoria: 'It had never been seen before by European eyes; but scenes so lovely must have been gazed upon by angels in their flight.' His second book was *The Zambesi and its Tributaries* (1865), in which he exposed the Portuguese slave trade. Other expeditions followed, and in 1865, encouraged by the Royal Geographical Society, he undertook to unravel the age-old mystery – the source of the Nile.

Years passed and nothing was heard from Livingstone. Rumours spread that he was held captive or had died of fever. 'Where is Livingstone?' read newspaper headlines. The public concern over the fate of their national hero inspired James Gordon Bennett, publisher of the *New York Herald*, to commission journalist and explorer Henry Stanley to 'Find Livingstone'. To lesser men this would have been a bit like trying to find a needle in a haystack, but, against all odds, Stanley 'found' Livingstone at Ujiji in Tanganyika (now part of Tanzania) in 1871. They explored the northern reaches of Lake Tanganyika together, and Stanley tried to persuade Livingstone to return to Europe with him, but Livingstone was resolved to solve the Nile problem.

Livingstone was found dead one morning in 1873 in the village of Old Chitambo, kneeling by his bedside, as if praying. His heart was buried by his followers, and his body was embalmed with salt and carried on a nine-month journey to the coast, where it was shipped to England and buried in Westminster Abbey.

SEE ALSO: Mungo Park.

FURTHER INFORMATION: Livingstone's birthplace was converted into a museum in 1929 and depicts his life from early childhood working in the cotton mills to his African adventures. New facilities include an art gallery, social history museum, themed gift shop and tearoom, jungle garden and riverside walks. David Livingstone Centre, Shuttle Row, 165 Station Road, Blantyre, South Lanarkshire, G72 9BY. Located just off the M74, junction

5, via A725 and A724. Open from Good Friday to 24 December. Tel: 01698 823140.

Website: www.undiscoveredscotland.co.uk/blantyre/livingstone centre

FURTHER READING: Tim Jeal, *Livingstone* (Pimlico, 1993); Oliver Ransford, *David Livingstone: Dark Interior* (J. Murray, 1978).

Cathkin Braes
Setting for 'The Vision of Cathkin Braes' by Edwin Morgan (1920–), poet, critic and translator

> One Saturday night in Glasgow in the 1970s, after the pubs had spilled out, I climbed on a bus to find the top deck swept up in a raucous sing-song, everything from 'Ah belang tae Glesca' to 'Bye Bye Blackbird' – the old Harry Lauder–Frank Sinatra repertoire. There was nothing unusual about it, except that in the middle of it all sat Edwin Morgan, hands clasped on his lap, silent and smiling, absorbing the city throb.
>
> James Campbell, *The Guardian*, 18 January 2003

Edwin Morgan became Glasgow's first official Makar (poet laureate) in 1999, and in 2004 he became the Scots Makar, the nation's first national poet. Both titles are endorsements of his unique talent. His achievements since his first book, *The Vision of Cathkin Braes and Other Poems* (1952), have been extraordinarily diverse and prolific, ranging from sonnets, concrete and sound poems, and essays to science fiction poems and translations. Endlessly innovative, he blends traditional forms with experimental and concrete poetry, often recalling the urban landscapes of his native land.

He was born an only child in Glasgow's West End on 27 April 1920, where his father was a clerk with a local firm of scrap merchants. His family later settled in Pollokshields and Rutherglen, and it was here that he spent his childhood. He attended Rutherglen Academy

Views of Glasgow and beyond from Cathkin Braes.

and later won a scholarship to Glasgow High School. During the war, he served in the Royal Army Medical Corps, an option he chose as a conscientious objector. He graduated from the University of Glasgow in 1947 and became assistant lecturer in English there in 1947, rising to titular professor in 1975.

The gloominess of *The Vision of Cathkin Braes and Other Poems* was left behind him as he matured as a poet, and his later work has an effervescence and flamboyance, culminating in *A Second Life* (1968), which included 'Glasgow Green', a reflection on the legitimacy of homosexual love. Morgan did not come out as gay until the age of 70 in 1990. His other works include *Sonnets from Scotland* (1984), *From the Video Box* (1986), *Collected Poems* (1990) and *You: Anti-War Poetry* (1991). *Crossing the Border* (critical essays) was published in 1990. His translations of Boris Pasternak, Alexander Pushkin and Frederico García Lorca are collected in *Rites of Passage* (1976). He has also adapted Edmond Rostand's *Cyrano de Bergerac* into demotic Glaswegian.

Always looking to the future and not dwelling too long on history and tradition, Morgan declared in a 1987 interview that we should not 'just be curators, tending the buildings erected in the past. Each generation ought to have a chance of fulfilling its ambitions and shaping the world in its own way. I don't like to think of people in the future wondering why we never achieved anything.'

FURTHER INFORMATION: Cathkin Braes Country Park covers 493 acres in the south-east of Glasgow. Originally known as the Cathkin Hills, the eastern part of the Country Park was gifted to the city in 1887 by millionaire James Dick, who stipulated that the space must be retained in a natural state and remain open for public enjoyment. Rich in history and a familiar landmark on the southern skyline, its elevation is 200 metres above sea level, the highest point in Glasgow. It offers views over the city and beyond, including the Gleniffer Braes and the Kilpatrick and Campsie ranges. The park is located approximately five miles south of the city centre immediately south of Castlemilk, north-east of Carmunnock village and west of the housing suburbs of Fernhill and Cathkin. The park is open 24 hours a day all year. Parking is available on Ardencraig Road, in lay-bys along Cathkin Road (B759) or at the viewpoint also on Cathkin Road east of Carmunnock village.

FURTHER READING: R. Crawford and H. Whyte, *About Edwin Morgan* (Edinburgh University Press, 1990).

North Lanarkshire

Wishaw

13 The Broadway
Childhood home of Liz Lochhead (1947–), poet and dramatist

> All that Shelley, Wordsworth and Keats. Pantheism doesn't
> mean much to someone growing up surrounded by heavy
> industry in a Lanarkshire steel town. Poetry was something
> pansily exotic and alien.
>
> Liz Lochhead, *Scottish International*, 1971

In what is the predominantly male domain of Scottish poetry, Liz
Lochhead has forged a unique place for herself as one of Scotland's
most popular poets and dramatists. Whether in the Glasgow
vernacular or English, her works overflow with irony and wit,
bursting out of their traditional genres in a voice that on the
one hand is indigenous, but at the same time reaches out and is
understood everywhere.

Born in 1947, her roots are in North Lanarkshire: 'We lived,
my mother, my father and I, in a single upstairs room in my
grandparents' house. My father's side. A big between-the-wars
council five-apartment. Roughcast. Pebbledash. Six in the block.
In the shadow of all the steelworks, Colvilles, Anderson Boyes,
the Lanarkshire – number 13, the Broadway, Craigneuk, Wishaw.
Whenever I heard on the radio the "Lullaby of Broadway" I thought
they were singing about us.'

When she was four, her family
moved to a council house in the
small mining village of Newarthill,
four miles from Motherwell.
She attended the local primary
school, which was 'staffed by a
collection of remarkably similar
mainly maiden ladies . . . so many
Miss Jean Brodies twenty years
beyond their prime'. Secondary
school was Dalziel High School in
Motherwell, where she 'decided
absolutely' she wanted to go to art
school. In her final year at high
school the budding art student
was desperate for freedom. She
dyed her hair a 'startling blonde',
grew her fringe, ringed her eyes

13 The Broadway, childhood home of Liz
Lochhead.

145

with mascara, wore black stockings and suede boots, and asked her mother if she resembled Marianne Faithfull. The day she left school she threw away her school tie under the cars at Motherwell Cross.

During her first year at Glasgow School of Art in 1965, she started to write poetry. Soon her writing began to gain more meaning than her painting, and she commented in 1971 that 'words have a meaning of their own, paint strokes don't . . . What I love is flat rhythms of ordinary speech, slabs of slang and worn turns of phrase used in a jokey, pun-like literal way.' She lectured in fine art for eight years before becoming a professional writer, and in the early 1970s she joined Philip Hobsbaum's influential writers' group in Glasgow, whose other members included Alasdair Gray, James Kelman and Tom Leonard.

Her first published work was a collection of poetry called *Memo for Spring* in 1972. Several collections followed, including *Dreaming Frankenstein and Collected Poems* (1984), *True Confessions and New Clichés* (1985) and *Bagpipe Muzak* (1991). She has also written plays inspired by literature and history, including *Blood and Ice* (1982), based on the life of Mary Shelley, *Dracula* (1989) and *Mary Queen of Scots Got Her Head Chopped Off* (1989), and in 1985 she translated Molière's *Tartuffe* into the Glasgow vernacular. Between 1986 and 1987 she was Writer in Residence at Edinburgh University and a year later Writer in Residence for the Royal Shakespeare Company.

SEE ALSO: Philip Hobsbaum.

Renfrewshire

Paisley

Canal Street
Castlehead Church
Grave of Robert Tannahill (1774–1810), poet, flautist and songwriter

> How sweet is the brier wi' its saft faulding blossom
> and sweet is the birk, wi' its mantle o' green;
> Yet sweeter, and fairer, and dear to this bosom,
> Is lovely young Jessie, the flower o' Dunblane.
>   Robert Tannahill, from 'The Flower o' Dunblane'

Robert Tannahill's songs were extremely popular in their day, and he once wrote, 'Perhaps the highest pleasure I have ever derived from these things has been in hearing as I walked down the pavement at night, a girl within doors, rattling away at one of them.' His work appeared in newspapers and magazines of the time, and in 1807 he published, by subscription, 900 volumes of his poems, which sold out in a matter of weeks. Three years later he burned all his manuscripts and drowned himself in the Glasgow, Paisley and Johnstone Canal.

The 'Paisley Poet' was born on 3 June 1774 in a small cottage in Castle Street, Paisley, the fourth of eight children of James Tannahill, a weaver, and Janet Pollick. He was a delicate child and had a limp from a slight deformity in his right leg. He did not appear to excel at school, and when he was 12 he was apprenticed to his father as a handloom weaver. Around this time he developed

a keen interest in reading and writing poetry. He was inspired by Robert Burns, especially 'Tam O' Shanter', and shortly after the publication of the poem in 1791, he walked to Alloway Old Kirk in Ayrshire, scene of the witches' orgy. During his stay in Ayrshire, he was inspired to write his first song, 'My Ain Kind Dearie, O'. He composed verses working at his loom in his father's weaving shop in Queen Street and fell in love with Jessie Tennant, the love of his life, for whom he wrote 'The Flower o' Dunblane'.

Jessie, alas, married another, and he remained a bachelor for the rest of his life.

Due to a slump in the weaving trade in 1800, Robert and his brother Hugh sought work in England for a couple of years but he returned to care for his mother on the death of his father in 1802. In 1805 he was instrumental in founding the Paisley Burns Club, which still survives today. He continued to work at his loom, while writing and composing songs with his flute. In 1807 he published a 175-page volume of his poems by subscription, earning him a profit of £20 at a time when the average wage for a weaver was around £15 a year. This gained him recognition throughout Scotland, and he was visited by James Hogg (1770–1835) in 1810. His best-known songs include 'The Braes o' Balquhidder', 'The Braes o' Gleniffer', 'O are ye Sleepin', Maggie' and 'The Flower o' Dunblane'.

Tragically, he suffered throughout his life from depression, and when his second volume of poems was rejected by a Greenock publisher and then by Constables in Edinburgh he burned the manuscript. Shortly afterwards he woke in the middle of the night and made his way to a culvert at Candren Burn, where he drowned himself. The spot (visible through railings in Maxweltown Street) is now known as Tannahill's Pool.

SEE ALSO: James Hogg, Alloway Old Kirk.

FURTHER INFORMATION: Robert Tannahill's grave is in the grounds of Castlehead Church, Canal Street, Paisley. In 1775 the Tannahills moved to a house in Queen Street, where he was brought up and worked at his loom. The house, which is still used by the Paisley Tannahill Club (0141 561 8078), can be viewed by appointment. Open-air concerts on Gleniffer Braes, the place he celebrated in one of his songs, raised money for a statue erected in 1883 in the grounds of Paisley Abbey.

The self-educated Alexander Wilson (1766–1813), regarded as the founder of North American ornithology, was also born in Paisley. He was an apprentice weaver and a packman, who hawked his wares around the town. In 1787 he became a burgess of Paisley, but as a poet he gained notoriety for his outspoken verse about mill owners. He was once imprisoned in Paisley's Tollbooth and was forced to burn a copy of one of his poems on its steps. In the 1790s he emigrated to America, where he first took work as a packman. During an 800-mile walk through the American countryside, he became fascinated by the flights and migrations of the birds he saw. He was subsequently employed as a schoolmaster and farmer, and between 1808 and 1813, with no training whatsoever, he wrote and illustrated his mammoth nine-volume *American Ornithology*. His statue stands outside Paisley Abbey.

The Iain Banks novel *Espedair Street* (1987) takes its name from a street in Paisley and is partly set in and around the town.

FURTHER READING: Irene Livingston, *Robert Tannahill: A Biographical Sketch* (Renfrew District Libraries, 1892).

Inverclyde

Greenock

Inverkip Street
The Old Cemetery
Grave of John Galt (1779–1839), novelist and pioneer in Canada

> From the lone shieling of the misty island
> Mountains divide us, and the waste of seas –
> Yet still the blood is strong, the heart is Highland,
> And we in dreams behold the Hebrides!
> Fair these broad meads, these hoary woods are grand;
> But we are exiles from our fathers' land.
> John Galt, from 'Canadian Boat Song' (1829)

It was unfortunate for John Galt that he had to write in the shadow of Sir Walter Scott, but although his books were not in the major league, his novels, or 'theoretical histories' as he preferred to describe them, were extremely sharp and observant. He did not write fashionable, romantic novels, but subtle, detailed regional stories of domestic life, often using a Scots vocabulary, and he was a shrewd witness of social change. He produced poems, dramas, historical novels and travel books but will be best remembered for *The Annals of the Parish* (1821) and its descriptions of events in the life of an Ayrshire minister across half a century.

He was born in Irvine on 2 May 1779, the son of a sea captain. When he was ten, his family went to live in Greenock, and in 1789 they moved to London. Here he studied law and set up a failed venture as a merchant. It was while travelling on the Continent between 1809 and 1811 for his health that he met Lord Byron, of whom he later published a life in 1830. In 1824 he was appointed secretary to the Canada Company, an organisation involved in the country's colonisation, and in 1827 he founded the town of Guelph (named after the ancestral family of George IV). Although Galt became quite celebrated in Canada, the Lieutenant-Governor of Ontario wasn't too impressed with him, as he removed him from his post and jailed him for negligence. He is said to have returned from Canada a ruined man in 1829, but fortunately he continued to write. Galt was not revered or even taken much notice of in his day, but his contribution to Scottish fiction is unique, and his depiction of small-town and village life is unequalled. His other works include *The Ayrshire Legatees* (1820), *The Provost* (1822), *The Entail* (1823), *Lawrie Todd* (1830) and *The Member* (1832).
SEE ALSO: Lord Byron.

FURTHER INFORMATION: The gates to this old cemetery are usually locked, but a plaque erected there informs one that this is the last resting place of John Galt.

FURTHER READING: John Galt, *Autobiography* (two volumes; 1833); J.W. Aberdein, *John Galt* (Oxford University Press, 1941); H.B. Timothy, *The Galts: A Canadian Odyssey* (McClelland & Stewart, 1984); I. Gordon, *The Life of a Writer* (University of Toronto Press, 1972).

Glasgow

Charing Cross

North Street
The Mitchell Library
One of the largest public reference libraries in Europe

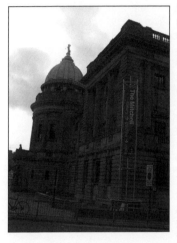

The Mitchell is named after the late Stephen Mitchell, a wealthy tobacco merchant, who left the sum of £67,000 to build and stock a public reference library for the people of Glasgow when he died in 1874. This is not something that would be morally acceptable today, but in Victorian times it was the norm. The library first opened in temporary premises in Ingram Street in 1877 with a stock of 14,000 books. Today its stock consists of 1.3 million books, 35,000 maps and thousands of photographs, newspapers and microfilms. Early in its history it established two special collections: the Scottish Poetry Collection and the Glasgow Collection, which contain 'copies of all books, pamphlets, periodical publications, maps, plans, pictorial illustrations, and generally all papers which in any way illustrate the city's growth and life'.

FURTHER INFORMATION: The Mitchell Library, North Street, Glasgow, G3 7DN. Tel: 0141 287 2999/2876.
Website: www.mitchelllibrary.org

Woodlands Road
Statue of Lobey Dosser, Rank Badjin and El Fideldo
Cartoon creations of Bud Neill (1911–70)

> The snow has fell
> Wee Josis nosis frozis well:
> Wee Josis frozis nosis skintit,
> Winter's diabolic intit.
> Bud Neill, from 'Winter's Came' (c. 1950s)

Cartoonist Bud Neill's hilarious trademark was two Glasgow 'wimmin' discussing life as seen from their corner of the universe, but it was the creation of the cartoon strip 'Lobey Dosser', which first appeared in the *Glasgow Evening Times* in January 1944, that captivated his readers and brought him fame. Scots loved the zany humour and antics of Lobey Dosser and his two-legged horse El Fideldo battling against the evil Rank Badjin. Other characters included Big Chief Toffy Teeth and former spy Red Skwerr.

In the early 1940s Bud Neill was working as a bus driver when he decided to send samples of his work to the *Glasgow Herald*, which led to the publication of a regular strip with their sister paper, the *Glasgow Evening Times*. In 1956 he moved to the *Daily Mail* and *Sunday Mail*, appearing lastly in the *Scottish Daily Express*. Bud Neill died at his home in Glenrothes, Fife, on 28 August 1970. In 1992 the *Glasgow Herald* raised money by public subscription for a statue to be erected to commemorate his much-loved characters. The statue was created for no fee by Tony Morrow and Nick Gillon, students of Duncan of Jordanstone College of Art. Not only is this statue the first one in Britain to be erected by public subscription since the reign of Queen Victoria, but it is also the only statue of a two-legged horse anywhere in the world.

SEE ALSO: *Glasgow Herald.*

FURTHER INFORMATION: The statue is across the street from the Uisge Beatha (Water of Life) pub at 232 Woodlands Road. With a gantry stocking over 125 single malts, this unusual pub is well worth a visit.

West End

731 Great Western Road
Auditorium of Òran Mór
Decorated with the artwork of Alasdair Gray (1934–), novelist, painter and playwright

> What's worth saying, these decades on, is that *Lanark*, in common with all great books, is still, and always will be, an act of resistance. It is part of the system of whispers and sedition and direct communion, one voice to another, we call literature. Its bravery in finding voice, in encouraging the enormous power of public, national, artistic, sexual and political imagination, is not something to take for granted.
>
> Janice Galloway, *The Guardian*, 12 October 2002

To describe Alasdair Gray as a Glaswegian reincarnation of the English poet, painter and mystic William Blake would be as close as you could probably get to pigeonholing him. Like Blake before him, Gray is not one to do things by halves. He doesn't just write books, he conceives them, enveloping them with his illustrations and typography, creating something that is unique and master-crafted.

The Òran Mór, formerly Kelvinside Parish Church.

The Òran Mór auditorium with artwork by Alasdair Gray.

Like Blake, Gray's origins were also humble and full of struggle. He worked for decades as an artist before *Lanark: A Life in Four Books*, his first novel, was published when he was in his late 40s in 1981 – it reputedly took him 28 years to write. Anthony Burgess once described Gray as 'the most important Scottish writer since Sir Walter Scott'. In quality perhaps, but in output he fails miserably. Scott wrote *Guy Mannering* in six weeks; Gray's *Book of Prefaces* (2000) took 18 years to write. He once told journalist A.J. Close that he 'would really like to die while engaged on a job, actually doing it and therefore leaving it unfinished'. 'Given his track record,' remarked Close, 'this seems more than likely.' However, with Gray, despite his lengthy gestation periods, it's worth the wait. *Lanark* was hailed as a landmark in Scottish fiction, and today he is at last recognised as one of Britain's leading writers.

He was born at 11 Findhorn Street, a three-roomed flat in Riddrie on Glasgow's Eastside, on 28 December 1934, to Alex Gray, a folding-box machine-cutting operator, and Amy Fleming, a former shop assistant. During the war, he was evacuated with his mother and younger sister to Auchterarder in Perthshire and Stonehouse in Lanarkshire, and in 1942 the family moved to Wetherby in Yorkshire, where his father managed a hostel for

munition workers. From 1947 to 1952 he attended Whitehill Secondary School in Hamilton, and from 1952 to 1957 he studied design and mural painting at the Glasgow School of Art. After training to be a teacher at Jordanhill College in 1960, he taught art in Glasgow schools for a couple of years, before attempting to make a living as an artist and writer. At the 1961 Edinburgh Festival he met, and later married, Inge Sørensen, with whom he had one son. They were divorced in 1970. In 1968 BBC television broadcast his play *The Fall of Kelvin Walker*, and various TV and radio plays followed throughout the 1970s.

From 1972 to 1974 he was invited to join the creative writing classes of the poet and critic Philip Hobsbaum at the University of Glasgow, later commenting that 'the best writing class I ever attended was run by Philip Hobsbaum. There I met many good local writers I had never met before, some of them now my closest friends, and several who (though unpublished then) are not only published now but are well known.' These unknown 'local writers' included James Kelman, Liz Lochhead, Tom Leonard and Jeff Torrington, all destined to become leading figures in contemporary Scottish writing.

Lanark received a lukewarm reception from the publishing world until the Edinburgh-based publisher Canongate had the confidence to publish this unique novel, which eventually received great critical acclaim. Other novels followed, including Gray's own personal favourite *1982, Janine* (1984), *The Fall of Kelvin Walker* (1985), *Something Leather* (1990), *McGrotty and Ludmilla* (1990), *Poor Things* (1992) and *A History Maker* (1994). He has also published a volume of poetry, *Old Negatives* (1989), and several volumes of short stories, including *Unlikely Stories, Mostly* (1983), *Lean Tales* (1985), written with James Kelman and Agnes Owen, *Ten Tales Tall and True* (1993) and *Mavis Belfrage: With Five Shorter Tales* (1996). In 1989 he published the autobiographical *Saltire Self-Portrait No. 4*.

Alasdair Gray has evolved into a writer of international standing, and his works have been translated into most European languages. In 2001 the University of Glasgow appointed Alasdair Gray, along with James Kelman and Tom Leonard, Professor of Creative Writing, attached to the School of English and Scottish Language and Literature.

SEE ALSO: University of Glasgow, James Kelman, Liz Lochhead.

FURTHER INFORMATION: Òran Mór (Gaelic for great music) is situated in the former Kelvinside Parish Church on the corner of Byres Road and Great Western Road. In 2003 Glasgow publican and property developer Colin Beattie turned the derelict building into a cultural centre, housing two pubs, two restaurants, a nightclub and an auditorium. Alasdair Gray was commissioned to decorate the auditorium, the ceiling of which consists of a depiction of the night sky with the constellations of the zodiac. The auditorium is above the bar and restaurant and is usually closed off when not in use, but a request to the staff for a quick peep is usually granted with pleasure.

Òran Mór, 731 Great Western Road, Glasgow, G12 8QX. Tel: 0141 357 6200.

Email: info@oran-mor.co.uk

Website: www.oran-mor.co.uk

Alasdair Gray's artwork can also be seen at the following venues: the back stairwell at the Ubiquitous Chip Restaurant,

12 Ashton Lane, Hillhead, Glasgow; the Palace Rigg Nature Reserve in Cumbernauld; and Abbots House local-history museum in Dunfermline. Several of his paintings are on display at the People's Palace on Glasgow Green, and the Scottish National Portrait Gallery has a collection of his self-portrait drawings. The National Library of Scotland holds the Alasdair Gray archive of personal papers, manuscripts and drawings.

FURTHER READING: P. Moores (ed.), *Alasdair Gray: Critical Appreciations and a Bibliography* (British Library Publishing, 2002); R. Crawford and T. Nairn (eds), *The Arts of Alasdair Gray* (Edinburgh University Press, 1991).

Gilmorehill

University Avenue
University of Glasgow
Alma Mater of Scottish men and women of letters since the fifteenth century

> George MacBeth said to me critically once, 'All your geese are swans.' I said, 'Well, it's just the reverse of reviewing and criticism: when it comes to books, treat the book as no good, until it proves itself otherwise. With students, assume they're good: let them prove they aren't.'
>
> Philip Hobsbaum, *The Dark Horse* magazine, 2002

With almost 16,000 undergraduate and 4,000 postgraduate students, the University of Glasgow is one of the UK's largest universities. Founded in 1451, and modelled on the University of Bologna, it is a university in the great European tradition. It began life in the crypt of Glasgow Cathedral, and in 1460 moved to accommodation in the High Street. In 1870, due to overcrowding and squalor in the city centre, it moved to its present magnificent and imposing site at Gilmorehill. Over the years its alumni have made an enormous contribution to Scottish literature, and include Adam Smith, James Boswell, Tobias Smollett, John Buchan, A.J. Cronin, James Bridie, Catherine Carswell, Alexander Trocchi, Janice Galloway, William Boyd, Christopher Brookmyre, William

McIlvanney, Helen MacInnes and Alistair MacLean.

In 1962 poet and critic Philip Hobsbaum (1932–2005) was appointed a lecturer at Queen's University, Belfast, but moved to the University of Glasgow as a reader in English literature in 1965, becoming a full professor in 1985. He is best remembered for launching and building a school of creative writing, about which he had very definite ideas. 'It should not be a separate department, as happens in several American universities,' he insisted. 'Students should

be taught not just how to read, and how to write critical essays, but how to write. People say, well, it can't be done, but it's done in music all the time.' Among the then unknown writers Hobsbaum fostered, often in meetings and readings held at his home, were Alasdair Gray, Liz Lochhead, James Kelman, Tom Leonard and Jeff Torrington. Gray dedicated his *Book of Prefaces* to Hobsbaum, 'poet, critic and servant of the servants of art'.

FURTHER READING: J.D. Mackie, *The University of Glasgow 1451– 1951: A Short History* (Jackson, 1954); P. Hobsbaum, *Essentials of Literary Criticism* (Thames & Hudson, 1983).

Hillhead

10 Bank Street
Childhood home of Alexander Trocchi (1925–84)
Cult writer and literary outlaw

> People didn't dislike Trocchi, but they felt he was dangerous.
> Edwin Morgan

Described by Allen Ginsberg as 'the most brilliant man I ever met', Alexander Trocchi was all but forgotten when he died in 1984, and the few that did remember him recollected him only as a heroin addict, pimp and author of pornographic novels. A product of the Beat Generation, Trocchi lived life in the fast lane, with abundant amounts of drugs and sex, laced with experimental writing. Like many writers before him, Trocchi lived the life of an exile in Paris in the 1950s – far from the Presbyterian grip of the land of his birth – where the rebels, drug takers and general bad boys of fiction have traditionally sought refuge and inspiration throughout literary history. He would probably still be wallowing in obscurity today, but following the popularity of Scottish writers like Alan Warner and Irvine Welsh, and the 2003 film adaptation of his novel *Young Adam* (1957), Alexander Trocchi returned from literary obscurity to widespread critical acclaim.

He was born in 1925, the youngest son of Alfredo Trocchi, a second-generation Italian immigrant, in Glasgow's Southside, where his father was a popular bandleader. During the Great Depression, the family's fortunes slumped, and they moved to Bank Street, close to the university, where they took in lodgers. Trocchi attended the University of Glasgow in 1947, studying English and philosophy. Poet Edwin Morgan, then a young lecturer, recalled him as a student who was 'extraordinarily magnetic, some would say manipulative – able to get what he wanted out of people. He was very charming, but with a hint of danger. Sometimes there were these dark looks from under his eyebrows, a sense of something different altogether. There was a depth to him that was impressive, strange and not quite sinister, but there was the sense that something unexpected could happen.'

After graduating, he was awarded a travelling scholarship, and together with his wife and two daughters he toured Europe, before choosing to settle in Paris, where he began his writing career with Maurice Girodias's infamous Olympia Press writing erotica. Abandoning his family, he found a new lover in Jane Lougee, the daughter of an American banker who financed the literary magazine *Merlin*, which was edited by Trocchi. *Merlin* lasted for five years, publishing Samuel Beckett, Jean Genet, Henry Miller, Eugène Ionesco and other greats of modernism. Meanwhile, he was getting heavily into opium and heroin. *Merlin* ceased publication when Trocchi's relationship with Lougee ended in 1955, and the following year he decamped to the United States, living in New York and Venice, California, the epicentre of the Beat Generation in southern California. He now had a new wife, who was also a heroin addict and who regularly prostituted herself to support their habit. When he was charged with supplying heroin to a minor, he fled the USA and settled in London, where he became a registered addict.

At a writers' conference during the Edinburgh Festival in 1962, Trocchi had a memorable public confrontation with Hugh MacDiarmid, who denounced him as 'cosmopolitan scum'. Edwin Morgan recalled that 'some wicked person had filled the water carafe with whisky, so it was a very merry occasion. Trocchi had taken heroin immediately prior to the afternoon's session', during which he claimed 'sodomy' as a basis for his writing. MacDiarmid summed up by declaring that he himself didn't conform to any Scottish stereotypes. Pointing at MacDiarmid's kilt, Trocchi said, 'Neither do I. Not even a kilt.'

In the 1970s, with his literary output drying up, he evolved into a counter-culture icon and antiquarian book dealer. His wife died from the results of heroin addiction in 1972, leaving Trocchi to bring up their two young sons, of whom one later died from leukaemia and the other committed suicide. Trocchi died in 1984. His ashes were stolen and have never been recovered.

His works include *Helen and Desire* (1954), *Carnal Days of Helen Sefaris* (1954), *White Thighs* (1955), *School for Wives* (1955), *Thongs* (1955), *Young Adam* (1957), *My Lifes and Loves* (1959), *Sappho of Lesbos* (1960), *School for Sin* (1960) and *Cain's Book* (1961).

SEE ALSO: Hugh MacDiarmid.

FURTHER READING: A.M. Scott, *Alexander Trocchi: The Making of the Monster* (Polygon, 1992); A.M. Scott (ed.), *Invisible Insurrection of a Million Minds: A Trocchi Reader* (Polygon, 1991); Gavin Bowd, *The Outsiders: Alexander Trocchi and Kenneth White* (Akros, 1998); A. Campbell and T. Niel (eds), *A Life in Pieces: Reflections on Alexander Trocchi* (Rebel Inc., 1997).

8 Bank Street
Childhood home of J.J. Bell (1871–1934), journalist, author and creator of Wee Macgreegor

'Wull I get a tert at Aunt Purdie's?' inquired Macgregor.

'Ye'll see whit ye'll get when ye get it,' replied his mother. 'An' mind, Macgreegor, ye're no' to be askin' fur jelly till ye've ett twa bits o' breid an' butter. It's no mainners; an' yer Aunt Purdie's rale parteeclar. An' yer no' to dicht yer mooth wi' yer cuff — mind that. Ye're to tak' yer hanky an' let on ye're jist gi'ein yer nose a bit wipe . . . An' if ye drap yer piece on the floor, ye're no' to gang efter it; ye're jist to let on ye've ett it . . .'

J.J. Bell, from 'Aunt Purdie's Tea-Party', *Wee Macgreegor* (1902)

J.J. Bell will be best remembered for his Wee Macgreegor sketches, which hilariously depicted an ordinary working-class family in turn-of-the-century Glasgow. The Robinsons typified the Glaswegian perception of things, with their witty vernacular, and became enormously popular with the reading public. The sketches originally appeared in the columns of the *Glasgow Evening Times*, and when published in book form in 1902 sales reached over 20,000 by the end of the year. The John Hassall drawing of Wee Macgreegor on the book's front cover appeared on lemonade bottles, match boxes, china, postcards, sardine tins and taiblet (tablet), Macgreegor's favourite sweet. The craze was such that the book was pirated in America, film contracts were signed and in 1911 it was adapted for the stage. The seed for Wee Macgreegor was reputedly planted in the early 1890s on board a Firth of Clyde excursion steamer on a Glasgow 'Fair Saturday', when Bell heard a distracted mother of five children address her eldest with the words, 'Macgreegor, tak' yer paw's haun', or ye'll get nae carvies [sugared caraways] to yer tea!' As with most bestsellers throughout literary history, publishers showed little initial interest. Bell actually offered the copyright to one publisher for a mere £5. It was only when he guaranteed £50 against possible loss that it actually went to press.

John Joy Bell was born in Bothwell Terrace, Glasgow, in 1871, the son of a tobacco merchant. He was schooled at Kelvinside Academy and Morrison's Academy, and attended the University of Glasgow, where he studied chemistry. He began writing as a student, and in 1896 he became editor of *Glasgow University Magazine*. In 1898 he joined the staff of *The Scots Pictorial* as assistant editor, and in the same year he published two books of poetry for children, *The New Noah's Ark* and *Jack of All Trades*. He was now writing regular columns for the *Glasgow Evening Times*, the *Weekly Herald* and *People's Friend*. His other works include *Songs of the Hour*, a collection of poetry inspired by the Boer War in 1900, various sequels of *Wee Macgreegor*, and in 1932 he wrote *I Remember*, a memoir of his Glasgow childhood. Bell is all but forgotten today, and his work is sometimes criticised for its mawkishness and cosy vernacular of the Kailyard, but his accurate descriptions of tenement life and humour in early twentieth-century Glasgow have never been equalled.

City Centre

11 Mitchell Lane
The Herald Building
Home of the *Glasgow Herald* from 1895 until 1980

> It may be tripe but it's my tripe – and I do urge other authors to resist encroachments on their brain-children and trust their own judgement rather than that of some zealous meddler with a diploma in creative punctuation who is just dying to get into the act.
>
> George MacDonald Fraser (1926–),
> former acting editor of *The Herald*

Jack 'The Hat' MacLean.

One of the oldest newspapers in Glasgow, *The Herald* began its life as the *Glasgow Advertiser* in January 1783. In 1802 it became the *Herald & Advertiser*, before becoming the *Glasgow Herald* on 26 August 1804. Its home from 1895 until 1980 was in a Charles Rennie Mackintosh-designed building in Mitchell Street. Over the years, along with its sister paper the *Glasgow Evening Times*, it has nurtured many literary talents. Among them was its former acting editor, historical novelist George MacDonald Fraser, whose greatest creation was Sir Harry Paget Flashman, brigadier-general, VC, KCB, KCIE. Fraser started writing *Flashman* at his kitchen table, and it was first published in 1969, but only after several years of publishers' rejections. *Flashman* evolved into a successful series of historical novels, but when the first novel was published many reviewers (mostly American) believed the 'Flashman Papers' to be a genuine historical document. 'The most important discovery since the Boswell Papers,' commented one. He has since written over 20 bestsellers, including the screenplay for James Bond's *Octopussy* in 1983.

The spy-thriller writer J.K. Mayo (pseudonym of Bill Watson, 1930–2005) worked for *The Herald* in his latter years, but he will be best remembered for his two historical novels, *Beltran in Exile* (1979), about the Crusaders, and *The Night on the Bridge* (1982). Jack Webster, one of Scotland's most popular writers, also had a long and distinguished career with *The Herald*. His autobiography *Grains of Truth* (1999) recollects his Aberdeenshire background and the celebrities he encountered over the years, including Charlie Chaplin and Muhammad Ali. 'Mr. Glasgow', journalist Jack House (1906–91), wrote over 70 books, many of them about the city, notably *Glasgow Old and New* (1965), *Square Mile of Murder* (2002) and his autobiography *Pavement in the Sun* (1967). Wit from the diary column of *Herald*

stalwart Tom Shields can be found in copious tomes all over Scotland. And, finally, the well-known figure of Jack 'The Hat' MacLean, the 'Urban Voltaire', has published many books, including several anthologies of his journalism, which ranges from sport to politics and from the arts to social observation. Jack is one of the last of the old 'hacks', and his base of operations is Heraghty's Bar on the south side of Glasgow. In 1996 he wrote his autobiography, the title of which came about as follows. In the early 1950s Sir Winston Churchill met the Irish politician Sean Lemass. The great statesman remarked upon the economic circumstances of Britain at the time. 'The situation in Great Britain,' quoth Churchill in his most grandiloquent tones, 'is serious but not hopeless.' Lemass responded instantly. 'Sure,' he said, 'it's exactly the opposite in Ireland.' Thus the title for Jack's autobiography *Hopeless But Not Serious* (Mainstream, 1996).

SEE ALSO: Bud Neill, J.J. Bell, Mitchell Library.

FURTHER INFORMATION: *The Herald* moved to more modern premises in Albion Street in 1980, and the Mitchell Street building is now the home of the Lighthouse, Scotland's National Architecture and Design Centre (0141 221 6362). It is open to the public and its café on the top floor offers stunning views of the city. The Mitchell Library stores original copies of *The Herald* in printed form, as part of the History and Glasgow collection. The entire run of *The Herald* is available on microfilm, dating from 1783 to the present day. An index to the paper is also available, contained on two reels of microfilm for the period 1889–1906 and in printed volumes dated 1906–1984.

FURTHER READING: H. Reid, *Deadline: The Story of the Scottish Press* (St Andrew Press, 2006).

Merchant City

112 Stockwell Street
The Scotia Bar
Favourite haunt of James Kelman (1946–), novelist, short-story writer and playwright

> I reached the age of 22, in the knowledge that certain rights were mine. It was up to me what I did. I had the right to create. I didn't have to write as if I was somebody not myself (e.g. an imagined member of the British upper-middle classes). Nor did I have to write about characters striving to become other persons (e.g. imagined members of the British upper-middle classes). I could sit down with my pen and paper and start making stories of my own.
>
> James Kelman

It would be an interesting creative-writing experiment to have James Kelman write as 'an imagined member of the British upper-

middle class', but it's as hard to visualise the Duke of Edinburgh with a pie and a pint or Margaret Thatcher drawing the raffle winner at a miners' welfare club. Kelman writes in the language of the streets, depicting working-class life in Scotland. It's not *Brideshead Revisited*. He sees no merit in class hierarchies. His language can be brutal, crude and penetrating, and the intensity of his vernacular can often repel a reader. 'There is even a novel written entirely in Glaswegian. Lacking a dictionary, I soon gave up,' remarked Richard Cobb, chairman of the Booker Prize judges, of James Kelman's first novel, *The Busconductor Hines* (1984). Kelman didn't win the prize that year, nor did he win when his novel *A Disaffection* was shortlisted in 1989, but in 1994 he won it by a 3–2 majority with *How Late It Was, How Late*. One of the judges said his book was 'crap' and another said the decision was 'a disgrace' and 'that the tone of the whole book for a Sassenach was a bit wearing'. In his Booker Prize acceptance speech Kelman, dubbed the Kafka of the Clyde, replied, 'My culture and my language have the right to exist, and no one has the authority to dismiss that right.'

He was born in 1946 in Govan, where his father was a picture restorer and framer. He was one of five brothers and had no passion for learning when he was at school but did enjoy reading and joined the Elder Library in Govan. Leaving school at 15, he started work as an apprentice in the printing industry, a trade he later abandoned when his family emigrated to the United States. The move was not a success, and on his return from the States he got a job as a shoemaker in Govan. All kinds of jobs followed: on building sites; in shops and factories; and on the buses in Glasgow, Manchester and London. He studied philosophy and English at Strathclyde University in the early 1970s but left without taking his degree. At around the same time he also attended the creative-writing classes of the poet and critic Philip Hobsbaum, where he met many equally unknown writers, including Liz Lochhead, Tom Leonard, Alasdair Gray and Jeff Torrington.

In 1973 he published his first collection of stories, *An Old Pub Near the Angel*, followed by *Not Not While the Giro* (1983). His other works include *A Chancer* (1985) and the short-story collection *Greyhound for Breakfast* (1987), which won the 1987

Cheltenham Prize. His third novel, *A Disaffection* (1989), about an alcoholic secondary-school teacher, won the 1989 James Tait Black Memorial Prize and was shortlisted for the Booker Prize. More short stories followed in *The Burn* (1991), and three plays were published in *Hardie and Baird & Other Plays* (1991). In 1994 his Booker Prize-winning novel *How Late It Was, How Late* was published. It portrays an unemployed Glaswegian labourer and ex-convict who sobers up after a two-day drinking binge to find himself blind. Other novels include *Translated Accounts* (2001) and *You Have to Be Careful in The Land of The Free* (2004). He has also written many plays for radio and theatre.

SEE ALSO: University of Glasgow, Alasdair Gray, Liz Lochhead, Tom Leonard, Jeff Torrington.

FURTHER INFORMATION: The Scotia Bar, built in 1792, claims to be the oldest pub in Glasgow, and along with its sister pub, the Clutha Vaults at 167–69 Stockwell Street, it was the last stop of the Cluthas (the Gaelic word for the Clyde) boats, or penny steamers, which took people to work down the river. In their early years these pubs were popular with steamer passengers, seamen and workers from the shipyards. In 1862 the Scotia Theatre Music Hall (later the Metropole) opened nearby, and the pubs were frequented by performers and theatre audiences. In the 1960s and early '70s the Scotia became a watering hole for writers, folk singers and socialist political groups. Today it is still a meeting place for those with a love of literature, music and politics.

The Scotia Bar, 112 Stockwell Street, Glasgow, G1 4LW. Tel: 0141 552 8681.

Gallowgate

209 Gallowgate
Site of the Original Saracen's Head

> Robert Tennant takes this opportunity to acquaint all ladies and gentlemen that he has built a convenient and handsome new inn . . . containing 36 fine rooms, now fit to receive lodgers. The bed-chambers are all separate, none of them entering through another, and so contrived that there is no need of going out of doors to get to them. The beds are all very good, clean and free from bugs.
>
> From the *Glasgow Courant*, October 1755, advertising the opening of the new inn

The original Saracen's Head was three storeys high and was built from stone taken from the ruined Bishop's Palace, adjacent to Glasgow Cathedral, and from Gallowgate Port. With few hotels in the city, the inn prospered, and it became the main arrival and departure point for London coaches. It had a ballroom, accommodation for 60 horses in its stables, and its reputation for service was such that many famous wordsmiths passed a night at this welcoming watering hole, including James Boswell and Samuel Johnson in October 1773, Robert Burns in 1778, James Hogg in May 1804, and Samuel Taylor Coleridge with Dorothy and William Wordsworth in 1803. Dorothy recorded in her journal that it was 'quiet and tolerably cheap'. A pub called the Saracen's Head stands near the site today, but the original building was demolished in 1904.

SEE ALSO: Robert Burns, James Boswell, Samuel Johnson, Dorothy and William Wordsworth, James Hogg.

Calton

8 Ross Street
Birthplace of Matt McGinn (1928–77), songwriter, activist and singer

> Noo the darin' wee Annie, she went tae the Janny,
> A pleasant wee man as a rule,
> And 'am pleased a' can tell that he rang his wee bell
> And he asked a' the weans in the school.
>
> Huv ye seen a rid yoyo, rid yoyo, rid yoyo,
> Huv ye seen a rid yoyo wi' a wee yellow string?
>
> Matt McGinn, from 'Red Yoyo'

Matt McGinn was one of the most important folk-song writers of the twentieth century, who sang not only about the struggle of his own people, but for downtrodden people everywhere. With a voice once described as a mixture of lumpy porridge and broken glass, he was the British folk and protest movement's equivalent of Woody Guthrie. In songs such as 'Coorie Doon', 'The Red Yoyo' and 'The Ballad of John MacLean', no topic escaped his pen. He wrote about everything he had experienced, from his life in factories and shipyards to football referees and the pill. He claimed he never sang a song that was not political, and no subject was taboo. Dressed in his tartan bunnet, he sang unaccompanied with a compassion and vitality that made every appearance – whether in the back room of a pub, or in the Carnegie Hall – unforgettable.

He was born on 17 January 1928 in a two-roomed ground-floor flat at 8 Ross Street (now demolished) in Glasgow's East End into a strict Catholic family consisting of five sisters and three brothers. Traditionally known as a room and kitchen, his home was cluttered with 'pictures of the Sacred Heart and the Virgin and tea plates with pictures of the Celtic team on them'. He attended Saint Alphonsus's in Greendyke Street, and in 1940 he was sent to Saint Mary's Approved School in Bishopbriggs for 18 months for breaking into a fruit shop in the Candleriggs. Shortly after his release, he discovered socialism from street-corner soapboxes and began reading Tom Paine and Karl

Marx. He joined the Communist Party in 1949 and met his future wife Jeanette at a Young Communist League meeting. They married in 1950 and had four children. He worked at various factories and shipyards, where he was frequently sacked for his political and union activities. It was while working at Nettlefold's, the woodscrew manufacturers in Hillington, that he won a Transport and General Workers' Union scholarship to Ruskin College in Oxford.

He studied for an Oxford

University diploma in economics and political science for two years, and then attended teacher-training college in Huddersfield. His folk-singing career was launched after winning a competition in Huddersfield's *Reynold's News*, which offered a prize for a song 'in the folk-song tradition'. McGinn won the competition with a song called 'The Foreman O'Rourke' about a man who murders his gaffer. From then on, with the anti-Polaris movement at its height, McGinn started writing a succession of anti-establishment songs. Pete Seeger and Ewan McColl recognised his talent and invited him to sing in clubs, concerts and on radio programmes. His songs soon began to be sung by many of the pioneers of the folk-song revival, including Tom Paxton and Dominic Behan. McGinn churned out scores of songs on every topic, usually with a political punch. His career as a performer spanned only 15 years, singing and telling stories in folk clubs, concert halls, miners' welfares, clubs and pubs. He sang for everyone, and although he may have lacked polish, he was a true working-class poet.

He once played on the same bill as Bob Dylan. Dylan's fee was $60, against McGinn's $200: '"Hey, Matt," enquired Dylan. "You got any nail clippers?" Needless to say, I did not have any. Very few Glasgow men carry them around with them.'

FURTHER INFORMATION: Matt McGinn died on 6 January 1977, aged 48, from smoke inhalation after falling asleep with a lighted cigarette in his hand. Some of his ashes were scattered on the grave of Marxist teacher and socialist republican John MacLean in Eastwood Cemetery on May Day, 1977. The remainder were scattered on Glasgow Green.

FURTHER READING: Matt McGinn, *Fry the Little Fishes* (Calder & Boyars, 1975); Matt McGinn, *McGinn of the Calton: The Life and Works of Matt McGinn* (Glasgow District Libraries, 1987).

Cathedral

Wishart Street
Glasgow Necropolis
Monument to William Miller (1810–72), laureate of the nursery and author of 'Wee Willie Winkie'

> Wee Willie Winkie rins through the toon,
> Up-stairs and doon-stairs, in his nicht-goon,
> Tirlin' at the window, cryin' at the lock,
> 'Are the weans in their bed? for it's now ten o'clock.'
> 'Hey, Willie Winkie, are ye comin' ben?
> The cat's singin' grey thrums to the sleepin' hen,
> The dog's speldert on the floor and disnae gie a cheep –
> But here's a waukrif laddie that wanna fa' asleep.'
>
> William Miller

One of the most popular nursery rhymes ever written, 'Wee Willie Winkie' was written by Glasgow carpenter and woodturner William Miller. Manuscripts belonging to Miller are held at the Mitchell Library, some of them written on the back of sheets of sandpaper. As a poet and a songwriter he is all but forgotten today, but his hypnotic rhyme is sung by thousands of parents all round the world as their children drift off to sleep. In 1842 he published *Whistle-Binkie: Stories for the Fireside*, and many of his stories were published in

magazines of the day. He was born in the Briggate, just a stone's throw from the monument erected by public subscription in Glasgow Necropolis. He died penniless and is buried in the city's Tollcross Cemetery in an unmarked grave.

FURTHER INFORMATION: William Miller's monument is located on the left about 50 yards up the path leading from the Bridge of Sighs above Wishart Street.

Govanhill

21 Ardbeg Street
Birthplace of R.D. Laing (1927–89), existentialist psychiatrist and author of *The Divided Self*

> His major achievement was that he dragged the isolated and neglected inner world of the severely psychotic individual out of the back ward of the large gloomy mental hospital and on to the front pages of influential newspapers, journals and literary magazines . . . Everyone in contemporary psychiatry owes something to R.D. Laing.
>
> Anthony Clare

R.D. Laing was one of the most controversial psychoanalysts of the twentieth century. He made his name in the 1960s with his radical views about schizophrenia and the publication of *The Divided Self* (1960), which went against the psychiatric orthodoxy of the time. He argued that psychiatrists should not attempt to cure the symptoms of mental illness but assist and support patients to regard themselves as going through an enriching and cathartic experience. He claimed that schizophrenics suffer from 'ontological insecurity'

21 Ardbeg Street, birthplace of R.D. Laing.

(the branch of metaphysics dealing with the nature of being), becoming 'petrified' and closed off by their failure to communicate with other people, and argued that they need a place in which to explore their own lives without fear, in order to find a stable identity. The primary responsibility for psychiatric breakdown, claimed Laing, lies with society and/or with the patient's immediate family.

He was born on 7 October 1927, in a three-room tenement flat at 21 Ardbeg Street, to Amelia Kirkwood and David McNair Laing, an electrical engineer with Glasgow Corporation. His mother, who was a distinct oddity with an aversion to sex, gave birth to her only son nine years after her marriage and made every attempt to disguise her pregnancy. Emotionally distant, she rarely gave her son any affection as a child. She kept herself apart from her neighbours and nothing much from the outside penetrated her cloistered world. 'Everyone in the street knew she was mad,' said Walter Fyfe, a neighbour and school friend of Laing. Fyfe recalled that their flat was always in darkness, with heavy curtains drawn. 'I think she wanted to create a world in which the outside didn't impinge – she wanted to protect him from that, from anything untoward.'

In 1932, aged four, Laing attended the nearby Sir John Cuthbertson School, and later went to Hutchesons' Grammar School until he was seventeen. He attended the University of Glasgow (1945–51), studying medicine. At the end of his five-year course his interests were moving towards neurology and psychiatry. His first posting of six months was with the West of Scotland Neurosurgical Unit in Killearn. In 1951 he was conscripted into the Royal Army Medical Corps and posted to the Army Psychiatric Unit at Netley near Southampton. Here he was exposed to the psychiatric remedies he would come to question and eventually oppose, including pickaxe lobotomies, electric-shock treatment and insulin coma therapy. On leaving the army he completed his psychiatric training at Gartnavel Royal Mental Hospital in Glasgow, qualifying as a psychiatrist in 1956.

Laing now began in earnest expounding his doctrine of 'antipsychiatry' while conducting research on schizophrenia at the Tavistock Clinic and Institute of Human Relations. He later directed the Langham Clinic in London, where he founded a therapeutic community in which the distinction between staff and patients was more or less eliminated. His revolutionary ideas and books took the world by storm and turned him into a kind of celebrity shrink and media guru.

Being a pop icon, however, took its toll, and when the drink and a heart condition finally killed him he left behind four widows and their children. He will be best remembered for humanising the profession, but sadly he never had a humanising or a loving relationship with his mother, something which he struggled with all his life. His short poem about his mother's conflicting moods says it all: 'Do you love me? Do you believe me? Believe me, you don't love me.'

His other works include *The Politics of Experience* (1967), *Knots* (1970), *The Politics of the Family* (1976), *Sonnets* (1980) and *The Voice of Experience* (1982).

FURTHER READING: John Clay, *R.D. Laing: A Divided Self* (Hodder & Stoughton, 1996); Adrian Laing, *R.D. Laing: A Life* (Sutton Publishing, 2006); R.D. Laing, *Wisdom, Madness and Folly: Making of a Psychiatrist* (Canongate, 2001).

Crosshill

34 Queen Mary Avenue
Childhood home of John Buchan, writer and statesman, and Anna Buchan (1877–1948), who wrote under the pen name O. Douglas

> The wall that circles the domain is of bricks, old, dim, and dirty ... Two valiant elms guard the corners, and midway a herd of little ashes and lindens form a thin grove, beneath which pale valley-lilies raise their heads in spring. What else is there? A privet-hedge, a lawn with wide borders of flowers, a minute shrubbery, two great beds by the house wall flanked by two birch trees, and little more. It is a place 'shorn and parcell'd', with just enough magnitude to give point to its littleness.
>
> John Buchan describing the garden at Queen Mary Avenue in an essay called 'Urban Greenery', from *Scholar Gipsies* (1896)

Rev. John Buchan and his family had lived in Pathhead in Fife from 1875 to 1888, where he was minister of the West Church. At the end of November 1888 the family moved to Glasgow when he was appointed minister to the John Knox Church in the Gorbals, the oldest Free Church in Glasgow. The reverend was no fire-and-brimstone preacher, but a gentle, dreamy, soft-hearted man, a sharp contrast to his wife Helen, who was a no-nonsense, bustling and energetic organiser. The Buchans now had five children (a sixth and last child was born in 1894), of which John was the eldest at thirteen. His mother, together with a maid, combined running the household with organising Women's Meetings and Bible classes, while her husband, when not leading the congregation in prayer, was trying desperately to increase his flock. 'Knox's congregation came from all parts of the city,' wrote Anna Buchan, 'from Maryhill to Pollokshaws, from Govan to Parkhead, and most of the people seemed to live on the top flat of the highest tenements, so Father had many a weary trek. It is not easy work to build up a congregation that has dwindled away.' In 1917 Anna Buchan (under her pen name O. Douglas) portrayed the life of a Glasgow minister and his family in her novel *The Setons*.

John won a scholarship to Hutchesons' Grammar School, then situated two miles away at Crown Street in the Gorbals, and in 1892 he attended the University of Glasgow. In October 1895 he wrote

34 Queen Mary Avenue, childhood home
of John and Anna Buchan.

his first novel *Sir Quixote of the Moors*, a historical yarn with strong overtones of Robert Louis Stevenson. 'I went to Glasgow young and I left young,' wrote Buchan in middle age. In October 1895, having won a scholarship, he left Scotland behind him and headed for Brasenose College, Oxford.

SEE ALSO: The John Buchan Centre, Childhood home of John Buchan (Kirkcaldy).

The John Knox Free Church, Gorbals.

FURTHER READING: M. Greene, *A Biography of John Buchan and His Sister Anna: The Personal Background of their Literary Work* (Edwin Mellen Press, 1990); J.A. Smith, *John Buchan and His World* (Thames & Hudson, 1979); A. Buchan, *Unforgettable, Unforgotten* (Hodder & Stoughton, 1945).

Gorbals

Gorbals Street
The Citizens' Theatre and the literary legacy of the Gorbals

> A crowd numbering close upon a thousand assembled on Glasgow Green to watch the fight between Razor King and big McLatchie . . . It is to be noted that a 'fair fight' between gang champions is one in which nobody interferes, at least as long as both men are on their feet. But it is fighting, not boxing. There are no rules and no rounds and no weapons except fists and feet. It is sheer primitive battle that ends – and that can only end – when one man is battered into senselessness.
>
> A. McArthur and H. Kingsley Long, from *No Mean City*
> (1935), chapter 11 'Fair Fight'

Glasgow's rapid industrial expansion gave birth to deplorable slum housing in many areas of the city. The worst was just south of the River Clyde in the Gorbals, a district which housed a predominantly Irish–Catholic and Jewish population. It became a breeding ground for squalor and violence, nurturing a slum underworld of gang fights, drunkenness and immorality, which culminated in the great gang battles of the late 1920s. It was not uncommon for 12 people to

be herded together in a single room. There were no baths or internal sanitation, and the high infant mortality rate was mainly caused by tenement congestion.

Arguably the most infamous area of Glasgow, the Gorbals figures in many different genres of literature. There is little doubt that the image conjured up by the area is one of crime and extreme violence, often involving organised gangs. This view of the Gorbals is captured in many works but most famously in the novel *No Mean City*, written by A. McArthur and H. Kingsley Long in 1935. It deals with the harsh, emotionally stunted slum world of the Gorbals, with its grinding poverty and the excoriating effects of brutal violence, and tells the story of Johnnie Stark, who becomes a gang leader known as 'Razor King'. It is a world in which there is nothing to do but work, drink, fight and breed. The novel offers up no hope and no solutions, portraying the tenement life of a 'slummie' as a form of ritual suicide. No wonder many local libraries and bookshops refused to stock it – the image the novel portrayed became a cliché for working-class Glasgow and was seen to damage the city's image around the world.

The title is a biblical quotation from the Book of Acts, in which Paul introduces himself as 'a Jew of Tarsus in Cilicia, a citizen of no mean city'. Unemployed baker Alexander McArthur (1901–47) submitted some of his stories on Gorbals' life to Longmans, who deemed them unpublishable, but they hired experienced London journalist H. Kingsley Long to collaborate with McArthur and knock them into shape. The resulting book was a cross between social document and pulp fiction, with not a breath of air or shred of humour to be found anywhere among its pages. It is still a hard-hitting read to this day.

Tragically, McArthur died in poverty, committing suicide by drowning himself in the Clyde. His second novel *No Bad Money* was published posthumously in 1969. In May 2006 the Citizens' Theatre Company staged Alex Norton's adaptation of *No Mean City*. It played to huge audiences, including residents of the New Gorbals, living in an environment a world away from the conditions depicted.

Other Gorbals-born writers who have contributed to the area's story over the years include Ralph Glasser with his *Gorbals Trilogy* (1997), short-story writer Edward Gaitens with his *Dance of the Apprentices* (1948) and Jimmy Boyle, the convicted murderer and prize-winning writer. A more recent view of the Gorbals, set in the 1960s as the demolishment of the slums continued, can be found

James Bridie.

in the first novel of Jeff Torrington, *Swing Hammer Swing!* (1992). This book, which took 30 years to complete and won the Whitbread Prize in 1992, shows us the world of Tam Clay, drunk, waster, patter merchant and urban philosopher, as he waits for the birth of his child and deals with the disappearance of his housing.

Today little remains of the original Gorbals and few landmarks remind us of the area's history. However, the Citizens' Theatre, one of the leading theatres in Britain, with an international reputation, remains firmly in its position in Gorbals Street. The Citizens' Theatre Company was formed in 1943 by a group of theatre-minded men, including the playwright James Bridie (1888–1951), who became the first president, Dr Tom Honeyman, who became the first chairman, and the writer Guy McCrone, who was the first managing director. First located in the Athenaeum Theatre, the company moved to the Royal Princess' Theatre in the Gorbals in 1945, which was then renamed as the Citizens' Theatre. The name comes from the manifesto drawn up in 1909 for the Glasgow Repertory Theatre:

> The Repertory Theatre is Glasgow's own theatre. It is a citizens' theatre in the fullest sense of the term. Established to make Glasgow independent from London for its dramatic supplies, it produces plays which the Glasgow playgoers would otherwise not have the opportunity of seeing.

The Royal Princess' Theatre building, designed by Campbell Douglas, a friend of the architect Alexander 'Greek' Thomson, was built in 1878. By the start of the twentieth century the theatre stood surrounded by some of the worst overcrowded slums in Europe. The Citizens' building was further altered in 1989 by the building of a new atrium foyer and in 1992 by the creation of the Stalls and Circle Studio spaces. Still to be seen in the foyer of the theatre today are the statues of William Shakespeare, Robert Burns and four muses which adorned the original building. They were sculpted by J. Mossman. Also preserved are four elephant heads (astonishingly now painted bright pink) and goddesses from the auditorium of the Palace Theatre, which was next door to the Citizens' and built in 1904.

In its early years under the control of James Bridie, the Citizens' Theatre promoted a range of Scottish plays, including some of Bridie's own. After the death of Bridie, a series of artistic directors, including Callum Mill and Ian Cuthbertson, introduced Glasgow audiences to a wider range of British and European theatre. The Citizens' reputation became truly international under the control of the triumvirate of Giles Havergal, Robert MacDonald and Philip Prowse, who were the theatre's directors from 1969 until they retired in 2003. They were responsible for the development of the visceral Citizens' style and a truly international repertoire.

The Citizens' Theatre Company has performed 24 world premieres, 22 British premieres and in a large number of European cities. The Citizens' Theatre is not merely positioned in the Gorbals, it reaches out to attract the residents of the area through a variety of initiatives, including free previews, subsidised ticket prices for locals and community-theatre projects. It remains a hugely important cultural landmark in the Gorbals.

FURTHER INFORMATION: The Citizens' Theatre. Tel: 0141 429 5561/0022.

James Bridie (pseudonym of Osborne Henry Mavor) was born in Glasgow on 3 January 1888. He went on to study medicine at the University of Glasgow and qualified as a doctor in 1913. Although he maintained a successful career in medicine, Bridie's real passion was for the theatre. However, it was not until he was 40 that he had his first real play, *The Sunlight Sonata*, produced by Tyrone Guthrie at the Lyric Theatre, Glasgow. Bridie's output as a playwright was truly prolific. He wrote some 40 plays altogether and built a reputation as one of Scotland's greatest playwrights. He may be regarded as the founder of modern Scottish theatre. Among his most successful plays is *The Anatomist* (1931), dealing with Dr Robert Knox and the murders of Burke and Hare, which he regarded as his masterpiece and took two years to complete. Although most of his plays opened in London, many were performed at the Citizens' Theatre. Bridie was also concerned to see that there was proper training for the theatre and helped found the first college of drama in Scotland in 1950. He was also involved in the establishment of the Edinburgh International Festival. Sadly, few of Bridie's plays are performed today and only two remain in print. Perhaps the creation of the National Theatre of Scotland will see this corrected.

West Dunbartonshire

Balloch

Cameron House
Family seat of Tobias Smollett (1721–71), historian and writer of picaresque comic novels

> I have seen Lake Garda, Albana, de Visco, Bolsetta and Geneva. Upon my honour I prefer Loch Lomond to them all.
>
> Tobias Smollett

Tobias Smollett was born at Dalquhurn House (now demolished), near Renton, but although he was born in Dunbartonshire and educated at the University of Glasgow, Scotland never really empathised with Smollett, who lived most of his life in London and later moved abroad for his health. But where Robert Louis Stevenson turned exile into legend, Smollett was probably too anglicised, too caustic, too prejudiced and too out of touch with his roots for Scotland to claim him as its own.

He was a surgeon's mate in the Royal Navy and later practised in London, but he spent most of his life as a man of letters. It was his picaresque novels which brought him fame, namely *Roderick Random* (1748), *Peregrine Pickle* (1751) and *The Expedition of Humphry Clinker* (1771). In 1753 he edited the *Critical Review*, but his criticism was so savage it led to his imprisonment for libel in 1760. He was a noted historian, writing his *History of England* in three volumes (1757–58); another major achievement was his translation of Cervantes' *Don Quixote* into English in 1755.

During the summer of 1766, he stayed with his sister Mrs Telfer, who occupied the second flat of 182 Canongate (now renumbered 22 St John Street) above the pend (tunnel), and it was here he wrote part of his last and most popular novel, *The Expedition of Humphry Clinker*. Written during the last two years of his life, the story is told by its characters through a series of letters on a journey encompassing Wales, London and Scotland – Edinburgh disgusts them by its filth.

For health reasons his last years were spent abroad, and he died in Livorno, Italy. Shortly before his death he visited his mother at St John Street, confiding to her that he was ill and not long for this world. To this she replied, 'We'll no' be very long pairted onie way. If you gang first, I'll be close on your heels. If I lead the way, you'll no be far ahint me.'

SEE ALSO: Dr Johnson.

FURTHER INFORMATION: Cameron House, an eighteenth-century baronial mansion on the south-west bank of Loch Lomond, became the Smollett family home after 1763. Boswell and Johnson stayed there during their Highland tour in 1773. In 1986 it was sold and developed into a luxury hotel and leisure resort. Memorabilia connected to Smollett can still be seen at the hotel. Cameron House Hotel, near Balloch, Loch Lomond, Dunbartonshire, G83 8QZ. Tel: 01389 755565.

A monument was erected to Smollett's memory by his cousin James in 1774 at Renton and is located on the main road near the village school. It is a round Tuscan column, 60-feet high, with a Latin inscription by Dr Johnson.

FURTHER READING: L.M. Knapp, *Tobias Smollett: Doctor of Men and Manners* (Princeton University Press, 1949); G.M. Kahrl, *Tobias Smollett: Traveller–Novelist* (1945).

Stirling

Loch Lomond and the Trossachs
National Park

Loch Katrine
Inspiration for Sir Walter Scott's *The Lady of the Lake*

> That d – d Sir Walter Scott, that everybody makes such a
> work about! . . . I wish I had him to ferry over Loch Lomond: I
> should be after sinking the boat, if I drowned myself into the
> bargain; for ever since he wrote his Lady of the Lake, as they
> call it, everybody goes to that filthy hole Loch Katrine, then
> comes round by Luss, and I have had only two gentlemen to
> guide all this blessed season.
>
> Loch Lomond ferryman after publication of Scott's
> *The Lady of the Lake*

It's difficult to imagine today a single narrative poem sparking the
enormous number of sightseers who descended in droves in their
post-chaises to the Trossachs after the publication of *The Lady of
the Lake* in 1810. A hotel was built at Callander especially to cater
for those wishing to visit Ellen's Isle on Loch Katrine. J.G. Lockhart
gives us a taste of the frenetic atmosphere in his *Life of Sir Walter
Scott*:

> The whole country rang with the praises of the poet –
> crowds set off to view the scenery of Loch Katrine, till
> then comparatively unknown; and as the book came out
> just before the season for excursions, every house and
> inn in that neighbourhood was crammed with a constant
> succession of visitors.

Scott began writing *The Lady of the Lake* in August 1809 while
holidaying in the Trossachs with his wife and daughter, and was
inspired by the shores and islands of Loch Katrine. The poem was
laid aside when three of his children fell dangerously ill with an
inflammatory fever, and only after they had fully recovered did
he complete the poem, which was eventually published on 8 May
1810. The poem chronicles the dispute between King James V and
the Douglas clan, and is ladled with stag hunts, battles, knights,
unrequited love and the stunning scenery of Loch Katrine. It broke
all records for the sale of poetry, selling twenty-five thousand copies
in eight months. Most of the critics were also ecstatic about it,

although the Rev. Francis Hodgson in the *Monthly Review* thought the 'composition careless and the language barbaric'. However, he was decidedly in the minority, and had he been visiting the Trossachs at that time, would no doubt have been trampled to death by the scrambling masses.

SEE ALSO: Dryburgh Abbey, Abbotsford, Ashestiel, County Hotel, Clovenfords Hotel, Gordon Arms, Dryburgh Abbey, Scott's View, Scott's Courtroom and Statue, Traquair House, Minchmoor, Waverley Lodge, Newark Castle, Tibbie Shiel's Inn, Melrose Abbey, College Wynd, George Square, North Castle Street, Scott Monument.

FURTHER INFORMATION: Loch Katrine is situated in the Loch Lomond and the Trossachs National Park, approximately 45 minutes from Stirling and 60 minutes from Glasgow. The nearest town is Callander (Tourist info: 08707 200628). Loch Katrine derives its name from the Gaelic 'Cateran', meaning a Highland robber, and is just under ten miles long and over one mile wide. It is also Clan McGregor country, and the clan graveyard is at the head of the loch, near Glengyle House, birthplace of Rob Roy. Sailings on the steamship *Sir Walter Scott*, which has been sailing on the loch since 1899, depart from the Trossachs Pier. Tel: 01877 376 315.

Fife

97–99 Main Street
Lodgings of Alexander Selkirk (1676–1721)
Daniel Defoe's inspiration for *Robinson Crusoe*

> It happened one day, about noon, going towards my boat, I
> was exceedingly surprised with the print of a man's naked
> foot on the shore, which was very plain to be seen in the
> sand. I stood like one thunderstruck, or as if I had seen an
> apparition.
>
> Daniel Defoe, from *Robinson Crusoe* (1719)

Alexander Selkirk, the Scottish sailor who was the inspiration
for Daniel Defoe's *Robinson Crusoe*, was born in the small fishing
village of Lower Largo in 1676. A statue to the world's most famous
castaway can be seen halfway along Main Street at numbers 97–99.
The building stands on the site of his brother's house, where Selkirk
once lodged, but it is not his birthplace. The exact location of his
birth is unknown, but it is believed to have been at Drummochie,
which is separated from the village by the estuary of the Keil
burn.

Selkirk was the seventh child and seventh son of John Selcraig,
a shoemaker and tanner, and his wife Euphan Mackie. Lower Largo
legend claims he was a wild and wayward character. The records
of Largo Kirk record that he was twice cited to appear before the
session to account for his conduct. Only once did he comply, and he
was publicly rebuked in church for his 'scandalous carriage'.

The Crusoe Hotel, Lower Largo harbour.

In 1703 he joined Captain Dampier's privateering expedition to the South Seas, engaging as sailing-master of the frigate *Cinque Ports*, on a voyage to pillage French and Spanish shipping. The frigate was under the command of Captain Stradling, a domineering bully of a man with whom Selkirk quarrelled incessantly. When the frigate reached the uninhabited island of Juan Fernández in the autumn of 1704, Selkirk had had enough of Stradling and demanded to be put ashore. It was a decision he immediately regretted and tried to reverse. With only his sea chest, containing his clothes and bedding, a cooking pot, a hatchet and knife, a flint and steel, and some powder, bullets and a musket, he was put ashore. The nearest point of human habitation was Valparaiso, 400 miles to the east. It would be four years and four months before he would speak to another living soul.

He was finally rescued in February 1709 by William Dampier, who was then pilot on a privateering expedition. Selkirk was appointed ship's mate, and for the next couple of years he took part in raids off the South American coast. He returned to London relatively well-off, as his share of the booty was around £800. Essayist Richard Steele wrote up Selkirk's story and published it under the misleading title of *The Englishman* in 1711.

Selkirk returned to Scotland but had obviously not fully adjusted from his years on Juan Fernández, as he spent much of his time alone. He never felt at ease living indoors and built a makeshift cave behind his brother's house. There is some doubt whether or not Defoe actually met Selkirk, but some sources claim the two encountered one another at the house of Mrs Demaris Daniel in Bristol, where Selkirk supposedly retold his adventures to Defoe and handed over his personal papers. Whatever the reality was, there seems little doubt that *Robinson Crusoe* was inspired by Selkirk. Defoe, however, extended his castaway's exile to 28 years and moved the island from the South Pacific, off the coast of Chile, to the Caribbean, off the coast of Venezuela. Defoe was nearly 60 when he wrote the book, which became a bestseller and was translated into many languages. Although a work of fiction, Robinson Crusoe is still believed by many to have been a real person. There are people on the island of Tobago who claim most sincerely to be his descendants.

FURTHER INFORMATION: No visit to Lower Largo is complete without a visit to the Crusoe Hotel down by the harbour, where you can sample the Juan Fernández Bar, with Man Friday's footprint highlighted in the floor, and eat in the Castaway Restaurant. The Crusoe Hotel, The Harbour, 2 Main Street, Lower Largo, Fife, KN8 6BT. Tel: 01333 320759.

FURTHER READING: D. Souhani, *Selkirk's Island: The True and Strange Adventures of the Real Robinson Crusoe* (Harcourt, 2002); G. Dingwall, *The Story of Alexander Selkirk* (Fifeshire Advertiser, 1951); J. Richetti, *The Life of Daniel Defoe: A Critical Biography* (Blackwell, 2005).

Kirkcaldy

The Manse
Smeaton Road
Childhood home of John Buchan and birthplace of Anna Buchan

> John once wrote, rather rudely, 'I never likit the Kingdom of Fife,' and certainly we never loved it as we loved the Borders, but looking back our life there was full of sunshine . . . Some time ago we crossed the Forth Bridge, anxious to see how much remained of the place we remembered so well. We found practically nothing. The big Manse garden had disappeared. The Manse itself was still there, but crushed among tenements . . . electric trams clanged through streets that had not existed in our day.
>
> Anna Buchan, *Unforgettable, Unforgotten* (1945)

John Buchan, father of the modern espionage novel and best remembered as the author of *The Thirty-Nine Steps*, was born at 20 York Place in Perth on 20 August 1875, the eldest child of Helen Masterton and Rev. John Buchan. Shortly after his birth his parents moved to Pathhead in Fife, then a small town between Dysart and Kirkcaldy, but now part of Kirkcaldy, where Rev. Buchan was appointed minister of the West Church (now demolished). The Buchans stayed at the Manse in Smeaton Road for twelve years, and four more children were born there. Anna Buchan recalled the house in her 1945 biography of the Buchan family, *Unforgettable, Unforgotten*:

Rev. John Buchan.

> One of the two windows looked across the garden and the field beyond and a jumble of roofs, to the grey water of the Firth of Forth and the Inchkeith Lighthouse. As the darkening fell, we children clustered round to watch the light come and go, convinced in our own minds that it was caused by a giant waving a lantern . . . Willie and Walter and I shared the night-nursery. John, the eldest, had a small room to himself, a sort of prophet's chamber, containing only a bed, chair, and a table. I did not envy him his lonely splendour.

When John was about four years old, he fell out of a carriage and the rear wheel struck his head, fracturing his skull. After surgery, he was bedridden for a year and carried a prominent scar on his left brow for the rest of his life. Local legend has it that the 39 steps in the book were inspired by the steps on the west side of Ravenscraig

Castle leading down to Pathhead beach, and the opening chapter of *Prester John* (1910) was supposedly set on the beach after young John heard an African minister preaching there. When Buchan was 13, his father became minister of John Knox Church in Glasgow, and from Kirkcaldy High School he was sent to Hutchesons' Grammar School, Glasgow, and later to the University of Glasgow. He won a scholarship to Brasenose College, Oxford, and in 1901 became assistant private secretary to the High Commissioner for South Africa. In South Africa he became involved in the running of concentration camps and the repatriation of prisoners following the end of the Boer War. Buchan returned to England and the Bar in 1903 and in 1907 married Susan Grosvenor.

A prolific writer from his youth, he wrote seven volumes of prose and poetry while still at Oxford. In 1914 he went to France as correspondent for *The Times* before being commissioned in the Intelligence Corps. In 1915 *The Thirty-Nine Steps* first appeared anonymously in *Blackwood's Magazine*, which began the first of the Richard Hannay novels and established him as a bestseller. Other fast-moving adventure stories followed, including *Greenmantle* (1916), *Huntingtower* (1922), *The Three Hostages* (1924) and *Witch Wood* (1927). He also wrote biographies, notably *Montrose* (1928) and *Sir Walter Scott* (1932). He was created a baron in the mid-1930s, choosing the title Lord Tweedsmuir of Elsfield, and in 1935 he was appointed governor general of Canada, where he died on Sunday, 11 February 1940 after injuring his head in a fall. His ashes are buried in St Thomas of Canterbury Churchyard, Elsfield, Oxfordshire.

Buchan's younger sister Anna was also a prolific novelist. *Olivia in India*, her first novel, was published in 1913, but she did not want to use her own name, claiming that her brother John 'had given lustre to the name of Buchan which any literary efforts of mine would not be likely to add to, so I called myself "O. Douglas"'. Anna was also educated at Hutchesons' Grammar School in Glasgow, and lived most of her life in Peebles, the setting for Priorsford in her novels. Other works included *The Setons* (1917), *Penny Plain* (1920), *Ann and her Mother* (1922), *The Proper Place* (1926), *The Day of Small Things* (1930), *Jane's Parlour* (1937) and *People Like Ourselves* (1938). She also wrote a biography of the Buchan family, *Unforgettable, Unforgotten*, and her own autobiography, *Farewell to Priorsford*, was published posthumously in 1950.

SEE ALSO: John Buchan Centre, Childhood home of John Buchan (Glasgow).

FURTHER READING: J.A. Smith, *John Buchan* (Oxford Paperbacks, 1985); J.A Smith, *John Buchan and His World* (Scribner, 1984); A. Lownie, *John Buchan: The Presbyterian Cavalier* (Pimlico, 2002); A. Buchan, *Unforgettable, Unforgotten* (Hodder & Stoughton, 1945).

Perth and Kinross

Auchterarder

Kenwood Park
Birthplace of James Kennaway (1928–68), novelist, playwright and screenwriter

> It is becoming more and more ludicrous to pretend that the point of my life is anything other than writing. All the day and half the night I think of nothing else. For days on end I'm totally immersed in the work. Where will it lead, except to megalomania, it's hard to see. But facts have to be accepted. The curse of it is that it gets out of hand. The only way to get away from the difficulties one's encountering in the work is to live hard, nearly to blaze.
>
> James Kennaway

At a dinner party at the Kennaways' a friend once remarked that she hadn't known where her husband had been all day and had been trying to reach him without success. James Kennaway's wife Sue, without any antipathy, casually remarked that she hadn't known where James had been for a fortnight. James Kennaway's wild, hard-drinking and turbulent life lasted only 40 years, but within those years he wrote many books and film scripts. However, it is for his outstanding first novel *Tunes of Glory* (1956) that he will be best remembered, in which a clash of wills in a Highland regiment between Lieutenant-Colonel Jock Sinclair, an El Alamein veteran, and Lieutenant-Colonel Basil Barrow, a 'by the book' officer, ends in tragedy. One goes insane and the other commits suicide. The book was successfully adapted for the screen in 1960, for which Kennaway wrote the screenplay. Both book and film became huge international successes.

He was born on 5 June 1928 into a comfortable middle-class family. His mother was a doctor and his father was a solicitor, who died when Kennaway was only 11. He attended public school at Trinity College, Glenalmond, and did his national service with the Queen's Own Cameron Highlanders in 1946. He also served with the Gordon Highlanders on the Rhine, whose 'petty squabbling for authority in the mess' planted the seed for *Tunes of Glory*. After the army, he went to Trinity College, Oxford, where he studied economics, philosophy and politics, and where he made the decision to become a writer. In the early 1950s he worked for the publisher Longmans and shortly afterwards married art student Sue Edmonds, with whom he had four children. His first published work was a long short-story in the magazine *Lilliput*, and from then on he wrote copiously for page and screen, remarking that his income fluctuated between £600 and £30,000 a year. His second novel, *Household Ghosts* (1961), was equally potent and also adapted for the stage and screen. Other works included *Some Gorgeous Accident* (1967) and the autobiographical *The Cost of Living Like This* (1969).

'I have no faith in tomorrow,' he once wrote. 'The idea that I shall see my children grown up is immediately, automatically dismissed.' Driving home from an evening with the actor Peter O'Toole on 21 December 1968, he died in a car crash after suffering a heart attack. He is buried in St Mary's Churchyard, Fairford, Gloucestershire.

FURTHER INFORMATION: Kenwood Park is between Abbey Road and Abbottsfield, on the south side of Auchterarder High Street. The Argyll and Sutherland Highlanders were initially willing to allow Stirling Castle to be used as a location for the film *Tunes of Glory* but refused permission, once they had read the script, on the grounds that the film would disgrace the regiment. The film was eventually shot at Shepperton Studios and at locations around Windsor Castle. The film-makers did get permission to use the castle as a backdrop, so long as they made it unrecognisable. After the film was released and became successful, the Argyll and Sutherland Highlanders requested permission to use it in their recruiting drive.

FURTHER READING: S. Kennaway, *The Kennaway Papers* (Jonathan Cape, 1981); T. Royle, *James and Jim: A Biography of James Kennaway* (Mainstream, 1983).

Kinnaird

Kinnaird Cottage
Where Robert Louis Stevenson wrote 'Thrawn Janet' and other tales

In the summer of 1881 Robert Louis Stevenson and his wife Fanny holidayed with his parents at Kinnaird Cottage above Pitlochry in the Vale of Atholl. They arrived on Friday, 7 June and stayed for two months. 'If we are to come to Scotland,' he wrote to his parents, 'I will have fir trees, and I want a burn, the firs for my physical, the water for my mental health.' Louis got his firs in abundance, and water from the heavens poured down on them relentlessly. In the Preface to *The Merry Men and Other Tales* Fanny describes what sounds like a typical Highland summer:

Although it was the seventh of June when we moved into the cottage, as yet we had nothing but cold rains and penetrating winds; and in all innocence (this being my first season in this beautiful and inclement region) I asked when spring would begin. 'This is the spring,' said my mother-in-law. 'And the summer,' I inquired, 'when will the summer be here?' 'Well,' returned my mother-in-law, 'we must wait for St Swithin's Day; it all depends on what kind of weather we have then.' St Swithin's Day came and went in a storm of wind and rain. 'I am afraid,' confessed my mother-in-law, 'that the summer is past, and we shall have no more good weather.' And so it turned out. Between showers she and I wandered over the moor and along the banks of the burn, but always with umbrellas in our hands, and generally returning drenched. My husband, who had come to the Highlands solely for the sunshine and bracing air, was condemned to spend most of his time in our small, stuffy sitting-room, with no amusement or occupation other than that provided by his writing materials. The only book we had with us, two large volumes of the life of Voltaire, did not tend to raise our spirits. Even these, removed by my husband's parents one Sunday as not being proper Sabbath Day reading, were annexed by the elder couple, each taking a volume. Thrown entirely on our own resources for amusement, we decided to write stories and read them to each other; naturally these tales, coloured by our surroundings, were of sombre cast.

With hindsight, perhaps we should be thankful for the rain that kept Louis housebound, as he wrote his classic ghost story 'Thrawn Janet' there and began work on *The Merry Men*. After two months of endless rain and wind, Louis's health again declined, and he experienced severe chest pains and vomited blood. On doctor's advice they moved to Braemar, where Louis began work on the book for which he will be best remembered – *Treasure Island*.

SEE ALSO: Braemar, The Edinburgh Book Lovers' Tour, The Literary Pub Crawl, Howard Place, Inverleith Terrace, Rutherford's Howff, Hawes Inn, W.E. Henley, The Writers' Museum, The *Kidnapped* Trail.

FURTHER INFORMATION: Kinnaird is approximately two miles north-east of Pitlochry, beyond Moulin on the road to Kirkmichael. The front wall of Kinnaird Cottage carries a plaque commemorating the visit of Robert Louis Stevenson.

FURTHER READING: L. Stott, *Robert Louis Stevenson and the Highlands and Islands of Scotland* (Creag Darach Publications, 1992).

Angus

9 Brechin Road
Birthplace of J.M. Barrie (1860–1937), novelist and dramatist

Oh, for an hour of Herod.
Anthony Hope's comment after watching
a performance of *Peter Pan*

J.M. Barrie (c. 1894).

Chiefly remembered today as the creator of *Peter Pan*, James Matthew Barrie rose from humble origins to become one of the most praised and successful dramatists of his day. Wealth and fame, however, failed to bring him happiness, and he spent much of his life trying to win the love denied him as a child. His generosity could be overwhelming, his affection intense and possessive. Small in stature, shy, secretive, and with unpredictable moods, Barrie was an odd and complex genius.

He was born on 9 May 1860 in Kirriemuir, the ninth child of Margaret Ogilvy and David Barrie, a hand-loom weaver. His parents had ten children in all: seven daughters and three sons. David, his mother's favourite son, died tragically, aged fourteen, in a skating accident when James was six. His mother was 'always delicate from that hour', he recalled, and constantly thinking of her boy who was gone. She never recovered from her loss, and throughout his childhood Barrie tried desperately to replace him, yearning for his mother's love.

He attended Glasgow Academy, Dumfries Academy and the local school in Kirriemuir. When he was 18, he entered Edinburgh University, the fees for which were paid by his elder brother Alec, with whom he shared lodgings at the top of a house at 14 Cumberland Street. His father sent him an allowance, which he supplemented by writing theatre reviews for the *Edinburgh Courant*. He lived frugally and kept pretty much to himself. A fellow student described him as 'a spare, short figure in a warm-looking Highland cloak'. In 1882 he received his degree and had his photograph taken in cap and gown, with 'hair straggling under the cap as tobacco may straggle over the side of a tin when there is difficulty in squeezing down the lid'.

He was writing regularly by this time, but apart from a few

Barrie's birthplace and the wash house.

articles written for the *Courant*, no one was interested in publishing his work. In 1883, more in desperation than as a career move, he started work as a leader writer for the *Nottingham Journal*, eventually moving to London in 1885, where he began freelancing. In 1888 he published *Auld Licht Idylls*, the first of his Kailyard stories, which was followed by *A Window in Thrums* (1889) and *The Little Minister* (1891). *Richard Savage*, his first play, was performed in London in 1891, and from this point onwards he wrote mainly for the theatre. J.M. Barrie was becoming a talent to be reckoned with.

In 1894 he married 32-year-old actress Mary Ansell, who discovered on her wedding night that Barrie was impotent, and, consequently, their marriage was never consummated. Barrie refused to discuss his problem or seek medical advice. Mary made the best of it, but, effectively, they ended up living separate lives, eventually divorcing in 1909.

Between 1901 and 1920 Barrie produced his most successful plays, including *Quality Street* (1901), *The Admirable Crichton* (1902), *Peter Pan* (1904), *What Every Woman Knows* (1908), *Dear Brutus* (1917) and *Mary Rose* (1920).

In 1897 he began a curious infatuation with Sylvia Llewelyn-Davies and her young sons, to whom he became an oppressive and domineering guardian, lavishing gifts, holidays, money and counsel. Sylvia and her husband died young, and Barrie unofficially adopted the five children; they became literally the 'Lost Boys'. One of them, Michael, photographed by Barrie in 1906, was the original inspiration for the Peter Pan statue in Kensington Gardens. Another of the boys, Peter, once described *Peter Pan* as 'that terrible masterpiece'.

The 'Little Scotchman' died on 19 June 1937 and is buried in the town cemetery on Kirrie Hill.

SEE ALSO: Rutherford's Howff.

FURTHER INFORMATION: After Barrie's death in 1937, his birthplace had a narrow escape when it was proposed that

Margaret Ogilvy, J.M. Barrie's mother.

the house be sold and dismantled stone by stone for a buyer in the USA. Fortunately for Scottish literary history, a local philanthropist bought it and donated it to the National Trust. The house is now a museum and includes manuscripts, diaries, photographs, Barrie's own writing desk, examples of the original costumes worn at the first production of *Peter Pan* and a contract which Barrie made with the six-year-old Princess Margaret after he had incorporated some words she had said to him into one of his plays. Outside is the communal wash house, reputedly the origin of the house the Lost Boys built in Neverland.

Barrie bequeathed the copyright of *Peter Pan* to the Great Ormond Street Hospital for Sick Children and immortalised his 'wee red toonie' (Kirriemuir) in *A Window in Thrums* (1889). A statue to Peter Pan can be seen in Kirriemuir High Street.

J.M. Barrie's Birthplace, 9 Brechin Road, Kirriemuir, Angus, DD8 4BX. Tel: 01575 572646. Open April to September.

FURTHER READING: J. Dunbar, *J.M. Barrie: The Man Behind the Image* (Collins, 1970); C. Asquith, *Haply I May Remember* (1950); C. Asquith, *Portrait of Barrie* (1954); V. Meynell (ed.), *Letters of J.M. Barrie* (1942); G. McCaughrean, *Peter Pan in Scarlet* (Oxford University Press, 2006); A. Birkin, *J.M. Barrie and the Lost Boys: The Real Story Behind Peter Pan* (Yale University Press, 2003).

Dundee

Riverside Drive

Memorial to William McGonagall (c. 1825–1902), writer of doggerel

> It must have been an awful sight,
> To witness in the dusky moonlight,
> While the Storm Fiend did laugh, and angry did bray,
> Along the Railway Bridge of the Silv'ry Tay,
> Oh! ill-fated Bridge of the Silv'ry Tay,
> I must now conclude my lay
> By telling the world fearlessly without the least dismay,
> That your central girders would not have given way,
> At least many sensible men do say,
> Had they been supported on each side with buttresses,
> At least many sensible men confesses,
> For the stronger we our houses do build,
> The less chance we have of being killed.
>   William McGonagall, from 'The Tay Bridge Disaster' (1880)

Described as the world's best bad poet, William McGonagall's popularity still flourishes, and his poetry is still published all over the world, proof that poetry, no matter how execrable, can still find an audience. The son of an Irish cotton weaver, he was born in Edinburgh but grew up in Dundee, to where his father had moved in search of work. For many years he lived in Paton's Lane (first at number 48 and later at number 19), near McGonagall Square, named in his memory. One of seven siblings, he worked from the age of eleven as a handloom weaver. He acted in amateur productions at Dundee's Royal Theatre and in 1878 published  his first collection of poems. He gave public readings to derisory applause, ducked missiles thrown at him and was labelled with the ridiculous sobriquet of 'Sir Topaz, Knight of the White Elephant of Burmah'. He sold his broadsheets in the street and once walked all the way to Balmoral, but Queen Victoria denied him an audience. He also tried his luck in London and New York but returned, as he had arrived, penniless. During his lifetime, he published over 200 poems, his best known being 'The Tay Bridge Disaster'. His *Poetic Gems* was published in 1890.

He may have died in poverty and be buried in a pauper's grave, but the memory of this eternal optimist, who disregarded everything that makes poetry worth reading, will live for ever. He was buried in Greyfriars Churchyard, Edinburgh, but the burial records give no clue as to where his remains are interred. Bob and Pat Watt, founders of the Edinburgh Friends of William McGonagall (0131 441 2580), raised money for a memorial plaque in the churchyard, erected on 6 October 1999.

Below is an appreciation of William McGonagall by Bob:

> William's parents were Irish migrants who followed the work. With their six children, of whom William was the youngest, they had lived in Mabole, Edinburgh, Paisley and the Orkney Islands, before settling in Dundee. When they arrived in the city, William was probably a teenager. There is some debate as to the date and place of his birth. Some sources say 1825, although he claimed it was 1830. In 1846 he married Jean King, with whom he had five sons and two daughters. Like his father, William became a handloom weaver. He was also a teetotaller and spent his leisure time reading. Considering he had little schooling, his ability to read and write were notable achievements. He read cheap editions of Shakespeare, focusing on *Macbeth*, *Richard III*, *Hamlet* and *Othello*. He would perform scenes on the factory floor for his workmates, who enjoyed his entertainments so much that they clubbed together and raised money for him to perform *Macbeth* at Mr Giles's Lindsay Street Theatre. Subsequent performances followed over the years on stage and in pubs and clubs around Dundee. William always carried an umbrella during performances – not for the rain, but to fend off the missiles people would throw at him. His appearances at Baron Zeigler's Circus and the Transfield Circus resulted in such riotous behaviour from the audiences that the magistrates banned his performances. William's treatment in Dundee was diabolical, but in all his writings there is not a bitter word against the city. Dundee has never been the epicentre of epiphanies, but William gave the city what it has never had before or since – a world-famous poet. History, travel, the great, the tiny, politics, love and national disasters are all immortalised in his rich range of poetry. Today the city has carved some of William's words in stone, but what he really deserves is a statue. Dundonians in history threw rotten fruit at him, proving they have it in their DNA to throw things. Why not throw money at a statue fund?

FURTHER INFORMATION: The McGonagall Memorial is engraved into the walkway of Riverside Drive on the west side of the town overlooking the Tay Bridge. The William McGonagall Collection is held at the Local History Centre of Dundee Central Library and includes news cuttings, correspondence (many of which are begging letters), manuscript poems and biography, broadsheets, and *Jack o' the Cudgel*, a new play in three acts dramatised by

McGonagall in July 1886. For further details contact the Local History Centre, Central Library, Wellgate, Dundee, DD1 1DB. Tel: 01382 431550.

The Dundee McGonagall Appreciation Society can be contacted through Alex Goick. Tel: 01382 223649.

The original Tay Bridge, then the longest bridge in the world, spanned two miles across the Tay estuary. On the evening of 28 December 1879, only nine months after it was opened, the central part of the bridge collapsed in a gale, plunging an express train into the river. The accident claimed 75 lives. The wrought-iron girders that remained standing after the disaster were incorporated into the structure of the present bridge, where they are still in use today.

To find McGonagall's memorial plaque at Greyfriars Churchyard in Edinburgh follow the path from the main entrance round the right-hand side of the church. Walk straight ahead and through the archway in the Flodden Wall. McGonagall's memorial is in the top-left corner.

FURTHER READING: William McGonagall, *Poetic Gems* (Duckbacks, 2006); C. Hunt, *William McGonagall: Collected Poems* (Birlinn, 2006).

Broughty Ferry

Brook Street
Brook Street House
Childhood home of Lewis Spence (1874–1955), poet and folklorist

> O that yon river micht nae mair
> Rin through the channels o' my sleep;
> My bluid has felt its tides owre sair,
> Its waves hae drooned my dreams owrre deep.
> Lewis Spence, from 'Great Tay of the Waves'

James Lewis Spence was born in Broughty Ferry in 1874, the eldest son of James E. Spence, and was educated at Collegiate School in Brook Street. Along with Hugh MacDiarmid, he was one of the founders of the Scottish Renaissance, whose purpose was to 'bring Scottish literature into closer touch with current European tendencies in technique and ideation'. Writing in classical Scots, his collections of poetry include *The Phoenix* (1924) and *Weirds and Vanities* (1927).

He travelled to Edinburgh in 1892 to study dentistry but ended up as a sub-editor on *The Scotsman* newspaper and later *The British Weekly* (1905–09). An ardent nationalist, he was one of the founders of the National Party of Scotland in 1928 and in the same year became the first nationalist to stand for election, although he lost his deposit. He was also a leading authority on ancient folklore and wrote many books on the subject, including the *Dictionary of Mythology* (1913), *Encyclopaedia of Occultism* (1920) and *The Magic Arts in Celtic Britain* (1945). He lived in Edinburgh at 34 Howard Place for many years and died in the city from a cerebral haemorrhage in 1955.

SEE ALSO: Hugh MacDiarmid.

South Baffin Street
Site of 'The Cottage'
Where Mary Shelley (1797–1851) stayed between 1812 and 1814, and where it is reputed she began writing *Frankenstein* (1818)

I lived principally in the country as a girl, and passed a considerable time in Scotland. I made occasional visits to the more picturesque parts; but my habitual residence was on the blank and dreary northern shores of the Tay, near Dundee. Blank and dreary on retrospection I call them; they were not so to me then. They were the eyry of freedom, and the pleasant region where unheeded I could commune with the creatures of my fancy. I wrote then – but in a most common-place style. It was beneath the trees of the grounds belonging to our house, or on the bleak sides of the woodless mountains near, that my true compositions, the airy flights of my imagination, were born and fostered.

Mary Shelley, from the introduction
to the 1831 edition of *Frankenstein*

Mary Shelley was born Mary Wollstonecraft Godwin in London on 30 August 1797, the only child of feminist and writer Mary Wollstonecraft and political writer and novelist William Godwin. Her mother died ten days after her birth, and together with her half-sister she was brought up by her father, who quickly remarried. Mary's relationship with her stepmother was strained. She did not receive any formal education but was schooled by her father. A sickly child, she was sent in the summer of 1812 to the Scottish seaside for her health, where she stayed with William Baxter, an acquaintance of her father who lived in Broughty Ferry. Baxter had four daughters and two sons, and Mary soon developed a special affection for his daughters Christina and Isabella, returning to Dundee for frequent visits between 1812 and 1814.

Legend has it that she began writing *Frankenstein* at the Baxters' house, a claim that's not too difficult to believe. The novel opens with Robert Walton's voyage exploring the 'wild and mysterious regions' of the Arctic wilderness, and Mary was daily surrounded by inspiration for such a haunting introduction. Dundee was a thriving whaling centre in 1812, full of whalers supplying oil for the burgeoning jute industry and lamp fuel. The port would be full of rugged seamen and the stench of blubber. And the city was no stranger to polar exploration, providing vessels for Captain Scott, Ernest Shackleton and Admiral Byrd. There is a northern Antarctic peninsula named Dundee Island. Even the streets Baffin Street and Whale Lane recall its whaling interests.

When she was 16, Mary eloped with the Romantic poet Percy Bysshe Shelley, whom she married in 1816. For many years she was eclipsed by the reputation of her more famous husband, but she was an extremely gifted and articulate writer, and two years after her marriage she wrote *Frankenstein: Or, the Modern Prometheus*, at the Villa Diodati on the shores of Lake Geneva, the seeds of which were probably planted in Dundee.

FURTHER INFORMATION: In 2004 a plaque was erected in South Baffin Street at the site of The Cottage commemorating Mary Shelley's connection with Dundee. The plaque is a replica of one that existed at the same site before it disappeared 40 years ago.

FURTHER READING: M. Seymour, *Mary Shelley* (Picador, 2001); M. Spark, *Mary Shelley: Child of Light* (Constable, 1993); B.T. Bennett (ed.), *Selected Letters of Mary Wollstonecraft Shelley* (Johns Hopkins University Press, 1995); P.R. Feldman and D. Scott-Kilvert (eds), *The Journals of Mary Shelley* (Oxford University Press, 1987).

23 Reres Road
Former home of Dudley Watkins (1907–69), strip cartoonist and illustrator

> Somebody once told me that reading the *Sunday Post* was a bit like having a bath in a tub of thin, lukewarm, porridge.
> George Rosie, former D.C. Thomson journalist

He gave the world the Broons, Oor Wullie, Desperate Dan, Lord Snooty, Biffo the Bear, and many more. They are loved by generations, but few know anything of the man who created them. A shy, reclusive and deeply religious man, Dudley Watkins never became a household name. His death went unnoticed, and no obituaries appeared in the national press, but he was arguably the greatest comic-strip artist of all time. He had the rare gift of being able to make people laugh, a talent that was never properly recognised in his lifetime.

He was born in Manchester on 27 February 1907, the son of a lithographic artist, and grew up in Nottingham in a strict Baptist household. At the age of six the mayor showered him with praise for his drawing depicting a town pageant and at eleven his work was displayed in the town castle. In his teens he attended evening classes at the local art school, and in the early 1920s he was employed by Boots the Chemist as a window-dresser, where his artwork was published for the first time in the company's staff magazine *The Beacon* in March 1923. That same year he was approached by a talent scout from D.C. Thomson, and after a brief spell as a full-time student at Nottingham Art School, he moved to their offices in Dundee in 1925 and remained with the company until his death in 1969.

The 'Three Js', the traditional summary of Dundee industry, represent 'jam, jute and journalism'. The third 'J' stands for D.C. Thomson, established in 1905 and renowned in history for its conservatism, its opposition to trade unions and denying employment to Roman Catholics. Its publications were aimed at the lower end of the publishing market, with a cosy, sentimental, down-to-earth quality and generous dollops of the vernacular. Thomson moved into the comic market in the 1920s with *Adventure*, *Rover* and *Wizard*, and in the early 1930s with *Skipper* and *Hotspur*.

Dudley Watkins began his career as a strip cartoonist on these comics, supplementing his salary by teaching life drawing at Dundee Art School. His colleagues recalled him as a quiet, amusing character, who was always well dressed and frequently sported a bowler hat, but, ultimately, he was an enigma. 'He never fitted in with the rest of the journalists,' commented a former Thomson editor, 'and eventually he didn't even bother coming into the office because he was more comfortable at home where he could dwell in his own little fantasy world . . . I do seem to recollect that he had no sense of humour, and also that when it came to religion, he could talk the hind legs off a donkey.'

On 8 March 1936 Thomson launched the 'Fun Section' in the *Sunday Post*, which introduced two new comic strips, Oor Wullie and The Broons. Dudley Watkins was given the job of breathing life into the characters and in so doing created a Scottish institution that is still going strong today. Written in the vernacular of their characters' unique language ('Help ma boab! Jings! Crivvens! Mighty me!'), they are understood only by Scots and ex-pats, remaining a linguistic mystery to the outside world. The following year saw the launch of *The Dandy*, which gave birth to Watkins' Desperate Dan, the grumpy cowboy who eats pies filled with entire cows in Cactusville, a cross between Scotland and the Wild West, where tram cars exist alongside stagecoaches. In July 1938 *The Beano* made its debut featuring Watkins' Lord Snooty and His Pals, and in 1947 he illustrated a series of adaptations of classic adventure novels, including Stevenson's *Treasure Island, Kidnapped* and *Catriona*. Artwork for *The Topper* and *The Beezer* comics followed during the 1950s.

Dudley Watkins' output for D.C. Thomson was prolific, and he could certainly lay claim to being one of the prime movers who made it one of the most successful newspapers in the world in its heyday. In September 1946 he became the only Thomson artist permitted to sign his work, an unique privilege even today.

Watkins was a member of the Church of Christ in Dundee, where he met Doris Taylor. The couple married in 1937 and had one son. He also created strip cartoons for religious publications, including the Young Warrior for the Worldwide Evangelisation Crusade, and he always kept a copy of the Bible beside his desk, a book he harboured dreams of illustrating in its entirety. There was no deep mystery about Dudley Watkins: he was just a quiet and devoutly religious man, who kept himself to himself in his own Bunkerton Castle. On the morning of 20 August 1969 his wife found him dead at his desk in front of a half-finished Desperate Dan strip. He had died of a heart attack, aged only 62.

FURTHER INFORMATION: Most of Watkins' artwork was created at Winsterley, his house at 23 Reres Road. His wedding took place at the Methodist Church, Ward Road, Dundee, and he is buried in Barnhill Cemetery, Broughty Ferry. Statues of Desperate Dan and Minnie the Minx, sculpted by Angus artists Tony and Susie Morrow in 2001, can be seen in Dundee High Street.

FURTHER READING: Anon., *D.C. Thomson Firsts* (Chimera-Posner Ltd, 1978); Anon., *Identification Guide to the D.C. Thomson and John Leng Children's Annuals 1921 to 1964* (published for private circulation, 1975); Alan Clark, *The Best of British Comic Art* (Boxtree, 1989); Denis Gifford, *Discovering Comics* (Shire Publications, 1991); Denis Gifford, *Happy Days: A Century of Comics* (Bloomsbury, 1988).

Aberdeenshire

Fettercairn

Burnside Road
Ramsay Arms Hotel
Site of Queen Victoria's secret visit in 1861

Queen Victoria (1819–1901) kept a diary from 1832, when she was 13, until just days before she died in January 1901. Her first diary was given to her by her mother to set down a holiday in North Wales, and thereafter she wrote daily entries for the rest of her life. What began as a record of holiday adventures matured over the years to state affairs and ministerial meetings – all of it competently written in an immensely readable style. On the suggestion of 'a near and dear relative' she consented to have her diaries published, and in 1867 the first edition of *Leaves from the Journal of our Life in the Highlands* appeared, although it was initially restricted to private circulation only. The following year it was released to the public and became an instant bestseller.

Victoria and Albert visited Scotland for the first time in 1842, visiting Edinburgh, Perth, Taymouth and Stirling. Both of them soon fell under its spell, captivated by the country and its people. Frequent holidays followed, and in 1848 they acquired a home of their own at Balmoral in Deeside. From there they would take off on 'Great Expeditions' with their family and explore the surrounding countryside by carriage or on horseback, with their faithful servant John Brown at the head. These expeditions could last for days, and riding a hundred miles a day was not unheard of. Often they stayed incognito at country inns, experiencing the simple country life. One such episode is recorded in her diary entry for Friday, 20 September 1861:

The inn at Fettercairn.

At a quarter-past seven o'clock we reached the small quiet town, or rather village, of Fettercairn, for it was very small – not a creature stirring, and we got out at the quiet little inn, 'Ramsay Arms', quite unobserved, and went at once upstairs. There was a very nice drawing-room, and next to it, a dining room, both very clean and tidy – then to the left of our bedroom, which was excessively small, but also very clean and neat, and much better furnished than at Grantown. Alice had a nice room, the same size as ours; then came a mere morsel of one, (with a 'press bed'), in which Albert dressed; and then came Lady Churchill's bedroom just beyond. Louis and General Grey had rooms in an hotel, called 'The Temperance Hotel', opposite. We dined at eight, a very nice, clean, good dinner. Grant and Brown waited. They were rather nervous, but General Grey and Lady Churchill carved, and they had only to change the plates, which Brown soon got into the way of doing. A little girl of the house came in to help – but Grant turned her round to prevent her looking at us! The landlord and landlady knew who we were, but no one else except the coachman, and they kept the secret admirably.

The evening being bright and moonlight and very still, we all went out, and walked through the whole village, where not a creature moved – through the principal little square, in the middle of which was a sort of pillar or Town Cross on steps, and Louis read, by the light of the moon, a proclamation for collections of charities which was stuck on it. We walked on along a lane a short way, hearing nothing whatever – not a leaf moving – but the distant barking of a dog! Suddenly we heard a drum and fifes! We were greatly alarmed, fearing we had been recognised; but Louis and General Grey, who went back, saw nothing whatever. Still, as we walked slowly back, we heard the noise from time to time – and when we reached the inn door we stopped, and saw six men march up with fifes and a drum (not a creature taking any notice of them), go down the street, and back again. Grant and Brown were out; but had no idea what it could be. Albert asked the little maid, and the answer was, 'It's just a band,' and that it walked about in this way twice a week. How odd! It went on playing some time after we got home. We sat till half-past ten working, and Albert reading, – and then retired to rest.

Saturday, 21 September 1861

Got to sleep after two or three o'clock. The morning was dull and close, and misty with a little rain; hardly anyone stirring; but a few people at their work. A traveller had arrived at night, and wanted to come up into the dining-room, which is the 'commercial travellers' room'; and they had difficulty in telling him he could not stop there. He joined Grant and Brown at their tea, and on his asking, 'What's the matter here?' Grant answered, 'It's a wedding party from Aberdeen.' At 'The Temperance Hotel' they were very anxious to know whom they had got. All, except General Grey, breakfasted a little before nine. Brown acted as my servant, brushing my skirt and boots, and taking any message, and Grant as Albert's valet.

At a quarter to ten we started the same way as before, except that we were in the carriage which Lady Churchill and the General had yesterday. It was unfortunately misty, and we could see no distance. The people had just discovered who we were, and a few cheered us as we went along.

Victoria and Albert out riding in their beloved Highlands.

SEE ALSO: Abbotsford.
FURTHER INFORMATION: Ramsay Arms Hotel and Restaurant, Burnside Road, Fettercairn, AB30 1XX. Tel: 01561 340334. Email: info@ramsayarmshotel.co.uk

Virtually no one in Fettercairn saw Victoria and Albert that night in September, 1861, but afterwards the village built a triumphal archway at the west end of the bridge to commemorate their visit, lest we forget.

FURTHER READING: D. Duff (ed.), *Queen Victoria's Highland Journals* (Bounty Books, 1994).

Arbuthnott

Laurencekirk
The Grassic Gibbon Centre
Devoted to the life and times of novelist Lewis Grassic Gibbon (1901–35)

> Laddie, what did you want to write all that muck for? You've the mind of a dirty midwife. It's the speak of the place, and I'm fair ashamed of ye.
> Mitchell's mother voicing her disapproval of *Sunset Song*

Lewis Grassic Gibbon's novel *Sunset Song* was voted the Best Scottish Book at the Edinburgh International Book Festival in August 2005. When it was first published in August 1932, it was hailed as the first great Scottish novel since the works of Galt, and his female character Chris Guthrie was said to be the most convincing character in Scottish fiction, so convincing that many thought that Lewis Grassic Gibbon was the nom de plume of a woman. Writers of the Scottish Renaissance, including Hugh MacDiarmid and Neil Gunn, embraced him. His mother may have thought the book was 'muck', but her dirty-minded son is now regarded as one of the greatest Scottish novelists of the twentieth century.

Lewis Grassic Gibbon was born James Leslie Mitchell on 13

February 1901 at the croft of Hillhead of Seggat (now derelict) in the parish of Auchterless on the north-west border of Aberdeenshire, the only son of James McIntosh Mitchell and Lilias Grant Gibbon, the daughter of a farm labourer. Lilias had two illegitimate sons by different fathers when James married her in 1898, and young James grew up with two half-brothers. Knowledge of his childhood is hazy, but in 1907 the family left Hillhead for Aberdeen, and the following year moved to a croft at Bloomfield on the Arbuthnott estate in what was then Kincardineshire, also known as The Mearns. He attended the village school, a three-mile walk away in Arbuthnott, where, in 1913, he was befriended by its schoolmaster Alexander Gray. Gray detected that Gibbon was gifted and nurtured his talents by loaning him books and offering him friendship, remarking that he was 'sensitive, lonely, introspective . . . He was the only boy I ever saw hoeing turnips with an open book in his hand . . . Not bothering much with the other boys' games and adventures, but always friendly and kind, especially to the younger ones.' His future wife, Rebecca Middleton, who lived at the nearby croft of Hareden, also portrayed a similar view of him when she wrote, 'He was a strange, unusual boy, and looked so very distant. I disliked him at first sight . . . I certainly never dreamed Leslie would one day marry me.'

His parents were unsympathetic to his talents, and in 1915, when he would normally have left school, they were reluctant to let him continue his education, but the following year he won a place at Mackie's Academy in Stonehaven. It proved to be a dismal experience for him, and he left after a year to become a junior reporter with the *Aberdeen Journal*. In 1919 he moved to Glasgow, where he was employed on the *Scottish Farmer* and where he joined the Communist Party. He was later dismissed by the magazine for fiddling his expenses, a sum of around £60, which he donated to the party. This was not petty cash – his wage was £2 5s (£2.25) a week, and £60 amounted to just over six months' salary – and the disgrace resulted in a failed suicide attempt. Any career in journalism was now out of the question, and in 1919 he joined the Royal Army Service Corps, where during the next three and a half years he was posted to the Middle East. In 1923 he enlisted in the RAF and served as a clerk until 1929.

His first published work appeared in the autumn of 1924 when he won a short-story competition in the magazine *T.P.'s & Cassell's Weekly*. In 1925 he married Rebecca Middleton and solemnised their union by purchasing a typewriter. They were to have two children. Living on his meagre RAF pay, and stationed at Uxbridge, he began writing short stories, which brought only rejection slips from publishers. 'Could I write or not? Was I merely boring an over-weary world?' he wrote. He sent a story called *The Ten Men of Sodom* to H.G. Wells for his opinion, not expecting any response. Wells replied, 'Very good story. Stick to it! You can do this sort of thing and will certainly come through.' With his confidence bolstered, he soldiered on, and in January 1929 the *Cornhill* magazine published it and asked for more of the same. The same year he left the RAF and became a professional writer.

His first published book was a Wellsian-type prophecy titled *Hanno, or the Future of Exploration*, published in 1928, followed by the novels *Stained Radiance* (1930) and *The Thirteenth Disciple* (1931). Between 1932 and 1934 he published a further five novels, including *Three Go Back* (1932) and *Spartacus* (1933). Works of history and anthropology also flowed from his pen. In 1931 the Mitchells moved to Welwyn Garden City, where *Sunset Song* was written in less than two months during the spring of 1932 and published in August of that year. The second volume, *Cloud Howe*, was published in 1933, and the third part, *Grey Granite*, followed in 1934. All three were published under the name Lewis Grassic Gibbon, taken from his mother's maiden name, and chart the life of heroine Chris Guthrie and, in parallel, Scotland's transition from rural to urban and industrial society. It is for these three novels that he is best remembered today; his other works are now largely forgotten, and his historical and anthropological works have no contemporary value. He was only a professional writer for five years, but his output was prolific, purely because he needed the money. Sadly, the only books he ever wrote that made any money were the trilogy of novels that became known as *A Scots Quair*.

He died from peritonitis following a perforated ulcer on 7 February 1935 at Welwyn Hospital. He was one week away from his 34th birthday. His ashes were buried in Arbuthnott Kirkyard.

SEE ALSO: Hugh MacDiarmid, Neil Gunn, John Galt.

FURTHER INFORMATION: The Grassic Gibbon Centre, Arbuthnott, Laurencekirk, AB30 1PB. Open March to October. Groups and school parties welcome by appointment. Tel: 01561 361668. Website: www.grassicgibbon.com

The Grassic Gibbon Centre is signposted from the A90 and A92, and is approximately two hours' drive north of Edinburgh and thirty minutes' drive south of Aberdeen.

FURTHER READING: I. Munro, *Leslie Mitchell: Lewis Grassic Gibbon* (Oliver & Boyd, 1966); D. Young, *Beyond the Sunset: A Study of James Leslie Mitchell* (Impulse Publications, 1973); Peter Whitfield, *Grassic Gibbon and his World* (Aberdeen Journals, 1994).

Cruden Bay

Bridge Street
The Kilmarnock Arms Hotel
Where Bram Stoker wrote the early chapters of *Dracula*

> . . . a dreadful fear came upon me, and I was afraid to speak or move . . . We kept on ascending, with occasional periods of quick descent, but in the main always ascending. Suddenly I became conscious of the fact the driver was in the act of pulling up the horses in the courtyard of a vast ruined castle, from whose tall black windows came no ray of light, and whose broken battlements showed a jagged line against the moonlit sky.
>
> Bram Stoker, from chapter one,
> 'Jonathan Harker's Journal', *Dracula* (1897)

A research trip for a production of *Macbeth* at London's Lyceum Theatre first brought Bram Stoker (1847–1912) to Cruden Bay in the late 1880s. Historical accuracy was required if they were to build convincing sets, and a research group toured the Highlands to observe its moors and castles. While journeying to Inverness, they came across Cruden Bay and the clifftop Slains Castle. Stoker loved the setting and returned alone in 1893 for a walking tour,

Bram Stoker in 1884.

taking lodgings at the Kilmarnock Arms Hotel. He returned in the summer of 1894 to introduce his family to this romantic idyll, and it was during an August holiday there in 1895 that he was inspired to write the immortal classic *Dracula*. The early chapters of the book, in which Jonathan Harker journeys to Castle Dracula, were written at the Kilmarnock Arms, and the final pages were written there the following summer.

There is no evidence that Slains Castle was the original inspiration for Castle Dracula, but most visitors to this desolate place will agree that it easily doubles for Transylvania and could not have failed to influence Stoker. However, when he first saw Slains Castle in the late 1880s it was still inhabited and was not the crumbling and foreboding ruin it is today – a result of the roof having been removed in the 1920s to avoid paying taxes. Built in 1664, it was the home of the Earls of Erroll, chiefs of the clan Hay, and its distinguished guests have included James Boswell and Samuel Johnson, who recalled their visit in *A Journey to the Western Islands of Scotland* (1775):

> The walls of one of the towers seem only the continuation of a perpendicular rock, the foot of which is beaten by the waves . . . I would not for my amusement wish for a storm, but as storms, whether wished or not, will sometimes happen, I may say without violation of humanity, that I would willingly look out upon them from Slains Castle.

In 1895 Stoker published *The Watter's Mou'*, about smuggling in Cruden Bay, which mentions the Kilmarnock Arms. In 1902 he

rented 'The Crookit Lum', a house overlooking the sea, which is still standing in nearby Whinnyfold, and became his summer retreat until his death in 1912.

SEE ALSO: Dr Johnson, James Boswell.

FURTHER INFORMATION: The Kilmarnock Arms Hotel, Bridge Street, Cruden Bay, by Peterhead, AB42 OHD. Tel: 01779 812213.

Slains Castle can be reached by footpath from the Main Street car park. Great care should be taken when visiting Slains Castle, which is situated perilously close to the cliff edge on the grassy headland known as The Bow.

FURTHER READING: D. Farson, *The Man Who Wrote Dracula* (St Martin's Press, 1975); B. Belford, *Bram Stoker: A Biography of the Man Who Wrote Dracula* (Knopf, 1996); H. Ludlam, *A Biography of Dracula: The Life Story of Bram Stoker* (Fireside Press, 1962).

Braemar

Glenshee Road
Stevenson's Cottage
Where Robert Louis Stevenson was inspired to write *Treasure Island*

> Fifteen men on a dead man's chest
> Yo-ho-ho, and a bottle of rum!
> Drink and the devil had done for the rest –
> Yo-ho-ho, and a bottle of rum!
>
> From *Treasure Island*, chapter three

The lovable rogue Long John Silver, and the crew of the *Hispaniola*, are now part of the popular consciousness. Inspired by Daniel Defoe, Edgar Allan Poe, Washington Irving and Captain Marryat, Stevenson's 'story for boys' is one of the great classics of children's literature, and much of it was written in Braemar. The Stevensons, along with Louis's parents, rented a cottage near Kindrochaid Castle in Castleton of Braemar in August 1881. They had previously been staying at a cottage near Pitlochry, but the weather was foul, and Louis's health suffered as a consequence. On doctor's advice they moved to Braemar, one of the highest villages in Scotland, where the clear air would hopefully mend his lungs. Neither Louis's health nor the weather improved, and to entertain his 12-year-old stepson Lloyd, he began drawing treasure maps and writing the story that would become *Treasure Island*:

'One more step, Mr Hands,' said I, 'and I'll blow your brains out! Dead men don't bite, you know,' I added with a chuckle.
J. L'Admiral (1885).

On a chill September morning, by the cheek of a brisk fire, and the rain drumming on the window, I began *The Sea Cook*, for that was the original title. I have begun (and finished) a number of other books, but I cannot remember to have sat down to one of them with more complacency.

He wrote the first 15 chapters of *The Sea Cook* at Braemar and finished the story in Davos, in eastern Switzerland. In September it was accepted by *Young Folks' Magazine*, whose editor, James Henderson, suggested changing the title to *Treasure Island*. The story was published in 17 instalments under the pseudonym 'Captain George North', beginning in October 1881. As a magazine story, it didn't make much of an impact. His wife Fanny didn't like the story, describing it as 'tedious', and was not keen on it being published as a novel. Fortunately for literary history, Louis was keen to publish and was staggered to be paid 'a hundred jingling, tingling, golden-minted quid' for it.

SEE ALSO: Kinnaird, The Edinburgh Book Lovers' Tour, The Literary Pub Crawl, Howard Place, Inverleith Terrace, Rutherford's Howff, Hawes Inn, W.E. Henley, The Writers' Museum, The *Kidnapped* Trail.

FURTHER INFORMATION: Approaching the village from the Aberdeen side on the A93, do not take the turning on the left into the village, but stay on the A93. Stevenson's Cottage is the second house on the left past St Margaret's Episcopal Church and is marked by a plaque. It is not open to the public.

FURTHER READING: L. Stott, *Robert Louis Stevenson and the Highlands and Islands of Scotland* (Creag Darach Publications, 1992).

Aberdeen

Skene Street

Aberdeen Grammar School
Statue of Lord Byron, English poet of Scottish antecedents

> The careless writer, the tormented face,
> The hectoring bully or the noble fool,
> But, just like Gordon or like Keith, a name,
> A tall, proud statue at the Grammar School.
>
> From *Home Town Elegy* (1944) by George
> Sutherland Fraser (1915–80), poet, critic and
> alumnus of Aberdeen Grammar School

Love affairs with both sexes, drinking bouts, bizarre athletic feats, his club foot, the scandal of his affair with his half-sister, who may have borne him a child, his exile in Italy and his romantic, some say farcical, death in the Balkans for a lost cause, are all part of the legend of Byron. His lover, Lady Caroline Lamb, accurately summed him up as 'Mad, bad and dangerous to know', but, sensationalism and cliché aside, Byron also left us some of the greatest poetry ever written. Poetry of such genius that it made Sir Walter Scott throw in the poetic towel and turn to novel-writing.

He was born George Gordon in London on 22 January 1788 and was lame from birth. His father was Captain John 'Mad Jack' Byron, generally considered to have been a wastrel, and his mother was Catherine Gordon of Gight, a mentally unstable Scottish heiress who claimed descent from King James I. In 1789 the family moved to Aberdeen, where six-year-old George attended Aberdeen Grammar School from 1794 to 1798. In Byron's day the school, which was believed to have been founded in 1263, was located at Schoolhill, near the site of the current Robert Gordon's College. During the years 1861 to 1863, the school moved to its current location in Skene Street.

To claim Byron as a Scottish poet would be stretching it, but he did say his love of mountainous terrain originated from his Scottish childhood, and his first sexual experience took place in Aberdeen, aged nine, in 1797. He recalled his Scottish roots in the satirical *Don Juan* (1819–24):

> But I am half a Scot by birth, and bred
> A whole one, and my heart flies to my head, –
> As 'Auld Lang Syne' brings Scotland one and all,
> Scotch plaids, Scotch snoods, the blue hills and the clear
> streams,

The Dee, the Don, Balgounie Brig's black wall,
All my boyhood feelings, all my gentler dreams
Of what I then dreamt, clothed in their pall,
Like Banquo's offspring.

Mad Jack deserted the family and died when Byron was three. When he was six, he became the direct heir to the Byron estate, and in 1798 mother and son moved south to the baronial seat of Newstead Abbey. He was educated at Harrow and Cambridge, and later set out on a grand tour of Europe, returning with copious stanzas, which were published under the title of *Childe Harold's Pilgrimage* in 1812. It was a literary triumph, and he became the darling of aristocratic and literary London. 'I awoke one morning and found myself famous,' he remarked after its instantaneous success. The 'Byronic hero' was born and became the archetype of European Romanticism, influencing artists as diverse as Alexander Pushkin, Ludwig van Beethoven, Johann Goethe and Stendhal. Other works included *Beppo* (1818), *A Vision of Judgement* (1822) and *Don Juan* (1819–24). In 1815 he married Annabella Milbanke, but the marriage collapsed after the birth of their daughter Ada the following year. By 1816 the concept of the Byronic hero was tarnishing. Mounting debts, doubts about his sanity and rumours of incest left him ostracised and resentful, and he left England for good. In 1824, after many affairs and adventures, his wild and extravagant life ended when he died of marsh fever at Missolonghi, preparing to fight with the Greek insurgents who had risen against the Turks. His body was refused by the deans of both Westminster and St Paul's and was buried in the family vaults at Hucknall Torkard in Nottingham.

FURTHER READING: Phyllis Grosskurth, *Byron: The Flawed Angel* (Hodder & Stoughton,1997); P. Quennell, *Byron, a Self-Portrait: Letters and Diaries, 1798 to 1824* (Oxford University Press, 1989); P. Quennell, *Byron: The Years of Fame* (Read Books, 2006); S. Coote, *Byron: The Making of a Myth* (Bodley Head, 1988).

Argyll and Bute

Dunoon

Cowal Gardens
Statue of Highland Mary, beloved of Robert Burns

> That same afternoon, while the poet was taking wine with
> Lord Daer at Catrine, earth was being shovelled over the body
> of Mary Campbell in Greenock Churchyard. The same grave
> contained her dead baby. Round the grave the men of the
> Campbells and the Macphersons were cursing the name of
> Robert Burns . . .
>
> Catherine Carswell, from *The Life of Robert Burns*

Early in 1786 Jean Armour became pregnant. She gave birth to
twins on 3 September – a boy and a girl. The girl died in infancy.
On hearing the news of her pregnancy, her father, who strongly
disapproved of her Ploughman Poet lover, tore up his daughter's
marriage attestation to Burns and despatched her to Paisley to
spend her confinement with relatives. He also obtained a warrant
to detain Burns in jail until he could find the funds to support the
children. Plans were also afoot to marry Jean off to an eligible, but
probably more importantly solvent, weaver. Burns already had one
illegitimate daughter by Elizabeth Paton, a servant girl. The farm at
Mossgiel was going from bad to worse and his rent was in arrears. He
felt a betrayed, desperate and hunted man. His life was in turmoil,
and it was time to take drastic action and emigrate to Jamaica.

He had accepted a job as a plantation bookkeeper in Port
Antonio, Jamaica, at £30 a year for three years, but did not have
the money to fund his passage, and so Gavin Hamilton suggested he

Auchamore Farm, birthplace of Highland Mary.
A garden centre now stands on the site.

publish some of his poems 'as a likely way of getting some money'. Burns went ahead and appealed for subscribers to 'defray the necessary Expence'. The end result was the publication on 3 April 1786 of *Poems, Chiefly in the Scottish Dialect*, which would eventually change everything for him.

Meanwhile, Gavin Hamilton's new nurse maid at 'the Castle' in Mauchline caught Burns's eye – the golden-haired Mary Campbell (1763–86) from the Gaelic-speaking Cowal coast of the Firth of Clyde, hence her nickname of Highland Mary. She was born at Auchamore Farm near Dunoon, the daughter of a local seaman, and was soon courting Burns on a regular, though clandestine, basis. Burns persuaded her to go to Jamaica with him, a scene recreated in his song 'Will Ye Go to the Indies, My Mary'. The two lovers quickly made their plans. They met under Stairaird Crag, where Mauchline burn flows into the River Ayr. With him on one bank and her on the other, they joined hands under the stream and solemnly pledged their troth. They then exchanged Bibles, and according to Scots law and the Christian gospel they were truly married. The next day, pregnant with Burns's child, Mary left for her parents' home in Campbeltown in Kintyre.

The first edition of *Poems, Chiefly in the Scottish Dialect* was a success and sold out within a month of publication. Burns made plans to seek a second edition in Edinburgh; if it didn't work out, he would board ship for Jamaica at Leith. Mary, meanwhile, had obtained a situation in Glasgow and was conveyed in her father's boat from Campbeltown to Greenock, along with her younger brother Robert. They stayed with a cousin of her mother's, a shipwright named Macpherson, to whom Robert was to be apprenticed. A party was held at the Macphersons' tenement to celebrate the youth's admittance to the craft. The next day Robert fell ill and began to shiver and vomit. Mary nursed him through his fever, but just as her brother started to improve, Mary developed his symptoms, the characteristic symptoms of 'putrid' or 'malignant' fever, known today as typhus. Shortly before her death, she gave birth to a premature baby, which died a couple of days later. Mary was buried with her infant at Greenock's old West Highland Churchyard. Her family destroyed all the letters and poems she received from Burns, and an attempt was even made to eradicate his name from the Bibles he had given her. Burns, of course, was devastated to hear of Mary's death and wrote to the Campbells, but no reply was ever received.

In 1792 Burns immortalised her in his song 'Highland Mary':

> O pale, pale now, those rosy lips,
> I aft hae kissed sae fondly!
> And closed for aye the sparkling glance
> That dwelt on me sae kindly:
> And mouldering now in silent dust
> That heart that lo'ed me dearly!
> But still within my bosom's core
> Shall live my Highland Mary.

SEE ALSO: Failford.

FURTHER INFORMATION: Over the years an air of mystery has surrounded Mary's cause of death. Did she die in childbirth, from typhus or from both? In 1920 the West Highland Churchyard in Greenock was cleared for building and Mary's grave was opened. Among the remains was part of an infant's coffin. She was re-interred in the new cemetery at Nelson Street West. Much gobbledegook has surrounded the story of Burns and Mary Campbell over the years. My source was mainly Burns's biographer Catherine Carswell (1879–1946), described by Alasdair Gray as 'the best'. She was the first to crack the romantic myth surrounding him and present him to the public warts and all, commenting, '*How furious* they will be to have RB brought out of the mist they have loved to keep about him!' A statue of Highland Mary, erected in 1896 on the 100th anniversary of the death of Robert Burns, stands in the grounds of the Cowal Gardens, beside the Castle House Museum. Tel: 01369 701422. Website: www.castlehousemuseum.org.uk

FURTHER READING: Catherine Carswell, *The Life of Robert Burns* (Canongate, 1998).

Inveraray

Glen Aray
Memorial to Neil Munro (1863–1930), novelist, journalist and creator of Para Handy

> Whatever they may say of me or mine, they can never deny
> but I had the right fond heart for my own countryside . . .
> Neil Munro, from *John Splendid* (1898)

All of Neil Munro's novels were extremely competent literary works, but they never eclipsed in popularity the exploits of the crew of the *Vital Spark* and their skipper Para Handy, who first appeared in print in the pages of the *Glasgow Evening News* in 1905. Although Munro himself thought the stories 'slight', and published them under the pseudonym 'Hugh Foulis', thus disassociating them from his more serious work, they have evolved over the years into a national institution, been adapted for stage, radio and television, and are without a doubt the works for which Neil Munro will be best remembered.

Neil Munro, 1907.

He was born the illegitimate son of Ann Munro, a kitchen maid, on 3 June 1863 at Inveraray. Shortly after his birth, his mother went to stay with her mother in a one-roomed house in McVicar's Land (now called Arkland II). Both were native Gaelic speakers. His mother was brought up in Glen Aray, an area that was the setting for many of Munro's stories, including *The Lost Pibroch* (1896). His mother worked for a time at Inveraray Jail and married the prison

At the *Vital Spark's* home port of Glasgow a sculpture by George Wylie of the famous puffer can be seen in the gardens of Kelvingrove Museum. 'There is more life in wan day in the Broomielaw of Gleska,' remarked Para Handy, 'than there is in a fortnight in Loch Fyne.'

governor on his retirement in 1875. Munro was educated at the parish school in Inverary, and his first job in 1877 was in a local law office, where one of the firm's lawyers became the inspiration for Dan Joyce in his novel *Daft Days* (1907). When he was 18, he became a reporter on *The Greenock Advertiser*, graduating through various local newspapers to become chief reporter of the *Glasgow Evening News* at the age of 23 and editor at the age of 55 in 1918.

Munro's first literary success was a series of short stories which first appeared in *Blackwood's Magazine* in 1893, and his first novel, *John Splendid,* was published in 1898. His other works include *Doom Castle* (1901) and *The New Road* (1914). In 1902 he retired from full-time journalism to concentrate on his writing, but continued to pen a weekly column for the *Glasgow Evening News*. It was this column that gave birth to his three sets of popular short stories laced with pawky West Coast humour: 'Archie, my droll friend'; 'Jimmy Swan, the joy traveller'; and the immortal 'Para Handy'.

It's ironic that the newspaper stories Munro dismissed as ephemeral should be the ones that have lasted and are still read today, while his historical novels, good as they are, gather dust on the shelves. Conan Doyle also wanted to be remembered as a writer of 'quality' historical fiction, and dismissed Sherlock Holmes, while John Buchan thought Richard Hannay just an 'entertainment'. The lesson here must be that, in the end, it is the reading public who decide what works shall endure and become a lasting testimony to their creators' talent, not their creators. Neil Munro died in Helensburgh on 22 December 1930 and is buried in Kilmalieu Cemetery, Inverary.

FURTHER INFORMATION: In 1935 *An Comunn Gaidhealach* (The Highland Society) erected a monument to Neil Munro at the head of Glen Aray bearing the Gaelic inscription *Sar Litreachas* (Excellent Literature). A memorial cairn was also erected on the knoll of Craig Dhu. At Inverary Maritime Museum, Inverary Pier, you can see *VIC72 – Eilean Eisdeal* (renamed *The Vital Spark* in 2006), the last working Clyde puffer, built in 1944. The Neil Munro Society can be contacted at brian@bdosborne.fsnet.co.uk

Website: www.neilmunro.co.uk

FURTHER READING: Neil Munro, *The Brave Days* (Porpoise Press, 1931); L. Lendrum, *Neil Munro: The Biography* (House of Lochar, 2004); S. Donald, *In the Wake of the Vital Spark: Para Handy's Scotland* (Johnston & Bacon, 1994).

Carradale

Carradale House
Former home of Naomi Mitchison (1897–1999), writer

It is always a bore being ahead of one's time.
Naomi Mitchison, from *Among You Taking Notes* (1985)

Socialist, feminist, traveller, birth-control and anti-nuclear campaigner, Naomi Mitchison broke all the rules, wrote over 70 books and lived until she was 101. Her work included poetry, plays, travel writing, children's fiction, short stories and biography, but she will be best remembered for her historical fiction.

She was born on 1 November 1897 at 10 Randolph Crescent, Edinburgh, the daughter of physiologist John Scott Haldane and suffragist Kathleen Trotter, and was brought up in Oxford. She attended the (boys) Dragon School, until she began to menstruate, when her education was continued at home with a governess. In 1916 she married her brother's friend Dick Mitchison. This marriage was a reputedly happy one but, nonetheless, an 'open one'. Dick became Labour MP for Kettering, Northamptonshire (1945–64), and was later Lord Mitchison. The couple had seven children.

Naomi Mitchison in the 1920s.

Inspired by a diary she kept of her dreams, and by Gibbon's *Decline and Fall*, she wrote her first book, *The Conquered* (1923), set during Caesar's Gallic Wars, which mirrored the situation in 1920s Ireland. Her epic historical novel *The Corn King and the Spring Queen* (1931) is set in the Greek city-states of Athens and Sparta, and a visit to the Soviet Union in 1932 produced *We Have Been Warned* (1935), depicting a rape, a seduction, an abortion and contraception. She travelled extensively, and in 1963 the Bakgatla of Botswana made her their Tribal Adviser and Mother. During her life, her friends included Neil Gunn, W.H. Auden, Doris Lessing, Aldous Huxley, Stevie Smith and E.M. Forster. She was also a good friend of the writer J.R.R. Tolkien, and she was one of the proofreaders of *The Lord of the Rings*.

Mitchison was actively involved in Scottish politics and stood as Labour candidate for the Scottish Universities in 1935. In 1937 she bought Carradale, an estate on the Mull of Kintyre, where she was still living and writing 50 years later, commenting, 'So long as I can hold a pencil, let me go on.'

FURTHER INFORMATION: Carradale is now a residential estate offering country retreat holidays and is reached by taking the B842 coast road down the east of the Kintyre peninsula. When you reach Carradale, the east and west sides of Carradale village are separated by the Carradale Estate. Carradale House, Carradale

Estate, Carradale, Argyll, PA28 6QQ. Tel: 01583 431234.
Email: enquiries@carradale.org.uk
Website: www.carradale.org.uk

FURTHER INFORMATION: Naomi Mitchison published three volumes of autobiography – *Small Talk* (1973), *All Change Here* (1975) and *You May Well Ask* (1979) – and two volumes of diaries – *Vienna Diary* (1934) and *Among You Taking Notes* (1985).

FURTHER READING: J. Calder, *The Nine Lives of Naomi Mitchison* (Virago Press, 1997).

Dalmally

Glen Orchy
Monument to the memory of Duncan Ban MacIntyre (1724–1812), Gaelic poet

My blessing with the foxes dwell,
For that they hunt the sheep so well.
Ill fare the sheep, a grey-fac'd nation
That swept our hills with desolation.
Duncan Ban MacIntyre, from 'Song to the Foxes'

Although regarded as one of the great Gaelic poets, Donnchadh Bàn Mac an t-Saoir never learned to read or write, but with the help of his extensive memory and the pen of his friend Rev. Donald MacNicol, Minister of Lismore, his verses are preserved for posterity. Born in Druim Liaghart in Glen Orchy, which was once a small crofting community on the shores of Loch Tulla, he worked as forester and gamekeeper, where his love of the countryside inspired his verse. He was also a soldier in the Argyll Regiment of Militia and fought for the Hanoverian forces during the Jacobite rising of 1745–46.

His poems include satires, love songs and drinking songs, but he will be best remembered for his poems about the Argyll–Perthshire border, namely '*Moladh Beinn Dobhrain*' ('The Praise of Ben Doran'), which describes his love of deer and deer hunting, and '*Oran Coire a Cheathaich*' ('The Song of Misty Corrie'). He moved to Edinburgh in 1767, where he became a member of the City Guard and served in the Breadalbane Fencibles. MacIntyre and his wife, together with some of his children and grandchildren, are buried in Greyfriars Kirkyard. A Gaelic service is held in Greyfriars Kirk every Sunday. A granite monument was raised by public subscription in 1859 on a hill (544 feet) two miles south-west of Dalmally.

FURTHER INFORMATION: The monument commemorating Duncan Ban MacIntyre can be reached from Dalmally, a small village spread along the Strath of Orchy, two miles east of the tip of Loch Awe. Near the railway station is the junction from which a narrow single-track road leads upwards through forested hills. The views from the monument, which is just under two miles from the village, take in Loch Awe and Ben Cruachan in the west, Ben Lui in the east, and the Glen Kinglass mountains to the north.

Cardross

Murray's Road
Rosebank Cottage
Birthplace of A.J. Cronin (1896–1981), novelist

> The rope strained, but did not break. She hung suspended,
> twitching like a marionette upon a string, while her body,
> elongating, seemed to stretch out desperately, one dangling
> foot straining to reach the floor, yet failing by a single inch to
> reach it . . .
>
> A.J. Cronin, from *Hatter's Castle* (1931)

Best remembered today for the stories that inspired the popular radio and TV series *Dr Finlay's Casebook*, Archibald Joseph Cronin was a practising doctor until the success of his first novel, *Hatter's Castle*, in 1931, which enabled him to give up medicine and concentrate on writing. A prolific novelist, many of whose books were bestsellers, he continued writing until his 80th year.

He was born on 19 July 1896 at Rosebank Cottage, Murray's Road, Cardross, the only child of Patrick Cronin, a clerk and commercial traveller, and Jessie Montgomerie. He was educated at Dumbarton Academy and the University of Glasgow, where he studied medicine. During the First World War, he served as a Royal Navy surgeon, and after the war he practised in a mining area of South Wales, where he was appointed Medical Inspector of Mines in 1924. His Welsh practice provided the inspiration for *The Stars Look Down* (1935) and his semi-autobiographical novel, *The Citadel* (1937), filmed by King Vidor in 1938 and said to have contributed towards the creation of the National Health Service through its exposure of medical malpractice. A master storyteller, most of his works have an autobiographical streak, with Dumbarton portrayed as fictional Levenford. His other works include *The Keys of the Kingdom* (1941), *The Adventures of a Black Bag* (1943), *The Green Years* (1944), *Shannon's Way* (1948), *The Spanish Gardener* (1950) and his autobiography *Adventures in Two Worlds* (1952). He married Agnes Gibson in 1921 and had three sons. He died in 1981 at Glion, near Montreux, Switzerland.

Isle of Jura

Barnhill
Where George Orwell (1903–50) wrote *Nineteen Eighty-Four*

> Barnhill, Isle of Jura. Remote house with unique charm where
> George Orwell wrote *Nineteen Eighty-Four*. Place to truly 'Get
> away from it all'. Overlooking sea. Deer graze on the lawn.
> Seals and otters swim in the bay. Excellent birdwatching.
> Four miles from the public road. No mains electricity. Price
> includes coal. Tel: 01786 850274.

George Orwell can be ranked among the great essayists of modern British culture. He was amusing, engaging and disturbing, with journalistic values reminiscent of Daniel Defoe and William Cobbett,

but he is chiefly remembered for his two political allegories of the 1940s: *Animal Farm* and *Nineteen Eighty-Four*. In *Nineteen Eighty-Four* Orwell created a nightmarish and Kafkaesque vision of a totalitarian world. Published by Secker & Warburg in 1949, it tells the story of Winston Smith and his efforts to challenge the oppressive state in which he lives. The book's impact on modern culture was so great that its phrases and terminology have passed into the English language, and the adjective 'Orwellian' has come to mean anything pertaining to or characteristic of a totalitarian society.

Born Eric Blair in Bengal in 1903, Orwell was a complex and enigmatic man. Educated at Eton, he served with the Indian Imperial Police in 1920s Burma. He returned to Europe, working in Paris and London in a series of low-paid jobs, struggling to launch his career as a writer. He reported on poverty, fought against the fascists in Spain and worked for the BBC during the Second World War. In September 1945, then an established writer, Orwell left London for two weeks' holiday on the island of Jura and stayed in a deserted crofter's cottage near the sea. Recently widowed, he mourned and mulled over his life, living a hermit's existence fishing and absorbing the local flora and fauna. During his stay, he came across Barnhill on the northern tip of the island close to the seashore. The house was in a run-down state, with no electricity, no telephone and no daily postal service, and involved a four-mile hike along a track to reach it from the island's only road. What it did offer in abundance was solitude and escape, and Orwell promptly set about leasing it from the local laird.

He returned to Jura in April 1946, a sick, consumptive, depressive, chain-smoking author, escaping the endless treadmill of journalism in a London he had grown to hate. A suitcase, a saucepan, a kettle and a typewriter were all he landed with on the island, and the laird's wife commented that he seemed 'a sad and lonely man, who looked as if he'd been through a great deal'. He was labouring under his new novel, which would eventually become *Nineteen Eighty-Four*, and after six months on Jura, little progress was made. Progress was made, however, on getting the house in order, maintaining the vegetable garden, keeping the erratic water supply running and overcoming the never-ending problem of trying to gather enough fuel.

Barnhill with its tent for harvest workers. Orwell completed and typed *Nineteen Eighty-Four* in the top-floor attic room.

He returned to London in the autumn of 1946, and apart from a couple of weeks at New Year, he did not return to Jura again until April 1947. Unwell and still 'struggling' with *Nineteen Eighty-Four*, he had completed only a third of a rough draft by the end of May, much less than he had hoped, but ill health shadowed him constantly. Visits from friends and the summer weather also held him back, but by the end of the summer his lungs were deteriorating rapidly and he was becoming seriously ill. By the end of October he was bedridden with 'inflammation of the lungs'. Tuberculosis was diagnosed by a chest specialist, and in mid-December he was removed to Hairmyres Hospital near Glasgow. By July his health was improving, and he returned to Jura. By the end of October, in what Orwell no doubt viewed as a race against time as his condition deteriorated, he completed the manuscript of *Nineteen Eighty-Four*. A stenographer was needed to type the manuscript up, but with winter closing in no one was keen to travel to a remote island in the Inner Hebrides, so Orwell began the 'grisly job' himself.

In January he returned to England, where he was admitted to a sanatorium in the Cotswolds. By this time the typescript of *Nineteen Eighty-Four* was with Secker & Warburg, the latter describing it as 'amongst the most terrifying books I have ever read'. On 13 October Orwell, still bedridden at the sanatorium, married former editorial assistant Sonia Brownwell in Room 65. By Christmas his condition had worsened and little more could be done for him. On 21 January an artery burst in his lungs, killing him almost instantly.

He is buried in the churchyard at Sutton Courtenay, but as an atheist he was not eligible for burial in consecrated ground. The vicar, however, was persuaded but had to convince the church wardens. They all agreed, save for one, who consented only after reading a copy of *Animal Farm*.

FURTHER INFORMATION: Jura is about thirty miles long from north to south, and about seven miles wide east to west, with a population of around two hundred. There is only one road, and the west side of the island is barren and uninhabited. The island has no direct ferry connections with the mainland. To reach Jura from the mainland take the ferry that leaves from Kennacraig on the Mull of Kintyre to the Isle of Islay (www.calmac.co.uk). Jura is then reached by a small vehicle ferry from Port Askaig on Islay, which takes around ten minutes to cross to Feolin on the southern tip of Jura. From here it's nine miles to Craighouse, the main village, where there is a pub, hotel and shop. Barnhill is a further 21 miles over the island's single-track 'Long Road'. The last four miles you will have to walk unless you have a four-wheel-drive vehicle. The only remaining fitting at Barnhill since Orwell's time is the ancient but roomy bath. The contact for those wishing to rent Barnhill for a holiday is Jamie Fletcher, Easter Lennieston, Thornhill, Stirling, FK8 3QP. Tel: 01786 850274. Email: lennieston@aol.com

FURTHER READING: G. Bowker, *George Orwell* (Little, Brown, 2003); D.J. Taylor, *Orwell: The Life* (Chatto & Windus, 2003); P. Youngson, *Jura: Island of Deer* (Birlinn, 2001).

Erraid

The *Kidnapped* Trail
Where David Balfour and Alan Breck begin their epic trek
across Scotland in Robert Louis Stevenson's *Kidnapped*

Kidnapped made its first appearance in *Young Folks Paper* (1 May 1886).

Among literary travellers, Robert Louis Stevenson remains peerless. From the Cévennes to the Adirondacks, New York to Monterey, Cologne to Calistoga, Samoa to Sydney, Tahiti to the Tuamotus, and from far-flung Pacific pearls like the Marquesas to the Gilberts, Stevenson knew them all.

His wanderlust first began in Scotland. He spent family holidays in the Borders and Bridge of Allan, and in Dumfries, Ayrshire and Galloway, where he took that long winter's walk in 1876. He knew both shores of the Forth well: North Berwick and Anstruther, Dysart and Gullane, Limekilns and South Queensferry, where David Balfour was kidnapped and where Stevenson, as a young man, swam and canoed. The mountains, history and tradition of the Highlands called loudly to him: in the Hebrides, Glencoe, the Trossachs and Balquhidder; in Wick and Pitlochry, where 'Thrawn Janet' was penned; and in Braemar, the birthplace of *Treasure Island*. His travels even took him to Scotland's outpost islands of Orkney and Shetland on the lighthouse steamer.

On all his travels Stevenson was observing and scribbling, absorbing locations, landscape, colour, accents and characters, and stowing away detail and atmosphere to be reproduced, often years later. All these elements came together in his classical historical novel *Kidnapped* as he followed the adventures of David Balfour and Alan Breck on a 300-mile trek – that turned into a manhunt – through some of Scotland's most remote and spectacular country. The plot may have been hatched in

Ian Nimmo, author of *Walking with Murder: On the* Kidnapped *Trail* (Birlinn, 2005).

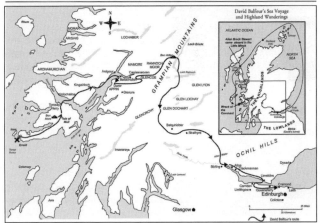

Stevenson's imagination, but the novel was built solidly on historical fact, the fiction seamlessly woven into the history.

The genesis of *Kidnapped* was in Inverness when Stevenson's father, the lighthouse builder Thomas Stevenson, purchased an old volume in a second-hand bookshop. It was entitled *The Trial of James Stewart*, the official record of the trial of a Jacobite clansman for shooting a government agent called Colin Campbell of Glenure in the Wood of Lettermore near Ballachulish in 1752. Earlier, Stevenson had expressed a desire to write a history of the Highlands, and his father thought the little volume would be useful historical background.

As he flicked through the pages, Stevenson was fascinated by the raw history. Colin Campbell's task after the 1745 Rebellion was to set and collect rents in the forfeited Stewart lands in Appin and among the Camerons in Callart. James Stewart was arrested, tried and hanged on grounds of complicity in the murder, but there was not a shred of evidence against him. The more Stevenson studied the case, the more convinced he became that this was a gross miscarriage of justice. It bore the hallmarks of political intrigue, with heavy overtones of a clan feud between sworn enemies, the Stewarts and the Campbells. Indeed, some historians have suggested the hanging of James Stewart was judicial murder.

As a trained advocate, Stevenson's view was that an innocent man had been hanged to ensure that the days of the clans – and therefore further Jacobite uprisings – were over for ever. He decided to use the background of the Appin Murder as the plot for *Kidnapped*, with the principals and witnesses in *The Trial of James Stewart* as his players. David Balfour was the only major fictional character, and the book was given further authenticity by routing it through the places mentioned in the trial or locations Stevenson knew so well and could describe in such detail.

For those with a taste for accuracy, David Balfour's journey began at Ashkirk in the Borders, a familiar village to him, although Stevenson names it Essendean. Essen Water and Essen Loch are both on the Ordnance Survey map, to make it all the more convincing. David headed along the old Borders drove roads, again well known to Stevenson, and eventually arrived at his bad old Uncle Ebenezer's dark House of Shaws on the west side of Edinburgh. Arguments continue about Stevenson's model for the towered Shaws, where David almost lost his life.

The seventeenth-century Hawes Inn is easily found at South

The 2007 cover image of Edinburgh UNESCO City of Literature's specially commissioned graphic novel of *Kidnapped* by author Alan Grant and illustrator Cam Kennedy.

Queensferry, almost below the Forth railway bridge. It was here David was banged on the head and then slung into the hold of Captain Hoseason's brig the *Covenant*, which was bound for the Carolinas, where David was to be sold into slavery. But heavy weather struck around Cape Wrath, and the captain decided to steer south. In thick fog in the Little Minch, they ran down a small boat. One man survived the collision by demonstrating great strength and agility, and David Balfour, acting as a forced cabin boy, clapped his eyes for the first time on the Jacobite courier and swordsman Alan Breck in all his French finery.

The *Covenant* foundered off Mull, and David Balfour, half-drowned, managed to kick and splash his way to the little islet of Erraid, off the most westerly point of the Ross of Mull, near Iona. In 1870, during his engineering student days, Stevenson spent three weeks on Erraid and knew every rock and cove. Erraid became David's island prison for a few days, because, as a countryman, he did not appreciate that he could have waded to the Mull mainland at low tide. Today Erraid is still a satellite island, but again such small points of accurate detail add authority to the *Kidnapped* fiction.

Stevenson had walked on Mull – with the twin peaks of Ben More his signposts – and had studied the old maps. He was able to direct David Balfour, as the 'Lad with the Silver Button', over the Torosay ferry, with the passengers taking turns at the oars and keeping the rhythm with Gaelic boat-songs. Today a modern car ferry plies the same route from Fishnish to Lochaline, but the Gaelic is muted.

Stevenson, of course, planned David's journey so that he could witness the killing of Glenure in Appin. By the wilds of Kingairloch he tramped, a little-known out-of-sight gem of Scotland, until he came to Loch Linnhe, where he was taken by boat to the murder scene at Lettermore. As he rested, David heard the sound of men and horses approaching through the birch trees and four travellers came into view. The big, imperious one with the red thatch was Colin Campbell. Seconds later the fatal shot rang from the hillside.

Stevenson visited Appin with his father to research *Kidnapped*, and his account of the assassination generally reflects the evidence presented in *The Trial of James Stewart*. But Stevenson deserted the historical fact at several points, just to remind readers that *Kidnapped* was a work of fiction, its historical accuracy not to be taken for granted.

A cairn marks the spot today where the 'Red Fox' met his end. A mile or so away at Cnap a' Chaolais, at the south end of the Ballachulish Bridge, a further dramatic cairn stands where James Stewart was 'hanged for a crime of which he was not guilty'. The remains of James's house at Acharn in nearby Duror are still visible, and all the place names associated with the Appin Murder and *Kidnapped* are there to be visited. The secret name of the man who shot Glenure – the Stewart Secret – has been handed down, generation by generation, in the area to this day.

At the murder scene David met up again with Alan Breck. Both were now prime suspects for the Appin Murder, and it was decided that they should take to the heather. Their route was out across Rannoch Moor, the largest, nastiest and most remote badland in Scotland. Rannoch Moor reaches south towards Schiehallion, east to Tyndrum and westwards to Ben Alder itself. Even today crossing the Moor is no small undertaking, and its harsh vastness has proved lethal on several occasions.

Near Ben Alder, the exhausted fugitives were ambushed by Cluny MacPherson's scouts and taken to Cluny's Cage, the secret hideout of the MacPherson chief, somewhere above Loch Ericht. The cave's one-time existence is beyond doubt, but the correct location remains unidentified. The rest of the *Kidnapped* route, however, was well indicated by Stevenson – across Loch Rannoch, by the heads of Glen Lyon, Glen Lochay and Glen Dochart, over a shoulder of Ben More above Crianlarich, and into the little village of Balquhidder. It was here that Alan Breck and the murderous Robin Oig MacGregor fought their duel by bagpipe. In Balquhidder Churchyard Robin Oig's father, the famous Rob Roy MacGregor, lies with his family.

All this was familiar territory to Stevenson. He guided his heroes by trails well known to him from childhood, by Strathyre and over Uam Var (Uamh Mor on the maps), down the Allan Water to Bridge of Allan and Stirling. The Stevensons holidayed for many years at Bridge of Allan, often at the Queen's or the Royal Hotel, and the *Kidnapped* locations are accurately and fondly remembered.

During the writing of *Kidnapped*, Stevenson's health was collapsing. His intention had been to incorporate both the Appin Murder and James Stewart's trial in the story, but it was proving unwieldy and his energy levels were failing him. His concerned friend Sydney Colvin suggested a sequel. James's trial, therefore, was eventually recounted in *Catriona*, with David cast as the missing witness.

After the adventure with the redcoat sentry at the old Stirling Bridge, when his heroes attempted to cross the Forth, Stevenson's illness impacted on the story and the ending was rushed. At Limekilns, nowadays in the shadow of the Forth bridges, Alison Hastie rowed them over to Carriden, and they walked to South Queensferry to meet the lawyer Rankeillor, before confronting his conniving Uncle Ebenezer – and at last David came into his inheritance.

David and Alan parted on Edinburgh's Corstorphine Hill with never a backwards glance, but at least Stevenson had the sure knowledge they would meet again in *Catriona*. Today sculptor Alexander Stoddart's magnificent statues of the two great friends mark the location.

Kidnapped was published in book form in 1886 and remains a national favourite. It marks Stevenson reaching full powers as a writer and is also an important social history. It has been turned into films, television, radio and stage plays, and in February 2007 Edinburgh UNESCO City of Literature Trust created three new editions of *Kidnapped* – a paperback, a simplified retold version and a new graphic novel. Thousands of copies of these books were given away to celebrate Stevenson, Edinburgh's status as a City of Literature and to bring the people of Edinburgh together to read.

Ian Nimmo

SEE ALSO: Howard Place, Inverleith Terrace, Heriot Row, Rutherford's Howff, Hawes Inn, W.E. Henley, The Writers' Museum, Kinnaird, Braemar.

FURTHER INFORMATION: Ian Nimmo explores his fascination with Stevenson's *Kidnapped* in detail in his book *Walking With Murder: On the* Kidnapped *Trail* (Birlinn, 2005). He is also former chairman of the Robert Louis Stevenson Club.

Website: www.robertlouisstevensonclub.org.uk

Highland

Sandaig
Site of Camusfeàrna
The house featured in *Ring of Bright Water* (1960) by Gavin Maxwell (1914–69), writer, traveller and conservationist

He has married me with a ring, a ring of bright water
Whose ripples travel from the heart of the sea . . .
  Kathleen Raine (1908–2003), from 'The Marriage of Psyche'

Ring of Bright Water, the story of how aristocrat adventurer and writer Gavin Maxwell came to share his isolated cottage in the west Highlands with a family of otters, remains one of the most popular wildlife books of the twentieth century, selling over a million copies worldwide. Written with great sensitivity and sense of place, it established Maxwell as one of the masters of natural-history writing. In his introduction to the story he evokes a sense of almost mystical harmony between man and nature:

> In writing this book about my home I have not given to the house its true name. This is from no desire to create mystery – indeed it will be easy enough for the curious to discover where I live – but because identification in print would seem in some sense a sacrifice, a betrayal of its remoteness and isolation, as if by doing so I were to bring nearer its enemies of industry and urban life. Camusfeàrna, I have called it, the Bay of Alders, from the trees that grow along the burn side; but the name is of little consequence, for such bays and houses, empty and long disused, are scattered throughout the wild sea lochs of the Western Highlands and the Hebrides, and in the description of one the reader might perhaps find the likeness of others of which he himself has been fond, for these places are symbols. Symbols, for me and for many, of freedom, whether it be from the prison of over-dense communities and the close confines of human relationships, from the less complex incarceration of office walls and hours, or simply freedom from the prison of adult life and an escape into the forgotten world of childhood, of the individual or the race.

Maxwell was born in the House of Elrig, near Monreith, Dumfries and Galloway, in October 1914, three months before his father

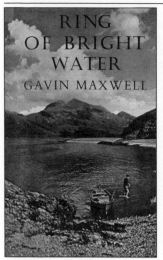

was killed at Antwerp. He was educated at Oxford University, and during the Second World War he served with the Special Operations Executive in the Highlands. Manic depressive, homosexual and intent on living life to the full, he experienced life as an explorer, a shark fisherman, a painter, a naturalist and a writer. It was shark fishing on Soay that inspired his first novel, *Harpoon at a Venture*, in 1952. In 1957 he published *A Reed Shaken by the Wind*, after living among the Marsh Arabs of Iraq with explorer Wilfred Thesiger.

South of Glenelg, amongst a small archipelago of islands, lies Sandaig, where Maxwell stayed in the lighthouse-keeper's cottage in the late 1950s with his otters and wrote *Ring of Bright Water*. The title was inspired by a poem written by Kathleen Raine, who was a frequent visitor to Sandaig and with whom Maxwell had an intense but platonic affair. The cottage was destroyed by fire in 1968, in which the otter Edal died, but the surrounding countryside remains very much as it was in Maxwell's time. The waterfall he said he would return to after his death still gushes nearby, the burn still flows into the sea and the rowan tree under which Kathleen Raine 'cursed' Maxwell still stands. His old boat trailer stands in the corner of a field, and the stunning views across the Sound of Sleet to Skye will never change.

His other works include *The Pains of Death* (1959), *The Otter's Tale* (1962), *The Rocks Remain* (1963), *Lords of the Atlas* (1966), the autobiographical *The House of Elrig* (1965) and *Raven Seek Thy Brother* (1968), sequel to *Ring of Bright Water*. A successful film adaptation was made of *Ring of Bright Water* in 1969, and the same year Gavin Maxwell died of cancer.

FURTHER INFORMATION: To reach Sandaig turn left off the A87 just past Sheil Bridge campsite, taking the unclassified road to Glenelg and Arnisdale. From here you will need OS Landranger map thirty-three to guide you over a distance of one mile. Park at grid reference NG784151 and take the forest track on your right. Follow the track through the trees until it crosses Allt Mor Shantaig (Big Sandaig Burn). Just before the bridge, turn right onto the path that follows the burn downhill towards the sea. The path emerges from the woods close to the shore. Use the stepping stones to cross the burn. Ahead of you are the remains of an old wall beside a dead rowan tree. Here lies the site of Sandaig (Camusfeàrna) with memorials to Gavin Maxwell (positioned in the location of his old writing desk) and his otter Edal.

The Bright Water Visitor Centre in Kyleakin, Skye, was established to create a wildlife sanctuary on the island of Eilean Bàn, Gavin Maxwell's last home, situated below the Skye Bridge. The 'Long Room' in his former home is now a museum devoted to his memory. For any enquiries about visiting or staying on the island, contact the Bright Water Visitor Centre, The Pier, Kyleakin. Tel: 01599 530040.

Email: enquiries@eileanban.org

FURTHER READING: D. Botting, *The Saga of Ring of Bright Water: The Enigma of Gavin Maxwell* (Neil Wilson Publishing, 2000); R. Frere, *Maxwell's Ghost* (Birlinn, 1999); Gavin Maxwell, *The House of Elrig* (Longmans, 1965).

Lynchat

Belleville House
Former home of James Macpherson (1736–96), poet and controversial 'translator' of Ossian

> Son of the noble Fingal, Ossian, Prince of men! What tears run down the cheeks of age? What shades thy mighty soul?
> Memory, son of Alpin, memory wounds the aged. Of former times are my thoughts; my thoughts are of the noble Fingal.
> From *Fingal: An Ancient Epic Poem, in Six Books* (1762)

As a poet James Macpherson is now forgotten, but the suspicions over the authenticity of his translations of ancient Celtic poetry will probably never die. In 1760 he published *Fragments of Ancient Poetry, Collected in the Highlands of Scotland, and Translated From the Gaelic, or Erse Language*. There was a vogue for Celtic poetry at that time, and his book received much praise. Macpherson claimed there were still more Celtic poetic gems waiting to be discovered, and in 1760 he was commissioned by the Faculty of Advocates in Edinburgh to conduct further research in the Highlands. This resulted in the publication of *Fingal: An Ancient Epic Poem, in Six Books* and *Temora: An Epic Poem, in Eight Books* (1763), supposedly written by Ossian – a legendary Irish Gaelic poet and warrior, and son of Fionn (Fingal) – who reputedly lived during the third century. Many oral ballads, lyrics and prose are attributed to him, but whether he composed them, or even existed, is debatable, although no one can deny that they are masterful works of literature.

The books became a literary phenomenon, and Macpherson was fêted in the literary salons of London; however, failure to produce evidence of his sources made many accuse him of being a hoaxer. One of his main detractors was Dr Johnson, whose caustic remarks about the Scots and Scotland are well known, and a belief that such poetic masterpieces could come out of its glens must have nettled him. Johnson demanded that Macpherson produce his original texts as proof of authenticity. Macpherson refused, which only increased people's suspicions, but to be fair to Macpherson, these poems were collected by him from an oral tradition, and most of it was never written down. He probably did embellish and tweak here and there (as did Homer and Walter Scott), but his translations were based on real Ossianic poems. Regardless, the controversy of Ossian as a Highland hoax, and Macpherson as the great hoaxer, still rages on today.

SEE ALSO: Dr Johnson.

FURTHER INFORMATION: Macpherson was born in Invertromie, Badenoch, in 1736. He attended Inverness Grammar School and was a student at the universities of Edinburgh and Aberdeen. In 1763 he was appointed surveyor-general of the Floridas, and in later life became a successful merchant and MP for Camelford. In the 1790s he retired to his estate near Kingussie, where he built Belleville House, close to his birthplace in Badenoch and situated approximately three miles north of Kingussie on the B9152, just beyond Lynchat. It is not open to the public. At his own request and expense he was buried in Westminster Abbey.

Ossian Hotel and Restaurant, The Brae, Kincraig, by Kingussie, Highland, PH21 1QD. Tel: 01540 651242.

Website: www.kincraig.com/ossian

FURTHER READING: H. Gaskill (ed.), *The Poems of Ossian and Related Works* (Edinburgh University Press, 1996); G. Black, *Macpherson's Ossian and the Ossianic Controversy* (New York, 1926); D. Thomson, *The Gaelic Sources of Macpherson's 'Ossian'* (Oliver & Boyd, 1952).

Daviot

Torguish House
Childhood home of Alistair MacLean (1922–87), adventure novelist

I'm an extraordinarily ordinary man. Basically I'm a person who tells stories – and what does that mean? How much is it worth?

Alistair MacLean

Popular and prolific adventure novelist Alistair MacLean was born in Shettleston, Glasgow, on 21 April 1922, the third of four sons of Mary Lamont and Rev. Alistair MacLean. The same year his family moved from the city to the idyllic village of Daviot near Inverness, where he was raised at Torguish House, an old three-storey manse of red sandstone close to the reverend's new kirk. He was educated at the local village school and Inverness Academy.

After his father's sudden death in 1934 from a cerebral haemorrhage, the family moved back to Glasgow to a tenement flat at Carrington Street, off the Great Western Road, and lived off Mrs MacLean's meagre kirk pension. Alistair won a bursary for Hillhead High School, and his first job on leaving school was in a Glasgow shipping office before joining the navy during the Second World War. After the war, he studied for an English language and literature degree at the University of Glasgow, and in 1954, while teaching at Gallowflat School (now an annexe of Stonelaw High) in Reid Street, Rutherglen, he entered a short-story competition in the Glasgow *Herald* newspaper, winning the first prize of £100.

In October 1955 he published his first novel *HMS Ulysses*, a drama of Second World War Russian convoys, written in only three months. By the end of the year it had sold over a quarter of a million copies. MacLean's second book – and the first to be filmed – was *The Guns of Navarone* (1957), the success of which enabled him to give up teaching for ever.

From then on he wrote a book almost every year for the next 30 years, many of which were adapted for the screen, including *The Satan Bug* (1962), *Ice Station Zebra* (1963), *Where Eagles Dare* (1967), *When Eight Bells Toll* (1966), *Puppet on a Chain* (1969), *Fear is the Key* (1961), *Caravan to Vaccarès* (1970) and *Bear Island* (1971).

A complex man who preferred anonymity to the glare of publicity, he was twice married and had three sons. He died in Munich in 1987 and was buried at a private funeral in Celigny, Switzerland, where he had lived in tax exile.

FURTHER INFORMATION: Torguish House, Daviot, Inverness. Tel: 01463 772208. Now a bed and breakfast, it is situated approximately four miles south of Inverness. The entrance is directly off the southbound carriageway of the A9.

FURTHER READING: Jack Webster, *Alistair MacLean: A Life* (Chapmans, 1991).

Dunbeath

The Terrace
Birthplace of Neil Gunn (1891–1973), novelist

> The wood had to be watched and its grasp avoided, while he passed through it. In fact his instincts so possessed the wood that to this day he can walk through it in his mind and feel the rough bark, see the crooked stem, slip in the brown earth, smell its exhalation, listen to its silence, and be unable to know where his own spirit ends and the wood begins.
>
> Neil Gunn, from *Highland River* (1937)

Neil Gunn will be best remembered for conveying the simple life and backgrounds of the Highland fishing and crofting communities he grew up amongst, describing in clear and lucid prose, with a kind of mystical awareness, a culture that has all but disintegrated today. Most of his books are about Highland people and their

Neil Gunn with Maurice Walsh at Tobermory, 1937.

Neil Gunn on a 500 cc Rudge Multi in the 1920s.

environment, and his most popular work, *The Silver Darlings* (1941), is a powerfully evocative story of the herring fishers of Caithness and Sutherland, displaced by the Clearances and forced to make the sea the source of their livelihood. The author of over 20 novels, several plays, a handbook on whisky and a travel book, he did not start writing seriously until his early 30s, but his work has earned him international acclaim.

He was born Neil Miller Gunn in Dunbeath on 8 November 1891 to Isabella Miller, a domestic servant, and James Gunn, a crofter–fisherman. James and Isabella had nine children, and Neil was the seventh child in a family of two sisters and seven brothers. James prospered as a fisherman and was a skipper with his own crew. In the late 1880s he built a slate-roofed, two-storey house on the village terrace, with a garden and a byre for the cow at the back. Neil attended the local village school until 1904, when he moved to St John's Town of Dalry in Kirkcudbrightshire to live with his sister and her husband; his education continued there under the guidance of tutors. In 1907 he sat the civil-service exam, which led to a job in London. In 1910 he became a customs and excise officer and was stationed in the Highlands, where he met and made friends with an Irish colleague called Maurice Walsh, who was also destined to become a prolific novelist. He began publishing various short stories, poems and essays in literary magazines during the 1920s, and his first novel, *The Grey Coast*, was published in 1926.

After the publication of *Highland River* in 1937, he resigned from the customs and excise to become a full-time writer, and so began his most productive period as a novelist and essayist. He was by now an ardent nationalist and, along with Hugh MacDiarmid and others, was a founder member of the Scottish National Party. He also became very much associated and involved with the writers of the Scottish Renaissance, including MacDiarmid, James Bridie, Naomi Mitchison, Eric Linklater, Edwin Muir and Lewis Grassic Gibbon.

His other works include *The Lost Glen* (1928), *Morning Tide* (1931), *Sun Circle* (1933), *Butcher's Broom* (1934), *Off in a Boat* (1938), *Wild Geese Overhead* (1939), *Young Art and Old Hector* (1942), *The Green Isle of the Great Deep* (1944), *The Well at the World's End* (1951), *Bloodhunt* (1952) and *The Other Landscape* (1954). His last work was *The Atom of Delight* (1956), a philosophical autobiography steeped in his love of solitude, loneliness and Zen Buddhism. Neil Gunn died on 15 January 1973 and is buried in Dingwall Cemetery.

FURTHER INFORMATION: Dunbeath is situated on the A9 between Helmsdale and Wick. Neil Gunn's birthplace is marked by a plaque on the house next to the local grocer's shop. The Dunbeath Heritage Centre (open Easter to October; 01593 731233) is located in the former village school where Neil Gunn began his schooling and contains a permanent exhibition of his life and work. A memorial sculpture to Neil Gunn was unveiled at Dunbeath harbour in 1991 by the Neil Gunn Society, featuring Kenn and the Salmon from *Highland River*. He is also remembered by a Memorial Viewpoint above Dingwall in Strathpeffer. In 1972 the Scottish Arts Council created the Neil Gunn Fellowship.

FURTHER READING: F.R. Hart and J.B. Pick, *Neil M. Gunn: A Highland Life* (Polygon, 1985).

Western Isles

Barra

Cille Bharra Cemetery
Eoligarry
Grave of Compton Mackenzie (1883–1972), novelist, poet, biographer, essayist, travel writer, journalist and secret agent

> Many romantic pages have been written about the sunken Spanish galleon in the bay of Tobermory. That 4,000-ton steamship on the rocks off Little Todday provided more practical romance in three and a half hours than the Tobermory galleon has provided in three and a half centuries. Doubloons, ducats, and ducatoons, moidores, pieces of eight, sequins, guineas, rose and angel nobles, what are these to vaunt above the liquid gold carried by the *Cabinet Minister*?
>
> Compton Mackenzie, *Whisky Galore* (1947)

For a successful writer, praised by Henry James and acknowledged as a major influence on F. Scott Fitzgerald, Compton Mackenzie is today curiously neglected. His main desire was to entertain his readers, and his portraits of couthy Highlanders are uproarious subtle parodies that never patronise.

He will be best remembered for his 1947 novel *Whisky Galore*, which was based on actual events that occurred in 1941 when the 8,000-ton cargo ship SS *Politician* ran aground in treacherous seas in the Sound of

Whisky Galore script conference on Barra, 1948: Compton Mackenzie, Monja Danischewsky (producer) and Alexander Mackendrick (director).

Eriskay, off the coast of Barra. Her cargo included pianos, bicycles, Jamaican banknotes and 22,000 cases of whisky. Mackenzie was commander of the Home Guard on Barra at the time and got his fair share of the 'liquid gold', unlike the pompous Captain Waggett in his novel. When working on the final draft for the script of the 1948 Ealing Studios film adaptation, Mackenzie grumbled, 'Another of my books gone west.' Producer Monja Danischewsky seemed of the same opinion, commenting, 'Well, I don't know . . . all I can see is a lot of elderly Scotsmen sitting by the fire and saying "och aye".' History has proved them both wrong. The film became an Ealing classic, and the novel is now ranked amongst the great Highland comedies.

He was born in West Hartlepool in 1863, the son of actor Edward Compton, and was educated at St Paul's School and Magdalen College, Oxford. He studied for the English Bar but abandoned law in 1907 to write his first play, *The Gentleman in Grey*. His first novel, *The Passionate Elopement*, was published in 1911. *Carnival* (1912) followed, but it was the publication of *Sinister Street* (1913) that won him acclaim. During the First World War he was recruited into the British Secret Service in Greece, an experience he later recounted in *Greek Memories* (1932). The book was immediately withdrawn, however, and all remaining copies destroyed. Mackenzie was charged with breaching the Official Secrets Act and fined £100.

After the war, he returned to novel-writing, producing *Rich Relations* (1921) and two novels about lesbian love, *Vestal Fire* (1927) and *Extraordinary Women* (1928). Between 1937 and 1945 he published the sextet *The Four Winds of Love*, and between 1963 and 1971 he produced his massive ten-volume autobiography *My Life and Times*.

Mackenzie was a staunch nationalist and a founder member of the Scottish National Party. He was also literary critic of the *Daily Mail* during the 1930s and was the founder editor of *Gramophone* magazine, now the oldest-surviving record magazine in the world. He lived for a period in Capri after the war and in 1934 built a house on the island of Barra. He was knighted in 1952. He died in Edinburgh on 30 November 1972 and is buried at Eoligarry on Barra. During his burial service, piper Calum Johnston, an old friend of Mackenzie, collapsed and died after playing a lament.

FURTHER INFORMATION: Compton Mackenzie's grave, marked by a plain cross, is in Cille Bharra Cemetery, which is situated on the hillside overlooking Eoligarry jetty.

FURTHER READING: A. Linklater, *Compton Mackenzie: A Life* (Chatto & Windus, 1987); R. Hutchinson, *Polly: The True Story Behind Whisky Galore* (Mainstream, 1998).

Bayble

52 Upper Bayble
Childhood home of Iain Crichton Smith (1928–98), poet and novelist

> I had no feeling for Scotland at all as a country except through football. I didn't feel myself as belonging to Scotland. I felt myself as belonging to Lewis. I had never been out of the island in my whole life; I had never even seen a train. Glasgow was as distant from me as the moon.
>
> Iain Crichton Smith, from *As I Remember* (1979)

A compassionate observer of Scottish culture who was imbedded in his Hebridean roots, Iain Crichton Smith's love for the Lewis of his youth surfaces and weaves its way into his numerous poems, books and plays. He wrote in both English and Gaelic, recalling the island's solitude and bleakness, where the world outside seemed unreal and alien. It was a place he loved because of its lack of modernity and reality, and which fed him the ideas and feelings that dominate his writing. 'I love it for its very bleakness, for its absences,' he once wrote. 'I think of it as a place beaten upon by winds,

an orchestra of gales, which bend the fences like the strings of a musical instrument.'

He was born in Glasgow on New Year's Day 1928, the second of three sons of John and Christina Smith. His father, a former merchant seaman, died of tuberculosis, and his mother, a former herring girl, decided to return with her sons to Lewis. He grew up in Bayble on the Point Peninsula, a Gaelic-speaking community steeped in a Presbyterian Calvinism, wedged between the moor and the sea, 'seven miles and a whole world away' from Stornoway. He attended the village school, where English was spoken, and later won a bursary to go to the Nicholson Institute in Stornoway. In October 1945, at the age of 17, he left Lewis for the first time in his life to attend Aberdeen University. 'I remember arriving in Aberdeen and seeing a beggar for the first time. I was deeply shocked,' he recalled. 'It was the first moral dilemma I had faced away from home . . . I stood there for a long time, not knowing what I was supposed to do.'

After a couple of years teaching in Dumbarton, he moved to Oban High School, where he remained for 22 years, teaching by day and writing by night. He published his first volume of poetry, *The Long River*, in 1955 while teaching English in Oban. By the time he took early retirement in 1977 he'd written sixteen books of poetry, five novels and seven collections of short stories.

His first novel, written in ten days and set in Strathnaver valley, near Durness, was *Consider the Lilies* (1968) and is his best-known work. It views the Highland Clearances through the consciousness of an old woman being evicted from her croft and betrayed by the Church. It was followed by *The Last Summer* (1969), a portrait of adolescence with strong autobiographical overtones. Other works include *My Last Duchess* (1971), *An End to Autumn* (1978), *Murdo and Other Stories* (1981) and *Selected Poems* (1982).

He married in 1977 and settled in Taynuilt, Argyllshire. The range and variety of his work was immense, and the lyrical quality of his writing is something that stays with you for a long time. His philosophy on old age is also worth noting: 'You don't grow wiser as you grow older,' he said. 'You just need to go to the toilet more often.'

Orkney

3 Mayburn Court
Former home of George Mackay Brown (1921–96), poet, novelist, playwright and short-story writer

> Every man and woman, however seemingly ordinary and unimportant, has by the mere fact of living set the whole web of human existence trembling, and has changed (however minutely) the history of the race.
>
> George Mackay Brown, from *An Autobiographical Essay* (1978)

The works of George Mackay Brown are inseparable from his Orcadian roots. Much of his inspiration came from farmers and fishing folk – 'the tillers of the earth and sea' as he called them. More Norse than Scots, his work is rooted in the ancient sagas and traditions of the islands which inspired him. He was like a medieval bard in a woolly jumper, rarely travelling beyond his hearth but knowing every stone in the universe. He once wrote that 'the whole world gathers about the parish pump', and that it is not necessary to stray very far from your own backyard to discover that any small community is a microcosm.

His lifelong home was Stromness, a small seaport that was once a haven for fishing fleets, and merchant and whaling ships. Many vessels, owing to the excellence of the harbour, called there for shelter,

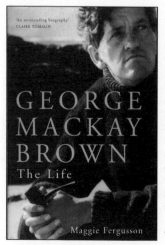

provisions and men, among them the ships of the Hudson's Bay Company. Market places and alehouses proliferated to cope with the trade coming from the North Sea and the Atlantic. Today this has all ended and only the annual invasion of summer tourists intrudes on its tranquillity, but as recently as the 1920s the single, narrow, twisting street of the town still throbbed with the atmosphere of a bustling seaport, peppered with drunken trawlermen, fishermen stringing creels, fish sellers, tinkers and the like.

It was into these surroundings that George Mackay Brown was

born on 17 October 1921. He later recalled that his birthplace was 'in a corner house whose upstairs window looked out over the street and whose door opened on to a fisherman's pier. Twice a day the sea comes and goes about the steps and the slipway of Clouston's pier: a blue-and-gray brimming, an ebb that leaves desolations of heaped red sea-weed.' He was the youngest of six children of John Brown, a postman and part-time tailor, and Mary Jane Mackay from Strathy in Sutherland. He apparently hated school but loved the stories told to him by his only sister Ruby – mostly love stories, in which most of the girls 'died of a broken heart' in the end. It was these stories, he always claimed, that planted the seeds of narrative and poetry in his mind. When he was 12, a severe bout of measles damaged his eyes and weakened his lungs, and in 1941 he was diagnosed with tuberculosis, which left him with recurring respiratory problems for the rest of his life.

He began writing poetry in the early 1940s and also began writing articles and news items for the local newspaper, the *Orkney Herald*, but 'had too much imagination to be a good correspondent'. He rarely left Orkney throughout his life, but in the summer of 1951 he met fellow Orcadian Edwin Muir, who was then warden of Newbattle Abbey, a further-education college near Dalkeith in Midlothian. On the strength of a story Brown had written in *The New Shetlander*, Muir took him on as a student for a year, becoming a great influence on him and encouraging him to write. Brown studied English at Edinburgh University from 1956 to 1960, and then did postgraduate work on Gerard Manley Hopkins. As a young student in Edinburgh, he befriended the poets of the Scottish Renaissance, including Sydney Goodsir Smith, Norman MacCaig and Hugh MacDiarmid, and frequented their watering holes at the Abbotsford and Milne's. By this time he was a hardened drinker and was once arrested for being 'drunk and incapable' in Edinburgh's Hanover Street. He was 'hooked on drink' for over 30 years, often teetering on the edge of alcoholism.

He self-published his first collection of poetry, *The Storm*, in 1954, and it was followed, thanks to efforts by Edwin Muir, by *Loaves and Fishes* in 1959. His other works of poetry include *The Year of the Whale* (1969) and *Selected Poems* (1977–1991). He also published several collections of short stories, including *A Calendar of Love* (1967) and *A Time to Keep* (1969). His first novel was *Greenvoe* (1972), followed by *Magnus* (1973). His work was published in the US and Japan, and translated into several languages. He was also awarded many prizes, including being shortlisted for the Booker Prize for his novel *Beside the Ocean of Time* (1994). He also influenced much of the music of composer Peter Maxwell Davies, providing several texts for musical settings.

He never married, and, apart from visiting Ireland and England, he never travelled abroad. He did, of course, suffer from agoraphobia, but, had he not, would sojourns in Montmartre, Chelsea or Greenwich Village have given us more? Most certainly they would have given us less.

SEE ALSO: Edwin Muir, Hugh MacDiarmid.

FURTHER INFORMATION: George Mackay Brown lived on the first floor at 3 Mayburn Court from the late 1960s until his death in 1996. It is marked with a plaque and is opposite Stromness Museum. His grave can be seen in Warbeth Kirkyard, where the inscription on his headstone reads 'Carve the runes then be content with silence'. The kirkyard is about 20 minutes' walk from the town, overlooking Hoy Sound.

FURTHER READING: George Mackay Brown, *For the Islands I Sing: An Autobiography* (John Murray, 1997); R. and B. Murray, *Interrogation of Silence: The Writings of George Mackay Brown* (John Murray, 2004); Maggie Fergusson, *George Mackay Brown: The Life* (John Murray, 2006).

Harray

The Merkister Hotel
Former home of Eric Linklater (1899–1974), novelist, poet and playwright

> 'There won't be any revolution in America,' said Isadore. Nikitin agreed. 'The people are all too clean. They spend all their time changing their shirts and washing themselves. You can't feel fierce and revolutionary in a bathroom.'
>
> Eric Linklater, from *Juan in America* (1931)

Eric Linklater in Uppsala, Sweden, in 1964.

Eric Robert Russell Linklater wrote over 20 novels, as well as short stories, travel writing, poetry, plays, autobiography and military history. His mock-heroic stories rivalled those of Compton Mackenzie, most notably his picaresque classic *Juan in America* (1931). He was born a Welshman at Penarth in the Vale of Glamorgan in 1899 to Robert Linklater, a master mariner from Mossetter, Harray, and Elizabeth Young, the daughter of a Swedish sea captain. The family moved back to Orkney when Eric was very young, and he always claimed it was his spiritual home. 'My knowledge of Orkney,' he once wrote, 'the love of Orkney which dominated and perhaps distorted so much of my life – I owe, not to my Orkney-born father, but to my neurotic, frequently exasperating and ultimately decisive mother.'

When war was declared in 1914, he was a medical student at Aberdeen University. He joined the Black Watch and was a sniper at the front line, seeing action at Passchendaele, the Somme and Ypres. He was nearly killed at Ypres when a German bullet shattered part of his skull, an injury that scarred him for life. After Ypres, he was billeted at Edinburgh Castle – which featured in *The Impregnable Women* (1938), his modern version of Aristophanes' *Lysistrata* – describing it in his 1934 novel *Magnus Merriman* as '. . . Scotland's castle, Queen Mary's castle and the castle of fifty thousand annual visitors who walk through it with rain on their boots and bewilderment in their hearts'. After the war, he transferred his studies from medicine to English literature, and after graduating he began a career in journalism, becoming assistant editor of *The Times* of India in 1925. In 1927 he returned to Aberdeen University as assistant to the professor of English. He wrote his first novel, *White Maa's Saga*, in 1929, a semi-autobiographical account of an

Merkister House in the 1950s.

Orcadian medical student. From 1928 to 1930 he went to the US on a Commonwealth fellowship, studying at Cornell and Berkeley, and his novel *Juan in America*, published in 1931, was based on his experiences there. It was reprinted nine times during its first year of publication and established him as a popular novelist. He stood, unsuccessfully, in the East Fife by-election of 1933 as the National Party of Scotland candidate, and after his marriage that same year returned to Orkney to live at Merkister House, Harray, where he remained until 1947. At the outbreak of the Second World War he commanded Fortress Orkney as a major in the Royal Engineers and founded the first newspaper for troops in Britain. It was during his work for the War Office recording the Italian campaign that he was inspired to write his story about an Italian peasant who eventually finds his courage in *Private Angelo* (1946). His other novels include *Juan in China* (1937), *The Ultimate Viking* (1955), *The Voyage of the Challenger* (1972) and his most popular children's book, *The Wind on the Moon* (1944). His autobiographical novels were *The Man on My Back* (1941), *A Year of Space* (1953) and *Fanfare for a Tin Hat* (1941). Eric Linklater died on 7 November 1974 and is buried in St Michael's Churchyard, Harray. Fellow Orcadian novelist George Mackay Brown summed up Linklater's contribution to literature in *The Orcadian* in 1954:

> Eric Linklater is not primarily a novelist or an essayist or a dramatist. He is above all else an enchanting prose poet. These fragments of wonderful singing prose are scattered all over his books, and through them English literature is permanently enriched.

FURTHER INFORMATION: Merkister House (now the Merkister Hotel) is located at Harray Loch on the West Mainland, three miles north-west of Kirkwall. Tel: 01856 771366. A plaque erected to Linklater's memory can be seen at the entrance.

FURTHER READING: M. Parnell, *Eric Linklater: A Critical Biography* (John Murray, 1984); A. Massie, *Eric Linklater* (Canongate, 1999); J.T. Firth, M. Buchan and S. Spence, *Harray, Orkney's Inland Parish* (published privately, 1975).

Appendices

Tour with the Author

The Literary Pub Crawl
The Edinburgh Book Lovers' Tour

Allan Foster, author of *The Literary Traveller in Scotland* and its companion volume *The Literary Traveller in Edinburgh*, leads regular literary walking tours around his home city of Edinburgh, the world's first City of Literature. Join him and visit the sites and haunts of Robert Louis Stevenson, Sir Arthur Conan Doyle, Robert Burns, J.K. Rowling, J.M. Barrie, Sir Walter Scott and others. Visit the birthplace of Sherlock Holmes and Long John Silver.

By day he leads The Edinburgh Book Lovers' Tour around Edinburgh's Old Town, and by night he leads the Literary Pub Crawl with a glass in his hand and a song in his heart through the city's Southside, visiting local pubs with a strong literary connection. Both tours offer a fascinating insight into the hidden world of literary Edinburgh. If you enjoyed the books, you'll love the tours!

Tel: 01573 223888/07989 546 791.
Email: allan@edinburghbookloverstour.com
Website: www.edinburghbookloverstour.com

Literary Festivals

Aberdeen
Word – Aberdeen's Book Festival
An eclectic mix of events featuring the finest writers from Scotland, the UK and beyond. As well as the main Word programme there is a Children's Word Festival, and a Gaelic and schools programme.

Email: word@abdn.ac.uk
Website: www.abdn.ac.uk/word

Ayrshire
Burns Festival
A major event celebrating Scottish life and culture in the heart of Burns country. The festival brings together international performers and local people to create a full programme of music, theatre and community events.

Email: info@burnsfestival.com
Website: www.burnsfestival.com

Borders
Borders Book Festival
Novelists, historians, poets, biographers, gardeners and cooks all head to the Borders in June to talk about their work. There is a lively children's programme and a series of events with over thirty writers, all of which takes place over four days in venues around Melrose in the Scottish Borders.

Email: info@bordersbookfestival.org
Website: www.bordersbookfestival.org

Dumfries and Galloway
Gaelforce
A multi-arts extravaganza extending throughout the autumn and across the south-west, with music events, book festivals, poetry and theatre performances, exhibitions, and street processions.

Email: rebeccac@dumgal.gov.uk
Website: www.gaelforceevents.co.uk

Wigtown
Scotland's National Book Town
The Scottish Book Town Festival is a ten-day autumnal celebration of the written word in Wigtown, our national book town. Wigtown also hosts a spring festival in April.

Website: www.wigtown-booktown.co.uk

Edinburgh
Edinburgh International Book Festival
The Edinburgh International Book Festival is the world's biggest book festival. The festival consists of hundreds of events, including a highly regarded children's programme, which has grown to become a leading showcase for children's writers and illustrators. The festival also runs its own independent bookselling operation – all proceeds from the sale of books are invested back into the

running of the event, run by a not-for-profit charity organisation that annually raises 80 per cent of its own funds.

Email: admin@edbookfest.co.uk

Website: www.edbookfest.co.uk

Festival of Scottish Writing

The annual Festival of Scottish Writing is a well-established highlight of the library year. Held over two weeks in May, the festival offers the chance to celebrate all that's best about Scottish writers and writing. It's just one of the many projects hosted by Edinburgh's City Libraries, who run regular and free events at their locations across the city.

Tel: 0131 242 8000

Leith Festival

This June festival is now a major arts and community event, featuring literature, poetry and drama, as well as music, dance and exhibitions.

Website: www.leithfestival.com

Scottish International Storytelling Festival

An October celebration of storytelling traditions from Scotland and around the world, with special guests, music, song, exhibitions and events for all ages in diverse locations across south-east and central Scotland. Guests from overseas join together with Scots-based tellers for a diverse programme of public events, workshops and schools visits. National Tell-A-Story Day also takes place during the festival, with community-based events all over Scotland, coordinated by the Scottish Storytelling Centre in Edinburgh.

Email: reception@scottishstorytellingcentre.com

Website: www.scottishstorytellingcentre.co.uk

Debut Authors Festival

The Debut Authors Festival in June is the only British festival dedicated to new writers, introducing the most exciting debut authors from Britain and beyond. They read from and talk about their work, looking particularly at issues concerning being a debut writer. These include how they chose what to write about, in which style or genre, their aims and influences, how they used their lives and experience to inform their work, how long it took them and how they found an agent and publisher.

Website: www.debutauthorsfestival.co.uk

Fife
StAnza – A Celebration of Poetry

The only regular festival dedicated to poetry in Scotland. Held in the ancient university town of St Andrews during the month of March, the festival presents world-class poets and writers performing in exciting, atmospheric venues. With workshops, readings, discussions and masterclasses.

Email: info@stanzapoetry.org

Website: www.st-andrews.ac.uk/standrews/stanza

Glasgow
Aye Write!

Aye Write! – Glasgow's annual book festival – celebrates the rich variety of Glaswegian writing and also brings the best of Scottish and international writers to the city. The programme includes workshops, readings and discussions and takes in a wide range of genres: poetry, prose, screenwriting, fiction, crime and children's books.

Email: lil@cls.glasgow.gov.uk

Website: www.glasgow.gov.uk/en/Visitors/AyeWriteGlasgows BookFestival

Highland
The Royal National Mod

Am Mòd Nàiseanta Rìoghail (The Royal National Mod) is Scotland's premier festival of Gaelic language, arts and culture and is held annually in October at a different location in Scotland. The Mod is a competition-based festival that celebrates the Gaelic language and culture through music, dance, drama, arts and literature. First held in Oban in 1892, the Mod has now grown to become the second-biggest festival in Scotland.

Email: info@the-mod.co.uk

Website: www.the-mod.co.uk

Orkney
The St Magnus Festival

Musical events are at the heart of the June programme, but the festival also encompasses drama, dance, literature and the visual arts. On the tenth anniversary of his death, the Orcadian writer George Mackay Brown was honoured at the 2006 festival, his work being celebrated in music, readings, theatre, films and exhibitions.

Email: info@stmagnusfestival.com

Website: www.stmagnusfestival.com

Perth and Kinross
The Word's Out!

Perth and Kinross's annual literary festival. A week-long celebration of the written and spoken word, which takes place towards the end of October each year.

Website: www.thewordsout.org.uk

Winter Words Festival

An annual programme of literary events run by the Pitlochry Festival Theatre.

Website: www.pitlochry.org.uk/page145.php

Shetland
Shetland Storytelling Festival

A gathering in the Northern Isles of local and visiting storytellers. Contact Lawrence Tulloch for more information on 01957 744201.

Western Isles
Stornoway – Faclan, The Hebridean Book Festival

Faclan is a four-day book festival rooted in writing about, from or relevant to the Hebrides, bringing together world-class authors in an inspiring Hebridean setting. The festival encompasses writing in both Gaelic and English, and features non-fiction, fiction, poetry and drama, providing an annual showcase of literature in the Hebrides. Every August/September.

Website: www.faclan.org

Literary Magazines

Anon

A poetry magazine that doesn't care who you aren't.
Editor: Mike Stocks
67 Learmonth Grove
Edinburgh
EH4 1BL

Cencrastus

The magazine for Scottish and international literature, arts and affairs.
Editor: Raymond Ross
Unit One, Abbeymount Techbase
Abbeyhill
Edinburgh
EH8 8EJ
Tel: 0131 661 5687
Email: cencrastus1@hotmail.com
Quarterly

Chanticleer

Editor: Richard Livermore
1 Alva Street (2FL)
Edinburgh
EH2 4PH

Chapman

Scotland's quality literary magazine.
Editor: Joy Hendry
4 Broughton Place
Edinburgh
EH1 3RX
Tel: 0131 557 2207
Email: chapman-pub@blueyonder.co.uk
Website: www.chapman-pub.co.uk
Thrice yearly

The Dark Horse

Founded in 1995, this is an international magazine committed to British and American poetry. It is published in Scotland.
Editor: Gerry Cambridge
c/o 3-B Blantyre Mill Road
Bothwell
South Lanarkshire
G71 8DD
Email: gjctdh@freenetname.co.uk
Website: www.star.ac.uk/darkhorse.html

The Drouth

A magazine dealing in informed critique, satire, film, theatre and prose.
The Drouth
PO Box 7419
Glasgow

G5 9WB
Tel: 0141 429 1805
Email: thedrouth@yahoo.co.uk
Website: www.thedrouth.com

Edinburgh Review

Scotland's leading biannual journal of ideas, the *Edinburgh Review* publishes essays, short fiction, poetry and reviews aimed at an educated reading public with an interest in critical thought.
Editor: Brian McCabe
22a Buccleuch Place
Edinburgh
EH8 9LN
Tel: 0131 651 1415
Email: edinburgh.review@ed.ac.uk
Website: www.edinburghreview.org.uk

Folio

Collections, research, events at the National Library of Scotland.
Editor: Jennie Renton
National Library of Scotland
George IV Bridge
Edinburgh
EH1 1EW
Website: www.nls.uk

Gath

An iris Ghàidhlig.
Editors: Dòmhnall E. Meek, Jò NicDhòmhnaill
27 Ceàrnag Sheòras/George Square
Dùn Eideann/Edinburgh
EH8 9LD
Email: d.e.meek@ed.ac.uk
Quarterly

Green Shoots

An occasional magazine of poetry, verse and prose by the people of Edinburgh. Available in hard copy from Edinburgh City Libraries and Information Services. If you are interested in contributing, contact community.information@edinburgh.gov.uk or 0131 242 8110. For further information visit the *Green Shoots* webpage.
Community Information Service
Central Library
George IV Bridge
Edinburgh
EH1 1EG
Website: www.edinburgh.gov.uk/CEC/Libraries/greenshoots/green shoots.html

island

A biannual literary magazine publishing poetry and prose poems, concrete poetry, essays and non-fiction fragments in themed issues. It is published by Essence Press.
Editor: Julie Johnstone
8 Craiglea Drive
Edinburgh
EH10 5PA

Email: jaj@essencepress.co.uk
Website: www.essencepress.co.uk

Lallans

Published twice a year, *Lallans* is the journal of the Scots Language Society. It includes poetry, fiction, reviews and articles in Scots.
Email: mail@lallans.co.uk
Website: www.lallans.co.uk

Northwords Now

A new writers' magazine for the north.
Email: info@hi-arts.org.uk
Website: www.hi-arts.co.uk
Quarterly

One O'Clock Gun

'First in, best dressed; original and still the best.' A double-sided broadsheet with 'cunning folds', published by:
Top Slot Publications
Edinburgh
Tel: 0796 946 3232
Email: paxedina@yahoo.co.uk

Product

This is a multi-arts magazine which promotes the work of writers and artists in Scotland, provides unique coverage of contemporary Scottish culture and encourages dialogue on arts and politics in Scotland.
Website: www.product.org.uk

Quarto

Newsletter of the National Library of Scotland.
National Library of Scotland
George IV Bridge
Edinburgh
EH1 1EW
Website: www.nls.uk

Saltire Magazine

The latest news, views and interviews from the Saltire Society, an organisation which saw the need in the 1930s to interest Scots in their own culture and preserve all that is best in Scottish tradition.
The Saltire Society
9 Fountain Close
22 High Street
Edinburgh
EH1 1TF
Email: saltire@saltiresociety.org.uk
Website: www.saltiresociety.org.uk

Scottish Review of Books

Editor: Alan Taylor
The Sunday Herald
9/10 St Andrew Square
Edinburgh
EH2 2AF
Quarterly

Scottish Studies

School of Scottish Studies
University of Edinburgh
27 George Square
Edinburgh
EH8 9LD
Tel: 0131 650 4156
Fax: 0131 650 4163
Email: ScottishStudies@ed.ac.uk
Annual

Textualities

An online literary and book-collecting magazine with a Scottish flavour. A print version of *Textualities* appears annually. Both website and magazine are based at:
Main Point Books
8 Lauriston Street
Edinburgh
EH3 9DJ
Tel: 0131 228 4837
Email: the.editor@texualities.net
Website: www.textualities.net

Tocher

Editor: Morag MacLeod
School of Scottish Studies
27 George Square
Edinburgh
EH8 9LD
Tel: 0131 650 3056

Understanding

Editor: Denise Smith
Dionysia Press
20A Montgomery Street
Edinburgh
EH7 5JS
Tel: 0131 478 2572

Variant

Free arts, culture and political magazine, published four times a year.
1/2 189b Maryhill Road
Glasgow
G20 7XJ
Tel: 0141 333 9522
Email: variantmag@btinternet.com
Website: www.variant.randomstate.org

Second-Hand and Antiquarian Bookshops

Aberdeen
Down's Bookshop
198 King Street, Aberdeen, AB24 5BH. Tel: 01224 646577

Old Aberdeen Bookshop
140 Spital, Old Aberdeen, AB24 3JU. Tel: 01224 658355

Oxfam Bookshop
5 Back Wynd, Aberdeen, AB10 1JN. Tel: 01224 642490

Winram's Bookshop
32/36 Rosemount Place, Aberdeen, AB25 2XB. Tel: 01224 630673

Aberdeenshire
Ballater
Deeside Books
18–20 Bridge Street, Ballater, AB35 5QP. Tel: 01339 754080

Dinnet
Jane Jones Books
The Old Shop, Dinnet, AB34 5JY. Tel: 01339 885662

Huntly
Orb's Bookshop
33A Deveron Street, Huntly, AB54 8BY. Tel: 01466 793765

Whitehills
The Bookcellar
5 West End, Whitehills, AB45 2NL. Tel: 01261 861150

Portsoy
Bookends
21 Seafield Street, Portsoy, AB45 2QT. Tel: 01261 842262

Angus
Arbroath
Books 'n' Things
5 Dishlandtown Street, Arbroath, DD11 1QX. Tel: 01241 431588

Forfar
Strathmore Books
136 East High Street, Forfar, DD8 2ER. Tel: 01307 469777

Argyll & Bute
Campbeltown
The Old Bookshelf
8 Cross Street, Campbeltown, PA28 6HU. Tel: 01586 551114

Colonsay
Colonsay Books
Portmore, Isle of Colonsay, PA61 7YP. Tel: 01951 200232

Dunoon
Well Read Bookshop
23 Argyll Street, Dunoon, PA23 7HH. Tel: 01369 706160
Helensburgh
McLaren Books
22 John Street, Helensburgh, G84 8BA. Tel: 01436 676453

Iona
The Iona Bookshop
Old Printing Press Building, Iona, PA76 6SL. Tel: 01681 700699

Ayrshire
Girvan
Ainslie Books
1 Glendoune Street, Girvan, KA26 0AA. Tel: 01465 715453

Borders
Galashiels
Books Plus
2 Channel Street, Galashiels, TD1 1BA. Tel: 01896 752843

Hawick
Books Plus
9 High Street, Hawick. Tel: 01450 375588

Waterspade Bookshop
23A Buccleuch Street, Hawick, TD9 0HH. Tel: 01450 378566

Kelso
Border Books
47–51 Horsemarket, Kelso, TD5 7AA. Tel: 01573 225861

McGregor Books
12 Bridge Street, Kelso, TD5 6JD. Tel: 01573 225309

Melrose
The Bookroom
1 Dingleton Road, Melrose, TD6 9QS. Tel: 01896 823337

Talisman Books
9 Market Square, Melrose. Tel: 01896 822196

Peebles
W.J. Whitie
71 High Street, Peebles, EH45 8AN. Tel: 01721 720169

West Linton
Linton Books
Deanfoot Road, West Linton, EH46 7DY. Tel: 01968 660339

Clackmannanshire
Alva
Stirling Book Byre
73 Stirling Street, Alva, FK12 5ED. Tel: 01259 769512

Dumfries and Galloway
Castle Douglas
Benny Gillies
31–33 Victoria Street, Kirkpatrick Durham, Castle Douglas, DG7 3HQ. Tel: 01556 650412
Douglas Books
207 King Street, Castle Douglas, DG7 1DT. Tel: 01556 504006

Dumfries
Crescent Books
32 Church Street, Dumfries, DG1 1DF. Tel: 01387 261137

Gatehouse of Fleet
Anwoth Books
Rutherford Hall, High Street, Gatehouse of Fleet, DG7 2HS. Tel: 01557 814774

Kirkcudbright
Solway Books & Gallery
14 St Cuthbert's Street, Kirkcudbright, DG6 4HZ. Tel: 01557 330635

Vailima Books
61 High Street, Kirkcudbright, DG6 4JZ. Tel: 01557 330583

Moffat
Moffat Book Exchange
5 Well Street, Moffat, DG10 9DP. Tel: 01683 220059

Stranraer
What the Dickens
14A Bridge Street, Stranraer, DG9 7HY. Tel: 0783 3571897

Thornhill
Fram Books
49 Drumlanrig Street, Thornhill, DG3 5LJ. Tel: 01848 331613

Whithorn
Pend Books
55 George Street, Whithorn, DG8 8NU. Tel: 01988 500469

Wigtown
451f
29 South Main Street, Wigtown, DG8 9HG. Tel: 01988 402515

AA1 Books at Windy Hill
Unit 3, Duncan Park, Wigtown, DG8 9JD. Tel: 01988 402653

Artyfacts
14 North Main Street, Wigtown, DG8 9HL. Tel: 01988 402020

The Book Corner
2 High Street, Wigtown, DG8 9HQ. Tel: 01988 402010

The Book End Studio
23 North Main Street, Wigtown, DG8 9HL. Tel: 01988 402403

The Bookshop
17 North Main Street, Wigtown, DG8 9HL. Tel: 01988 402499

The Book Vaults
Wigtown House Hotel, 19 Bank Street, Wigtown, DG8 9EH. Tel: 01988 402025

The Box of Frogs Children's Bookshop
18 North Main Street, Wigtown, DG8 9HL. Tel: 01988 402255

Byre Books
24 South Main Street, Wigtown, DG8 9EH. Tel: 0845 458 3813

Cauldron
3 High Street, Wigtown, DG8 9HH. Tel: 01988 402417

G.C. Books Ltd
Unit 10, Bladnoch Bridge Estate, Wigtown, DG8 9AB. Tel: 01988 402688

M.E. McCarty
13 North Main Street, Wigtown, DG8 9HL. Tel: 01988 402062

The Old Bank Book Shop
7 South Main Street, Wigtown, DG8 9EH. Tel: 01988 402111

ReadingLasses Book Shop
17 South Main Street, Wigtown, DG8 9EH. Tel: 01988 403266

Tideline Books
12 North Main Street, Wigtown, DG8 9HL. Tel: 01745 354919

Transformer
26 Bladnoch, Wigtown, DG8 9AB. Tel: 01988 403455

Dundee
Big Bairn Books
17 Exchange Street, Dundee, DD1 3DJ. Tel: 01382 220225

Edinburgh
Andrew Pringle Bookseller
62 West Port, Edinburgh, EH1 2LD. Tel: 0131 228 8880

Armchair Books
72 West Port, Edinburgh, EH1 2LE. Tel: 0131 229 5927

Aurora Books
6 Tanfield, Edinburgh, EH3 5DA. Tel: 0131 557 8466

Barnardo's Bookshop
45 Clerk Street, Edinburgh, EH8 9JQ. Tel: 0131 668 3142

The Book Swop
28 Bruntsfield Place, Edinburgh, EH10 4HJ. Tel: 0131 229 9451

Bookworm
210 Dalkeith Road, Edinburgh, EH16 5DT. Tel: 0131 662 4357

Duncan & Reid
5 Tanfield, Edinburgh, EH3 5JS. Tel: 0131 556 4591

Edinburgh Books
147 West Port, Edinburgh, EH3 9DP. Tel: 0131 229 4431

G.J. Thomson
60 West Port, Edinburgh, EH1 2LD. Tel: 0131 229 7534

The Hospice Bookshop
233 Morningside Road, Edinburgh, EH10 4QT. Tel: 0131 447 9008

Main Point Books
8 Lauriston Street, Edinburgh, EH3 9DJ. Tel: 0131 228 4837

McNaughtan's Bookshop
3A–4A Haddington Place, Edinburgh, EH7 4AE. Tel: 0131 556 5897

The Old Children's Bookshelf
175 Canongate, Edinburgh, EH8 8BN. Tel: 0131 558 3411

The Old Town Bookshop
8 Victoria Street, Edinburgh, EH1 2HG. Tel: 0131 225 9237

Oxfam Bookshop
116 Nicolson Street, Edinburgh, EH8 9EJ. Tel: 0131 667 9150

Oxfam Bookshop
25 Raeburn Place, Edinburgh, EH4 1HU. Tel: 0131 332 9632

Peter Bell
68 West Port, Edinburgh, EH1 2LD. Tel: 0131 229 0562

Pickering's Books
30 Buccleuch Street, Edinburgh, EH8 9LP. Tel: 0131 662 8570

Second Edition
9 Howard Street, Edinburgh, EH3 5JP. Tel: 0131 556 9403

The Shelter Bookshop
106 Raeburn Place, Edinburgh, EH4 1HH. Tel: 0131 315 0221

Southside Books
58 South Bridge, Edinburgh, EH1 1LS. Tel: 0131 558 9009

Telfer & Bolton
2 Summer Place, Edinburgh, EH3 5NR. Tel: 0131 556 7857

Tills Bookshop
1 Hope Park Crescent, Edinburgh, EH8 9NA. Tel: 0131 667 0895

Word Power
43 West Nicolson Street, Edinburgh, EH8 9DB. Tel: 0131 662 9112

Fife
Ceres
First Friends
19 Main Street, Ceres, KY15 5NA. Tel: 01334 828405

Glenrothes
Mitchell's Bookshop
26 Woodside Way, Glenrothes, KY7 6DF. Tel: 01592 758737

Newport-on-Tay
Mair Wilkes Books
3 St Mary's Lane, Newport-on-Tay, DD6 8AH. Tel: 01382 542260

St Andrews
Bouquiniste
31 Market Street, St Andrews, KY16 9NS. Tel: 01334 476724

Quarto Bookshop
8 Golf Place, St Andrews, KY16 9JA. Tel: 01334 474616

Glasgow
Book Nook
140 Queen Margaret Drive, Glasgow, G20 8NY.

Caledonia Bookshop
483 Great Western Road, Glasgow, G12 8HL. Tel: 0141 334 9663

Cooper Hay Rare Books
182 Bath Street, Glasgow, G2 4HG. Tel: 0141 333 1992

Oxfam Bookshop
330 Byres Road, Glasgow, G12 8AP. Tel: 0141 338 6185

Pulp Fiction
7 King's Court, King Street, Glasgow, G1. Tel: 01698 817931

Thistle Books
61 Otago Street, Glasgow, G12 8PQ. Tel: 0141 334 8777

Voltaire & Rousseau
12–14 Otago Lane, Glasgow, G12 8PB. Tel: 0141 339 1811

Highland
Dingwall
Mercat Books
6 Church Street, Dingwall, IV15 9SB. Tel: 01349 865593

Broadford
The Borealis Shop
The Old Pier Road, Broadford, IV49 9AE. Tel: 01471 822669

Fort William
Ben Nevis Book Corner
Springbank, Monzie Square, Fort William, PH33 6AG. Tel: 01397 703456

Inverness
Books Etc.
8 Market Hall, Inverness, IV1 4JP. Tel: 01463 712040

Leakey's Second Hand Bookshop
Greyfriar's Hall, Church Street, Inverness, IV1 1EY. Tel: 01463 239947

Thurso
Tall Tales Bookshop
Princess Street, Thurso, KW14 7HF. Tel: 07900 284 488

Ullapool
The Olde Moss Bookshop
6 MacLeod House, Royal Park, Ullapool, IV26 2XT. Tel: 01854 613317

North Lanarkshire
Newmains
Really Rare
82 Manse Road, Newmains. Tel: 07932 354150

South Lanarkshire
Biggar
Atkinson Pryce Bookshop
27 High Street, Biggar, ML12 6DA. Tel: 01899 221225

Moray
Fochabers
Marianne Simpson
61–63 High Street, Fochabers, IV32 7DU. Tel: 01343 821192

Forres
The Moray Bookshop
Logie Steading, Forres, IV36 2QN. Tel: 01309 611373

The Well of Lost Plots
142 High Street, Forres, IV36 1NP. Tel: 01309 676576

Orkney
Kirkwall
Moira McCarty
54 Junction Road, Kirkwall, KW15 1AG. Tel: 01856 870860

Perth and Kinross
Aberfeldy
Freader's Books
8 Dunkeld Street, Aberfeldy, PH15 2DA. Tel: 01887 829519

Blair Atholl
Atholl Browse
By the station, Blair Atholl, PH18 5SG. Tel: 01796 481530

Blairgowrie
Blairgowrie Books
3 Meadow Place, Wellmeadow, Blairgowrie, PH10 6NQ. Tel: 01250 875855

Comrie
Comrie Rare Books
Mallochs Buildings, Drummond Street, Comrie. Tel: 01764 681520

Glendoick
Scribe
The Old School, Glendoick, PH2 7NR. Tel: 01738 860870

Renfrewshire
Greenock
Westwords
14 Newton Street, Greenock, PA16 8UJ. Tel: 01475 892467

Paisley
Abbey Books
16 Gordon Street, Paisley, PA1 1XD. Tel: 0141 887 7303

Shetland
Lerwick
The Shetland Times Bookshop
71–79 Commercial Street, Lerwick, ZE1 OAJ. Tel: 01595 695531

Stirling
Bridge of Allan
Bridge of Allan Books
2 Henderson Street, Bridge of Allan, FK9 4HT. Tel: 01786 834483

Callander
King's Bookshop
91–93 Main Street, Callander, FK17 8BQ. Tel: 01877 339449

Stirling
Second Edition
30 The Arcade, King Street, Stirling, FK8 1AX. Tel: 01383 410197

Stirling Books
18 Maxwell Place, Stirling, FK8 1JU. Tel: 01786 461816

Western Isles
Stornoway
The Baltic Bookshop
8–10 Cromwell Street, Stornoway, HS1 2DA. Tel: 01851 702082

Hebridean Jewelry
63 Cromwell Street, Stornoway, HS1 2DD. Tel: 01851 702372

Index